1001 SIE® Exam Practice Questions

by Steven M. Rice

SIE® Exam: 1001 Practice Questions For Dummies®

Published by: **John Wiley & Sons, Inc.,** 111 River Street, Hoboken, NJ 07030-5774, www.wiley.com

Published simultaneously in Canada

For general information on our other products and services, please contact our Customer Care Department within the U.S. at 877-762-2974, outside the U.S. at 317-572-3993, or fax 317-572-4002. For technical support, please visit https://hub.wiley.com/community/support/dummies.

Wiley publishes in a variety of print and electronic formats and by print-on-demand. Some material included with standard print versions of this book may not be included in e-books or in print-on-demand. If this book refers to media such as a CD or DVD that is not included in the version you purchased, you may download this material at http://booksupport.wiley.com. For more information about Wiley products, visit www.wiley.com.

Library of Congress Control Number: 2023939002

ISBN 978-1-394-19524-4 (pbk); ISBN 978-1-394-19525-1 (ebk); ISBN 978-1-394-19526-8 (ebk)

SKY10049500_062123

Table of Contents

Introduction

This book is designed for people like you who are getting prepared to tackle the Securities Industry Essentials (SIE) Exam. Although the Securities Industry Essentials Exam is not as difficult as some of the other securities exams, it'll be rough if you don't prepare adequately. It is not enough for you to have a good grasp on the material covered on the SIE; you also need to have completed enough practice questions to go in to take the *real deal* with confidence.

No doubt tackling test questions is a skill. I have tutored many students who could just about recite an SIE, Series 65, or Series 7 book, but when it came down to answering questions, they were lost. The only way to get better is to answer a lot of questions. You need to learn how to break questions down, focus on the last sentence in the question, and eliminate wrong answers.

Although the book is broken down into chapters and sections, you can jump around the book to whatever topic you need help with. Even though the book is broken down into logical chapters, when you take the real SIE Exam, the questions are not going to be in chapter order; they will be jumbled. If you would like to get somewhat of a feel for the real exam, you may want to randomly grab 75 questions encompassing all of the different chapters and subchapters. Maybe you can even answer every 13th question or so, starting with number 1 the first time, 2 the second time, and so on.

This is your book, so feel free to either take a question and go look at the answer and explanation or complete a section before looking at the answers and explanations. Either way you do it, make sure that you give your best effort in answering each question before looking at the answer. Also, keep your eyes from wandering to the answers and explanations for questions you haven't completed yet.

Work hard and give yourself the best opportunity to pass the Securities Industry Essentials Exam on the first (or next) attempt.

What You'll Find

The 1,001 Securities Industry Essentials Exam practice problems in the book are divided into 12 chapters with several subsections. Each chapter provides an abundance of question types you are likely to face when taking the real exam. As on the real exam, some questions will take you a few seconds to answer, and some will take you a couple of minutes. Remember, the real exam weights the questions, so the more difficult ones are worth more, and the easier ones are worth less.

The last chapter of the book provides the answers and detailed explanations to all the problems. If you get an answer wrong, give it a second attempt before reading the explanation. Eliminating answers that you know are wrong will have a big impact on your score as compared to just "C"ing your way through (just choosing the answer "C" for every answer you're not sure of).

Beyond the Book

This product also comes with an online Cheat Sheet that helps you increase your odds of performing well. Go to www.dummies.com and type "SIE Exam: 1001 Practice Questions For Dummies cheat sheet" in the search box. Here, you'll find articles that will help you prepare for the SIE.

Where to Go for Additional Help

I wouldn't say that any part of the Securities Industry Essentials is overly difficult, but the exam itself is tough. The problem is that there is soooo much to remember. Remembering everything and not confusing rules and numbers makes it a little tougher than exams you faced when you were in high school.

In addition to getting help from people who have recently passed the Securities Industry Essentials Exam, securities teachers (like me), or tutors (like me), you can find a variety of questions and study materials online. A simple online search often turns up heaps of information. You can also head to www.dummies.com to see the many articles and books that can help you in your studies.

This book gives you 1,001 practice questions and answers in order for you to prepare yourself for the SIE Exam. If you need more in-depth study and direction, check out the latest edition of *Securities Industry Essentials Exam For Dummies*, which I also wrote. Here, you'll find in-depth coverage of all the topics and concepts presented in the SIE Exam along with full-length practice exams.

1

Tackling the Questions

IN THIS PART . . .

Underwriting securities (Chapter 1)

Equity securities (Chapter 2)

Corporate and U.S. government debt securities (Chapter 3)

Municipal bonds (Chapter 4)

Packaged securities (Chapter 5)

DPPs and REITs (Chapter 6)

Options (Chapter 7)

Customer accounts (Chapter 8)

Securities analysis (Chapter 9)

Orders and trades (Chapter 10)

Taxes and retirement plans (Chapter 11)

Rules and regulations (Chapter 12)

Chapter 1

Securities Underwriting: The Process and the Team Players

A good place to start is at the beginning. Prior to corporations "going public," they must register and have a way of distributing their securities. The Series 7 exam tests your ability to understand the registration process, the entities involved in bringing new issues to market, and the types of offerings. In addition, you're expected to know which securities are exempt from Securities and Exchange Commission (SEC) registration.

The Problems You'll Work On

As you work through this chapter, be sure you can recognize, understand, and, in some cases, calculate the following:

- The process involved with bringing new issues to market
- The different types of offerings
- Exempt securities and transactions

What to Watch Out For

Read the questions and answer choices carefully and make sure that you

- Watch out for words that can change the answer you're looking for, such as EXCEPT, NOT, ALWAYS, and so on.
- Recognize that there's a difference between *exempt securities* and *exempt transactions.*
- If you're not certain of the correct answer, try to eliminate any answers that you can. Doing so may make the difference between passing and failing.

1–35 Bringing New Issues to Market

1. Which of the following securities acts covers the registration and disclosure requirements of new issues?

(A) The Securities Act of 1933

(B) The Securities Exchange Act of 1934

(C) The Trust Indenture Act of 1939

(D) All of the above

2. The Securities Act of 1933 was enacted to

(A) require full and fair disclosure regarding sales of new securities to the public

(B) regulate the exchanges and the over-the-counter market in trades of outstanding securities

(C) require broker-dealers and registered reps to be licensed

(D) all of the above

3. The federal security law that provides rules for securities traded in the secondary market is

(A) the Trust Indenture Act of 1939

(B) the Securities Exchange Act of 1934

(C) the Securities Act of 1933

(D) FDIC

4. The Securities Exchange Act of 1934 created rules regarding all of the following EXCEPT

(A) the extension of credit in margin accounts

(B) transactions by insiders

(C) the registration of securities

(D) the handling of customer accounts

5. Which of the following securities is exempt from the Trust Indenture Act of 1939?

I. T-bonds

II. GO bonds

III. Equipment trust bonds

IV. Revenue bonds

(A) I only

(B) II and III

(C) I, II, and IV

(D) I, III, and IV

6. The Trust Indenture Act of 1939 regulates all of the following EXCEPT

(A) debentures

(B) collateral trusts

(C) mortgage bonds

(D) Treasury bonds

7. Which of the following information must be included in the registration statement to the SEC when registering new securities?

I. the issuer's name and description of its business

II. what the proceeds of sale will be used for

III. financial statements

IV. the company's capitalization

(A) I and III

(B) I, II, and III

(C) I, III, and IV

(D) I, II, III, and IV

8. What is the underwriting arrangement that allows an issuer whose stock is already trading publicly to time the sales of an additional issue?

(A) shelf registration

(B) a standby underwriting

(C) a negotiated offering

(D) an Eastern account underwriting

9. SEC Rule 415 outlines rules for

(A) primary offerings

(B) shelf offerings

(C) secondary offerings

(D) IPOs

10. KO Corp., a new company, has held back some of its shares for later use. According to shelf distribution rules, KO can sell the shares over the course of the next ________ without having to reregister the shares.

(A) 180 days

(B) 270 days

(C) 1 year

(D) 3 years

11. The cooling-off period for a new issue lasts approximately how many days?

(A) 20

(B) 30

(C) 40

(D) 60

12. Under the Securities Act of 1933, the SEC has the authority to

I. approve new issues of common stock

II. issue stop orders

III. review registration statements

(A) I and II

(B) II and III

(C) I and III

(D) all of the above

13. Zamzow, Inc., has filed a registration statement and is currently in the cooling-off period. Zowie Broker-Dealer is the lead underwriter for Zamzow and is in the process of taking indications of interest. Which TWO of the following are TRUE regarding indications of interest?

I. They are binding on Zowie.

II. They are binding on customers.

III. They are not binding on Zowie.

IV. They are not binding on customers.

(A) I and II

(B) III and IV

(C) I and IV

(D) II and III

14. A corporation in the process of issuing stock has not filed a registration statement with the SEC. An account executive may do which of the following relating to the new issue?

(A) Accept money from customers.

(B) Obtain indications of interest.

(C) Guarantee to customers that they will be able to purchase 1,000 shares of the new issue.

(D) Nothing.

15. A tombstone ad would include all of the following names EXCEPT

(A) selling group members

(B) syndicate members

(C) the syndicate manager

(D) the issuer

16. Which of the following are types of state securities registration?

I. filing
II. communication
III. qualification
IV. coordination

(A) I, III, and IV
(B) II, III, and IV
(C) I, II, and III
(D) I, II, III, and IV

17. This type of state registration is used for securities that are exempt from SEC registration but require state registration.

(A) Filing
(B) Coordination
(C) Qualification
(D) Notification

18. This type of state registration is used for established companies that have previously sold securities within the state.

(A) Notification
(B) Coordination
(C) Qualification
(D) (A) or (B)

19. This type of state registration is used for corporations who wish to register their securities with the SEC and states at the same time.

(A) Filing
(B) Coordination
(C) Qualification
(D) Notification

20. The main function of an investment banker is to

(A) advise an issuer on how to raise capital
(B) raise capital for issuers by selling securities
(C) help issuers comply with the laws of the Securities Act of 1933
(D) all of the above

21. A group organized to underwrite municipal or corporate securities is called

(A) a market maker
(B) a dealer's group
(C) a syndicate
(D) a posse

22. All of the following would be found in a final prospectus EXCEPT

(A) the issuer's business plan and what they intend to do with the proceeds of sale
(B) the underwriter's agreement
(C) the effective date
(D) the offering price

23. Which of the following types of underwriting agreements specify that any unsold securities are retained by the underwriters?

(A) mini-max
(B) firm commitment
(C) all-or-none (AON)
(D) best efforts

24. Which of the following documents details the liabilities and responsibilities of each firm involved in the distribution of new securities?

(A) the registration statement
(B) the letter of intent
(C) the agreement among underwriters
(D) the code of procedure

25. Which of the following is NOT a type of bond underwriting?

(A) Mini-max
(B) Best efforts
(C) Standby
(D) AON

26. Silversmith Securities is the lead underwriter for 2 million shares of HIJ common stock. Silversmith has entered into an agreement with HIJ to sell as many shares of their common stock as possible, but HIJ will cancel the offering if the entire 2 million shares are not sold. What type of offering is this?

(A) Firm commitment

(B) All-or-none

(C) Mini-max

(D) Best efforts

27. In this type of securities underwriting a certain minimum dollar amount of securities must be sold for the offering not to be cancelled.

(A) Firm commitment

(B) Mini-max

(C) All or none

(D) None of the above

28. A registered rep may use a preliminary prospectus to

(A) solicit orders from clients to purchase a new issue

(B) show prospective investors that the issue has been approved by the SEC

(C) obtain indications of interest from investors

(D) accept orders and payments from investors for a new issue

29. Who is responsible to make sure the information placed in a prospectus is accurate?

(A) The managing underwriter

(B) The selling group

(C) The SEC

(D) FINRA

30. All of the following are included in the preliminary prospectus EXCEPT

I. the public offering price

II. the financial history of the issuer

III. the effective date

(A) I only

(B) I and II

(C) II and III

(D) I and III

31. A red herring is also known as a

(A) tombstone advertisement

(B) final prospectus

(C) preliminary prospectus

(D) stop order

32. A preliminary prospectus

(A) may be used to help obtain indications of interest

(B) may not be sent to potential investors during the cooling-off period

(C) is also known as the pink sheets

(D) includes the final offering price

33. Which of the following is included in a preliminary prospectus?

I. The purpose of the funds being raised by the offering

II. Financial statements

III. A written statement in red citing that the prospectus may be amended and a final prospectus issued

IV. The final offering price

(A) I and II

(B) I, II, and III

(C) II and IV

(D) I, II, III, and IV

34. Which of the following is TRUE?

I. The registrar is responsible for making sure that a corporation's outstanding shares do not exceed the quantity of authorized shares.

II. The transfer agent is responsible for making sure that a corporation's outstanding shares do not exceed the quantity of authorized shares.

III. The registrar maintains records of a corporation's stock and bond owners plus mails and cancels old certificates as necessary.

IV. The transfer agent maintains records of a corporation's stock and bond owners plus mails and cancels old certificates as necessary.

(A) I and III

(B) I and IV

(C) II and III

(D) II and IV

35. Which of the following is a function of a transfer agent?

(A) Underwriting shares in new corporate stock offerings

(B) Preparing corporate balance sheets

(C) Advising municipalities regarding the debt structure of new issues

(D) Sending out proxies

36–43 Types of Securities Offerings

36. The first time a corporation ever issues securities to the public is called a(n)

(A) IPO

(B) first-market trade

(C) rights offering

(D) none of the above

37. HIJ Corporation is issuing common stock through an IPO that will trade on the OTCBB when it is first issued. Broker-dealers who execute orders for clients in HIJ common stock must have a copy of a final prospectus available for how long?

(A) 25 days after the effective date

(B) 30 days after the effective date

(C) 40 days after the effective date

(D) 90 days after the effective date

38. Pluto Broker-Dealer is offering an IPO that will not be listed on the NYSE, NASDAQ, or any other exchange. How long after the effective date must Pluto provide a final prospectus to all purchasers?

(A) 20 days

(B) 30 days

(C) 40 days

(D) 90 days

39. A corporation is offering 1 million shares of its common stock to the public. Of those shares, 600,000 are authorized but previously unissued, while insiders of the company are selling the other 400,000 shares. What type of offering is this?

(A) IPO

(B) Primary

(C) Secondary

(D) Combined

40. WXY Corporation is offering a large block of treasury stock. What type of offering is this?

(A) IPO

(B) Primary

(C) Secondary

(D) Split

41. The first time a corporation issues stock is called a(n)

(A) primary offering

(B) secondary offering

(C) split offering

(D) initial public offering

42. Another name for a combined offering is a _______________ offering.

(A) split

(B) dual

(C) secondary

(D) coupled

43. A primary offering would do which of the following?

I. Increase the number of shares outstanding.

II. Decrease the number of shares outstanding.

III. Raise additional capital for the issuer.

IV. Include selling treasury stock.

(A) I, III, and IV

(B) II, III, and IV

(C) I and IV

(D) I and III

44–61 Exempt Securities and Transactions

44. All of the following are exempt securities under the Securities Act of 1933 EXCEPT

(A) Treasury bonds

(B) municipal general obligation bonds

(C) REITs

(D) public utility stocks

45. Which of the following securities is exempt from SEC registration?

(A) Corporate term bonds

(B) Warrants

(C) General obligation bonds

(D) None of the above

46. Which TWO of the following are nonexempt securities under the Securities Act of 1933?

I. Variable annuities

II. Fixed annuities

III. Non-negotiable CDs

IV. Oil and gas limited partnerships

(A) I and III

(B) I and IV

(C) II and III

(D) II and IV

47. Which of the following securities are exempt from SEC registration?

I. Revenue bonds

II. Treasury bonds

III. Variable annuities

IV. Securities issued by not-for-profit organizations

(A) I, II, and IV

(B) II, III, and IV

(C) II and IV

(D) I, II, III, and IV

48. Under the Securities Act of 1933, all of the following securities must be offered by a prospectus EXCEPT

(A) variable annuities

(B) mutual funds

(C) UITs

(D) TIPS

49. Which of the following securities are exempt from the full registration requirements of the Securities Act of 1933?

(A) Corporate convertible bonds

(B) Closed-end funds

(C) Real estate limited partnerships

(D) Commercial paper

50. Which of the following are exempt transactions?

I. Private placements

II. Securities issued by the U.S. government

III. Municipal bonds

IV. Intrastate offerings

(A) II and III

(B) II, III, and IV

(C) I and IV

(D) I, II, III, and IV

51. A Rule 147 offering is

(A) an offering of securities only within the issuer's home state

(B) an offering of securities worth no more than $75 million within a one-year period

(C) an offering of securities to no more than 35 unaccredited investors within a one-year period

(D) also known as an interstate offering

52. A Regulation D offering is

(A) an offering of securities only within the issuer's home state

(B) an offering of securities worth no more than $75 million within a one-year period

(C) an offering of securities to no more than 35 unaccredited investors within a one-year period

(D) also known as an interstate offering

53. Which of the following is not an offering that is exempt from the full registration requirements of the Securities Act of 1933?

(A) Regulation D

(B) Regulation A+

(C) Regulation T

(D) Rule 147

54. All of the following would be considered accredited investors EXCEPT

(A) financial institutions

(B) joint investors with a combined income of at least $200,000 for the current year and previous two years

(C) corporations with a net worth of at least $5 million

(D) investors with a net worth of at least $1 million excluding primary residence

55. Which of the following is TRUE of Regulation A+ Tier 2 offerings?

(A) They are limited to 35 unaccredited investors each year.

(B) They are issued without using a prospectus.

(C) They are limited to raising up to $20 million per year.

(D) They are also known as private placements.

56. Which of the following is true?

(A) Public securities offerings are typically exempt from SEC registration.

(B) All securities offerings are exempt from SEC registration.

(C) No securities offerings are exempt from SEC registration.

(D) Private securities offerings are typically exempt from SEC registration.

57. Which of the following are considered accredited investors?

(A) Financial institutions

(B) Investors with a net worth of $1 million or more excluding primary residence

(C) Rural business investment companies

(D) All of the above

58. Under Rule 144, what percentage of outstanding shares may a control person sell every 90 days?

(A) 1%

(B) The average weekly trading volume for the previous 4 weeks

(C) Either (A) or (B)

(D) Neither (A) nor (B)

59. SEC Rule 144 regulates

(A) the sale of control stock

(B) the sale of new securities

(C) the sale of equity securities worth $75 million or less in a one-year period

(D) the conversion of convertible preferred stock into common stock

60. Sig Hillstrand has held shares of Greenhorn restricted stock for more than one year. Greenhorn has 4 million shares outstanding. The most recently reported weekly trading volumes for Greenhorn are as follows:

Week Ending	Trading Volume
May 27	35,000
May 20	50,000
May 13	40,000
May 6	45,000
Apr 29	50,000

What is the maximum number of shares that Sig can sell under Rule 144?

(A) 35,000

(B) 46,250

(C) 44,000

(D) 42,500

61. Which of the following securities is subject to the anti-fraud provision of the Securities Act of 1933?

(A) U.S. government securities

(B) Common stock issued by any corporation

(C) Private placements under Regulation D

(D) All of the above

Chapter 2

Equity Securities: Corporate Ownership

To be a corporation, you must have stockholders. Both common and preferred stock are considered *equity securities* because they represent ownership of the corporation. A majority of most registered representatives' commission is earned by selling equity securities because, historically, equity securities have outpaced inflation.

Although this isn't the largest section on the Series 7 exam, it does relate to many other chapters, such as packaged securities and options.

The Problems You'll Work On

In this chapter, you're expected to understand and calculate questions regarding the following:

- The specifics of common stock
- The difference between common stock and preferred stock
- The reason for American depositary receipts (ADRs), rights, and warrants

What to Watch Out For

Read the questions and answer choices carefully, and be sure you

- Don't assume an answer without reading each question and answer choice completely (twice if necessary).
- Watch out for key words that can change the answer (EXCEPT, NOT, and so on).
- Eliminate any incorrect answer choice that you can.
- Look at questions from the corporation's or the investor's point of view depending on how the question is worded.

62–97 Common Stock

62. Which of the following would be owners of a corporation?

I. Common stockholders
II. Debenture holders
III. Participation preferred stockholders
IV. Equipment trust bondholders

(A) I and III
(B) II and IV
(C) I, III, and IV
(D) II, III, and IV

63. Equity securities include

(A) TIPS
(B) debentures
(C) preferred shares
(D) GO bonds

64. Regarding investments, which of the following is true?

(A) Bonds represent ownership in an issuing corporation.
(B) Warrants and bonds represent ownership in an issuing corporation.
(C) Stocks represent ownership in an issuing corporation.
(D) Warrants represent ownership in an issuing corporation.

65. AylDec Corporation has just decided to go public. AylDec will issue

(A) preferred stock
(B) common stock
(C) term bonds
(D) warrants

66. Poor Outlook Corporation has just declared bankruptcy. Remaining assets would be distributed in which way (from first to last)?

(A) IRS, unpaid workers, general creditors, preferred stockholders, secured creditors, subordinated debenture holders, common stockholders
(B) Common stockholders, general creditors, preferred stockholders, subordinated debenture holders, secured creditors, IRS, unpaid workers
(C) Unpaid workers, IRS, secured creditors, general creditors, subordinated debenture holders, preferred stockholders, common stockholders
(D) IRS, unpaid workers, secured creditors, subordinated debenture holders, general creditors, preferred stockholders, common stockholders

67. In the event of corporate bankruptcy, preferred stockholders have priority claim of assets over

(A) unpaid workers
(B) debenture holders
(C) the IRS
(D) common shareholders

68. Common stockholders have which of the following rights and privileges?

I. The right to receive monthly audited financial reports
II. The right to vote for cash dividends
III. The right to vote for stock splits
IV. A residual claim to assets at dissolution

(A) I and II
(B) III and IV
(C) I, III, and IV
(D) II, III, and IV

69. Common stockholders have the right to vote for all of the following EXCEPT

I. cash dividends
II. stock dividends
III. stock splits
IV. members of the board of directors

(A) I, II, and III
(B) III and IV
(C) I and II
(D) IV only

70. Which of the following investors would have the right to vote for corporation board of director positions?

(A) Preferred stockholders
(B) Commons stockholders
(C) Bondholders
(D) Both (A) and (B)

71. ABCD Corporation's common shareholders would have the right to vote for

I. members of the board of directors (BOD)
II. cash dividends
III. stock dividends
IV. stock splits

(A) II and III
(B) I and III
(C) I and IV
(D) II and IV

72. An investor who holds common stock has

I. limited liability
II. unlimited liability
III. voting rights
IV. no voting rights

(A) I and III
(B) I and IV
(C) II and IV
(D) II and III

73. Cain Weidman owns 1,000 shares of HIT Corp. HIT issues stock with cumulative voting. What is the maximum number of votes that Cain can cast for one candidate if the board of directors of HIT has four vacancies?

(A) 100
(B) 250
(C) 1,000
(D) 4,000

74. An individual owns 2,000 shares of TUV common stock. TUV has four vacancies on the board of directors. If the voting is cumulative, the investor may vote in any of the following ways EXCEPT

(A) 4,000 votes for two candidates each
(B) 5,000 votes for one candidate and 3,000 votes for another candidate
(C) 3,000 votes each for three candidates
(D) 2,000 votes for four candidates each

75. This type of voting gives smaller shareholders (in terms of shares) a better chance to gain representation on the board of directors (BOD).

(A) Statutory
(B) Cumulative
(C) Regular
(D) Break-up

76. As a stockholder, Ayla Rice would really like to attend the vote for board of director members. Unfortunately, her schedule will not allow her to attend in person. Which of the following is true?

(A) Ayla can vote by proxy.
(B) Ayla will have to wait until the next vote.
(C) Ayla can show up to the location to cast her vote in person as long as it's within two weeks of the vote.
(D) Ayla will lose her right to vote for the next two years.

77. All of the following are possible ways to vote for the board of directors of a corporation EXCEPT

(A) in person

(B) by telephone

(C) by mailed proxy

(D) by online proxy

78. Which of the following does NOT describe treasury stock?

(A) Treasury stockholders have no voting rights.

(B) It is stock that was previously authorized but still unissued.

(C) It is issued stock that has been repurchased by the company.

(D) It has no dividends.

79. Treasury stock is

(A) U.S. government stock

(B) local government stock

(C) authorized but unissued stock

(D) repurchased stock

80. Macrohard Corp. was authorized to issue 2 million shares of common stock. Macrohard issued 1.1 million shares and subsequently repurchased 150,000 shares. How many of Macrohard's shares remain outstanding?

(A) 150,000

(B) 900,000

(C) 950,000

(D) 1.85 million

81. Which of the following changes the par value of a common stock?

(A) A cash dividend

(B) A stock dividend

(C) A stock split

(D) All of the above

82. The par value of a common stock is

I. used for bookkeeping purposes

II. one dollar

III. adjusted for stock splits

IV. the amount investors receive at maturity

(A) I and III

(B) I, II, and III

(C) II, III, and IV

(D) I, II, III, and IV

83. The amount over par value that an issuer receives when selling stock is called

(A) a bonus

(B) equity surplus

(C) surplus over par

(D) additional paid in capital

84. Tender offers typically ______________ the price of the outstanding shares of a corporation.

(A) increase

(B) decrease

(C) do not affect

(D) cannot be determined

85. Which of the following changes the par value of a stock?

(A) A rights offering

(B) The issuer repurchasing some of its outstanding stock

(C) A stock split

(D) A cash dividend

86. TUV Corporation declares a 4-for-3 stock split; an investor who owns 600 shares would receive ______________ additional shares.

(A) 100

(B) 200

(C) 400

(D) 600

87. Dana Black, an investor, purchased 1,000 shares of ABC at $40. If ABC announces a 5-for-4 split, what is Dana's position after the split?

(A) 800 ABC at $50

(B) 1,250 ABC at $32

(C) 1,250 ABC at $50

(D) 800 ABC at $32

88. An investor owns 100 shares of DEF common stock at the current market price of $40 per share. If DEF conducts a 1-for-2 reverse split, what would be the investor's position after the split?

(A) 50 shares at $20 per share

(B) 50 shares at $80 per share

(C) 200 shares at $20 per share

(D) 200 shares at $80 per share

89. Declan K. owns 2,500 shares of common stock of AylDec Corporation. Which of the following actions would dilute Declan's equity?

I. A primary share offering (registered)

II. A stock split

III. Payment of a stock dividend

IV. A secondary share offering (registered)

(A) I only

(B) II only

(C) I, II, and IV

(D) I, II, III, and IV

90. Which of the following is true regarding cash dividends?

I. They are decided by a shareholder vote.

II. They are decided by the board of directors.

III. They are guaranteed.

IV. They are not guaranteed.

(A) I and III

(B) I and IV

(C) II and III

(D) II and IV

91. TUVW Corp. declared a $0.40 dividend to their shareholders of record. Future dividend payments

(A) are not guaranteed

(B) are guaranteed to be paid although the amount needs to be decided

(C) will be $0.40 per share

(D) are guaranteed to be at least $0.40 per share

92. A listed stock closed at $24.95 on the business day prior to the ex-dividend date. If the company previously announced a $0.30 dividend, what will be the opening price on the next business day?

(A) $24.35

(B) $24.65

(C) $24.95

(D) $25.25

93. ABCDEF Corporation will be paying a cash dividend to its common stockholders. On what date will the market price of ABCDEF be reduced to reflect the dividend?

(A) The declaration date

(B) The ex-date

(C) The record date

(D) The payment date

94. The ex-dividend date as related to cash dividends is

I. the date that the stock price is reduced by the dividend amount

II. the date that the stock price is increased by the dividend amount

III. one business day before the record date

IV. one business day after the trade date

(A) I and III

(B) I and IV

(C) II and III

(D) II and IV

95. What is the main reason a corporation would split its stock?

(A) To bring in additional funds

(B) To increase the overall market value of its stock

(C) To decrease the amount of dividend paid per share

(D) To increase the demand for its stock

96. One of your customers owns 1,000 shares of DIM common stock at $24. DIM declares a 20% stock dividend. On the ex-dividend date, your customer will own

I. 1,000 shares

II. 1,200 shares

III. stock at $20 per share

IV. stock at $24 per share

(A) I and III

(B) I and IV

(C) II and III

(D) II and IV

97. EYEBM Corp. shares are trading at $55 per share when it declares a 5% stock dividend. After EYEBM pays the dividend, one of your clients who owned 500 shares now owns

(A) 500 shares valued at $57.73 per share

(B) 525 shares valued at $55.00 per share

(C) 550 shares valued at $55.00 per share

(D) 525 shares valued at $52.38 per share

98–125 Preferred Stock

98. Which of the following are advantages of holding straight preferred stock over common stock?

I. A fixed dividend

II. More voting power

III. Preference in the event of issuer bankruptcy

IV. The ability to receive par value at maturity

(A) I and II

(B) II and IV

(C) I and III

(D) I, III, and IV

99. Preferred stock has

I. characteristics of debt securities

II. no characteristics of debt securities

III. characteristics of common stock

IV. no characteristics of common stock

(A) I and III

(B) I and IV

(C) II and III

(D) II and IV

100. Preferred dividends may be paid in the form of

I. cash

II. stock

III. product

(A) I only

(B) I and II

(C) I and III

(D) I, II, and III

101. As interest rates rise, prices of outstanding preferred stock will likely

(A) fall

(B) rise

(C) fluctuate

(D) remain stable

102. Which TWO of the following are TRUE of preferred stock?

I. Holders have voting rights.

II. Holders do not have voting rights.

III. In the event of corporate bankruptcy, preferred stock is senior to common stock.

IV. In the event of corporate bankruptcy, preferred stock is junior to common stock.

(A) I and III

(B) I and IV

(C) II and III

(D) II and IV

103. Which of the following is true of a preferred stock dividend?

(A) It is variable and based on the consumer price index (CPI).

(B) It is fixed and based on the par value.

(C) It is variable based on the current market value.

(D) It is fixed and based on the current market value.

104. Preferred stockholders have

(A) preemptive rights

(B) voting rights

(C) both (A) and (B)

(D) neither (A) nor (B)

105. A preferred stock dividend is based on a percentage of

(A) its market price

(B) its par value

(C) the Consumer Price Index

(D) the current T-bill rate

106. Which two of the following are true of straight preferred shares?

I. They are cumulative.

II. They are non-cumulative.

III. They have no provision for missed dividends to be paid at a later date.

IV. They provide for any missed dividends to be paid at a later date.

(A) I and III

(B) I and IV

(C) II and III

(D) II and IV

107. LMNOP Corporation has past due dividends on their cumulative preferred stock. Which of the following is true?

(A) LMNOP can choose to resume current dividends when they are able and write off the past due dividends.

(B) Common stockholders must continue to receive dividends even though the dividends on their cumulative preferred stock are in arrears.

(C) They continue to accumulate on the company's books until they can be paid.

(D) The past due dividends must be paid within 90 days of a common dividend being paid.

108. Any corporation that has issued cumulative preferred stock

(A) must pay the current preferred dividend before paying interest on their bonds or dividends on their common stock

(B) must pay any past and current preferred dividends before paying any dividends on its common stock

(C) must pay only the current dividend on their preferred stock before paying a dividend on their common stock

(D) must pay only the current dividend with no liability for any missed dividends

109. A company has previously issued 4% of $100 par cumulative preferred stock. Over the first three years, the company paid out $9 in dividends. If the company announces a common dividend in the following year, how much does it owe preferred stockholders?

(A) $3

(B) $4

(C) $7

(D) $16

110. A corporation has issued 6% $100 par cumulative preferred stock. It paid $4 in dividends the first year and $3 in dividends the second year. If the corporation wants to declare a dividend for common shareholders the following year, how much must the company pay per share to its cumulative preferred stockholders?

(A) $5

(B) $6

(C) $11

(D) $14

111. A customer owns AylDec Corporation 6% cumulative preferred stock. AylDec has not paid a dividend yet this year, and they also missed the previous two years. If the AylDec wishes to pay a dividend to their common shareholders, how much must they pay this customer per share first?

(A) $24

(B) $18

(C) $12

(D) $6

112. One of your clients wants to purchase preferred stock but wants to reduce the risk of inflation. You should recommend

(A) straight preferred stock

(B) callable preferred stock

(C) cumulative preferred stock

(D) convertible preferred stock

113. ABCD Corp. issued convertible bonds. Holders of those bonds can

(A) convert their bonds for a set number of non-convertible bonds at any time

(B) convert their bonds for a fixed number of shares of ABCD common stock

(C) convert their bonds for 10 shares of ABCD straight preferred stock

(D) convert their bonds into non-convertible bonds and receive a premium for doing so

114. Which of the following types of preferred stock will most likely increase in value or decrease in value in line with the issuer's common shares?

(A) Convertible preferred

(B) Straight preferred

(C) Participating preferred

(D) Adjustable rate preferred

115. If interest rates remained relatively stable over the last year, which of the following types of preferred stock was likely the most volatile during that period?

(A) Adjustable rate

(B) Callable

(C) Participating

(D) Convertible

116. What is the advantage to a corporation issuing callable preferred stock as compared to non-callable preferred stock?

(A) It allows the issuer to take advantage of high interest rates.

(B) The dividend rate on callable preferred stock is lower than that of non-callable preferred stock.

(C) It allows the issuer to issue preferred stock with a lower fixed dividend after the call date.

(D) Callable preferred stock usually has a longer maturity date.

117. Missy Love Corp. has called in its 7% callable preferred shares. Holders of these shares should expect that

(A) the shares will likely be sold to other investors

(B) the shares will continue trading in the market

(C) dividend payments will continue to be paid until the shares are turned in

(D) dividend payments will stop once the shares have been called

118. With everything else being equal, which of the following preferred stock would pay the highest dividend?

(A) Straight preferred

(B) Cumulative preferred

(C) Participating preferred

(D) Callable preferred

119. HIJ Corp. issued 6% callable preferred stock many years ago. Interest rates have been steadily declining over the past few years to where HIJ Corp. could issue 4% callable preferred stock now. What is HIJ Corp. likely to do?

(A) HIJ will likely lower the dividend on their outstanding callable preferred stock to 4%.

(B) HIJ would likely call their outstanding 6% callable preferred stock.

(C) HIJ would likely leave their 6% callable preferred stock in the market and issue new callable preferred stock at a lower coupon rate.

(D) HIJ will attempt to convince the holders to convert their 6% callable preferred shares into common stock.

120. With everything else being equal, a preferred stockholder would expect ____________ preferred stock to pay the highest dividend.

(A) convertible

(B) straight

(C) callable

(D) cumulative

121. This type of preferred stock may pay a dividend that is higher than the stated dividend.

(A) Variable-rate

(B) Participating

(C) Senior

(D) Convertible

122. TUV Corporation has continued their winning ways and have had another stellar year. As such, TUV's board of directors has decided to pay their 5% participating preferred shareholders participating to 8% not only their 5% dividend but their full participating dividend this year. These preferred shareholders will receive

(A) an additional dividend of 3%

(B) an additional dividend of 5%

(C) an additional dividend of 4%

(D) an additional dividend of 8%

123. Which of the following is true regarding the dividend rate on variable preferred stock?

(A) The interest rate is often tied to the returns on S&P 500 index funds.

(B) The interest rate is based off of the Consumer Price Index.

(C) The interest rate is often tied to a benchmark rate like the Treasury bill rate.

(D) The interest rate increases the longer the variable preferred stock is held.

124. This type of stock is most likely to have a more stable price.

(A) Variable rate preferred

(B) Convertible preferred

(C) Participating preferred

(D) Callable preferred

125. When interest rates are steadily increasing, which of the following types of preferred stock would most likely pay a higher divided?

(A) Adjustable rate

(B) Convertible

(C) Callable

(D) Participating

126–141 ADRs, Rights, and Warrants

126. An ADR is

(A) a receipt for a foreign security trading in the United States

(B) a receipt for a foreign security trading in the United States and overseas

(C) a receipt for a U.S. security trading overseas

(D) a receipt for a U.S. security trading in the United States and overseas

127. All of the following are benefits of investing in ADRs EXCEPT

(A) the dividends are received in U.S. currency

(B) transactions are completed in U.S. currency

(C) it has low currency risk

(D) it allows U.S. investors to invest overseas

128. All of the following are characteristics of American depositary receipts EXCEPT

(A) they help U.S. companies gain access to foreign dollars

(B) investors do not receive the actual certificates

(C) investors can't vote

(D) dividends are paid in U.S. dollars

129. Which of the following securities backs an American depositary receipt (ADR)?

(A) U.S. corporate debt securities

(B) Common stock

(C) U.S. government bonds

(D) Foreign debt securities

130. Why do U.S. investors typically purchase American depositary receipts (ADRs)?

(A) As a hedge against currency risk

(B) Because U.S. investors will receive tax credits for purchasing ADRs

(C) Because typically foreign investments are more stable than U.S. investments

(D) As a way to diversify a portfolio

131. Which TWO of the following are TRUE?

I. ADRs are priced in U.S. currency.

II. ADRs are priced in foreign currency.

III. The price of ADRs fluctuates throughout the day like common stock.

IV. ADRs trade like mutual funds, and the price of trades is not determined until the end of the day.

(A) I and IV

(B) II and III

(C) II and IV

(D) I and III

132. Which of the following best describes ADRs?

I. They are receipts for foreign securities trading in U.S. markets

II. They are receipts for U.S. securities trading in foreign markets

III. They are used to help finance foreign corporations

IV. They are used to help finance U.S. corporations

(A) I and IV

(B) I and III

(C) II and IV

(D) II and III

133. All of the following are TRUE about rights offerings EXCEPT

(A) they are short-term

(B) each share of outstanding common stock receives one right

(C) they typically have a standby underwriter

(D) rights are automatically received by preferred stockholders

134. A corporation needs to raise additional capital. Which of the following would help the corporation meet its goal?

(A) Declaring a stock dividend to existing shareholders

(B) A rights distribution to existing shareholders

(C) Calling in their convertible bonds

(D) Splitting their stock 2 for 1

135. Which of the following statements are true?

I. Rights are short term.

II. Rights are long term.

III. Warrants are short term.

IV. Warrants are long term.

(A) I and IV

(B) II and III

(C) II and IV

(D) I and III

136. All of the following are true about warrants and rights EXCEPT

(A) They are securities regulated by the SEC.

(B) They allow investors to buy stock at a fixed price.

(C) They allow investors to buy unissued stock at a discount from market price.

(D) They are marketable securities.

137. Which of the following is true of rights offerings?

(A) It gives existing shareholders the right to purchase more shares at a discount if the issuer is offering more shares.

(B) It gives existing shareholders the right to purchase more shares at the current market price if the issuer is offering more shares.

(C) It gives existing shareholders the right to purchase more shares at a premium if the issuer is offering more shares.

(D) Each rights offering is unique, and the shares could be purchased at a discount, the current market price, or at a premium depending on the issuer.

138. All of the following securities may pay a dividend EXCEPT

(A) warrants

(B) common stock

(C) American Depositary Receipts (ADRs)

(D) participating preferred stock

139. Which of the following is NOT TRUE regarding warrants?

(A) They are marketable securities.

(B) They offer investors a long-term right to buy stock at a fixed price.

(C) They have voting rights.

(D) Investors do not receive dividends.

140. All of the following are TRUE of warrants EXCEPT

(A) they have a longer life than rights

(B) they are non-marketable securities

(C) they are typically issued in units

(D) the exercise price is above the current market price of the common stock when issued

141. Which of the following are TRUE regarding warrants?

I. Warrants are often issued with a corporation's other securities to make an offering more attractive to investors.

II. Warrants provide a perpetual interest in an issuer's common stock.

III. Holders of warrants have no voting rights.

(A) I and II

(B) I and III

(C) II and III

(D) I, II, and III

Chapter 3

Debt Securities: Corporate and U.S. Government Loans

When issuers want to borrow money from the public, they issue debt securities. These issuers include corporations, local governments (municipal bonds), and the U.S. government. Unlike equity securities, holders of debt securities are creditors, not owners.

The Problems You'll Work On

In this chapter, you'll work on questions regarding the following:

- Understanding the different types of bonds
- Determining bond prices and yields
- Comparing the different types of bonds
- Seeing the benefits and risks of convertible bonds
- Recognizing the different types of U.S. government securities and their tax benefits
- Comparing money market instruments

What to Watch Out For

Keep the following tips in mind as you answer questions in this chapter:

- Be aware of words that can change the answer you're looking for, such as EXCEPT or NOT.
- Don't jump too quickly to answer a question. Make sure you read each question and answer choice completely before choosing an answer.
- Make sure you understand which type of bond the question is talking about prior to answering because there are many differences.
- Double-check your math when doing calculations.

142–178 Types of Bonds

142. Corporations that sell bonds are taking the position of a(n)

(A) borrower

(B) loan shark

(C) investment banker

(D) creditor

143. An investor who purchases a corporate bond is

I. borrowing money from the issuer

II. lending money to the issuer

III. a creditor

IV. an owner

(A) I and III

(B) I and IV

(C) II and III

(D) II and IV

144. Dee Plump, an investor, owns a TUB 5% convertible bond purchased at 103 with five years until maturity. If they hold the bond until maturity, Dee will receive

(A) $970

(B) $1,000

(C) $1,015

(D) $1,030

145. ABC Corporate Bonds are quoted at 101⅜. How much would an investor purchasing ten of these bonds pay?

(A) $1,013.75

(B) $1,013.80

(C) $10,137.50

(D) $10,138.00

146. Which is the only yield found on the indenture of a bond?

(A) Nominal yield

(B) Current yield

(C) Yield to maturity

(D) Yield to call

147. An investor owns ten 6% corporate bond purchased at 102 with 7 years until maturity. If holding the bonds until maturity, the investor would receive?

(A) $10,000

(B) $10,200

(C) $10,000 plus $300 interest

(D) $10,000 plus $600 interest

148. The indenture of a corporate bond includes all of the following EXCEPT

(A) the coupon rate

(B) the credit rating

(C) the name of the trustee

(D) the maturity date

149. A corporate bond with a 5.5% coupon rate would make

I. annual interest payments of $55

II. annual interest payments of $5.50

III. semiannual interest payments of $2.75

IV. semiannual interest payments of $27.50

(A) I and III

(B) I and IV

(C) II and III

(D) II and IV

150. Ayla K. has 100 DEF corporate bonds with a coupon rate of 4½%. The bonds were purchased at 98% of $1,000 par each. How much interest will Ayla receive the next time she gets paid?

(A) $2,205

(B) $2,250

(C) $4,410

(D) $4,500

151. Mr. Bear purchased a bond with a 6% coupon rate. Mr. Bear will

(A) receive $6 annual interest until the bond matures

(B) receive $60 semiannual interest until the bond matures

(C) receive $60 annual interest until the bond matures

(D) earn $60 per year interest, which is not paid until maturity

152. An investor purchased a 4% corporate bond at 98 with ten years to maturity. If the bond is currently trading at 101, how much interest will the investor receive next time he gets paid?

(A) $19.60

(B) $20.00

(C) $20.20

(D) $40.00

153. A corporate bond indenture would include which of the following?

I. The nominal yield

II. The rating

III. Any collateral backing the bond

IV. The yield to maturity

(A) I and II

(B) I and III

(C) I, III, and IV

(D) III and IV

154. Which of the following is true regarding different types of debt security maturities?

(A) A balloon maturity uses components of not only term maturities but also serial maturities.

(B) A term maturity uses components of not only balloon maturities but also serial maturities.

(C) A series maturity uses components of not only balloon maturities but also term maturities.

(D) A series maturity uses components of not only balloon maturities but also serial maturities.

155. Term bonds are quoted according to

(A) a percentage of dollar price

(B) its nominal yield

(C) its yield to call

(D) its yield to maturity

156. This type of bond is structured so that the entire issue matures at one time.

(A) Serial

(B) Term

(C) Balloon

(D) All of the above

157. The type of security that is most likely to have a sinking fund is a

(A) series bond

(B) term bond

(C) serial bond

(D) none of the above

158. Which type of bond issue has an equal amount of debt maturing each year?

(A) Term

(B) Series

(C) Serial

(D) Balloon

159. Which type of bond issue pays off a portion of the bond principal prior to the final maturity, but the largest portion is paid at the final maturity date?

(A) Series

(B) Term

(C) Balloon

(D) Serial

160. Bonds can be issued with all of the following maturity types EXCEPT

(A) series

(B) term

(C) balloon

(D) serial

161. HIJ Corp. has issued $30 million worth of convertible mortgage bonds, which are convertible for $25. The bonds are callable beginning in March 2020, while the maturity date is March 2040. The bond trades at 98, and the stock trades at $24. The bonds are secured by

(A) rolling stock

(B) the full faith and credit of HIJ Corp.

(C) securities owned by HIJ Corp.

(D) a lien on property owned by HIJ Corp.

162. Corporations may issue which of the following debt securities?

I. Equipment trust bonds

II. Mortgage bonds

III. Double-barreled bonds

IV. Revenue bonds

(A) I and IV

(B) I and II

(C) II, III, and IV

(D) I, II, III, and IV

163. The type of secured bond typically issued by transportation companies is called

(A) a guaranteed bond

(B) a mortgage bond

(C) an equipment trust bond

(D) a collateral trust bond

164. Which of the following is true of equipment trust certificates?

(A) The titles to the assets backing the issue are held in trust.

(B) The equipment backing the issue is held in trust.

(C) If the issuer defaults on the issue, the assets can be repossessed and sold by the trustee.

(D) Both (A) and (C).

165. A collateral trust bond is

(A) mainly issued by transportation companies

(B) backed by stocks and bonds owned by the issuer

(C) issued by corporations in bankruptcy

(D) backed by the assets of a parent company

166. Which of the following BEST describes a guaranteed bond?

(A) One that is mainly issued by transportation companies

(B) One that is backed by the assets of another company

(C) One that is issued by corporations in bankruptcy

(D) One that is backed by stocks and bonds held by the issuer

167. A type of bond backed by no assets except a written promise by the issuer that the principal and interest will be paid on time is a(n)

(A) equipment trust bond

(B) mortgage bond

(C) collateral trust bond

(D) debenture

168. WHYWHY Corp. has issued subordinated debentures. Which of the following is true regarding those debentures in the event of bankruptcy?

(A) It has a claim that is lower than other debt securities but higher than the issuer's preferred stock.

(B) It has a claim that is lower than all other debt securities and higher than the issuer's common stock.

(C) It has a claim that is lower than all other debt securities, preferred stock, and common stock.

(D) It has a claim that is lower than only the common and preferred stock.

169. All of the following are secured debt securities EXCEPT

(A) collateral trust bonds

(B) equipment trust bonds

(C) investment grade debentures

(D) mortgage bonds

170. You have a customer who is risk-averse and wants to start investing in bonds. Which of the following should you NOT recommend?

(A) TIPS

(B) income bonds

(C) AAA rated corporate bonds

(D) T-bonds

171. Which of the following types of bonds trade without interest payments unless declared by the issuer's board of directors?

(A) Callable bonds

(B) Debentures

(C) Income bonds

(D) Puttable bonds

172. Bad Luck Corporation is attempting to emerge from a bankruptcy. Issuing which of the following types of bonds would help them reach their goal?

(A) Equipment trust bonds

(B) Debentures

(C) Mortgage bonds

(D) Adjustment bonds

173. One of your new clients has listed income as their biggest investment objective. Which of the following would you least likely recommend?

(A) U.S Treasury bonds

(B) Mortgage bonds

(C) Income bonds

(D) Participating preferred stock

174. The coupon rate on an existing bond

(A) moves in the direction of current interest rates

(B) moves in the opposite direction of current interest rates

(C) remains fixed

(D) can move up or down depending on the performance of the DJIA

175. An investor purchased a 5% corporate bond at par. Since their purchase, interest rates have been on a steady decline. The market price of their bond likely

(A) decreased

(B) increased

(C) remained the same

(D) cannot be determined

176. The indenture of a corporate bond includes the

(A) current yield

(B) yield to maturity

(C) yield to call

(D) nominal yield

177. If a Treasury bond is priced at par, which of the following is true?

(A) The current yield is equal to the yield to maturity.

(B) The current yield is greater than to the yield to call.

(C) The yield to maturity is less than the yield to call.

(D) The current yield is less than the yield to maturity.

178. To determine the current yield on a bond, you can divide the

(A) semi-annual interest by the market price

(B) semi-annual interest by the par value

(C) annual interest by the market price

(D) annual interest by the par value

179–208 Price and Yield Calculations

179. What is the current yield on a T-bond with an initial offering price of $1,000, a current market price of $101.16, and a coupon rate of 4.25%?

(A) 4.19%

(B) 4.25%

(C) 4.37%

(D) 4.41%

180. A 4% bond is purchased at 92 with 25 years until maturity. What is the current yield?

(A) 3.65%

(B) 4%

(C) 4.35%

(D) 4.66%

181. DEF mortgage bonds are trading for $1,100. If they pay a semiannual interest of $35, what is the current yield?

(A) 3.18%

(B) 3.5%

(C) 6.36%

(D) 7%

182. A 7% bond has a basis of 4.30%. The bond is trading at a

(A) discount

(B) par

(C) premium

(D) cannot be determined

183. A 6% bond is trading at 104. What yield could an investor expect if purchasing the bond at the current price and holding the bond until maturity?

(A) 6%

(B) Above 6%

(C) Below 6%

(D) Cannot be determined

184. Which of the following bonds may be purchased at the cheapest price?

(A) A 5% bond yielding 7%

(B) A 6% bond yielding 6%

(C) A 7% bond yielding 4%

(D) A 5% bond yielding 3%

185. Which of the following is TRUE of bonds selling at a discount?

I. The market price is lower than par value.

II. The current yield is greater than the coupon rate.

III. Interest rates most likely declined after the bonds were issued.

IV. The yield to maturity is greater than the current yield.

(A) I and III

(B) II and III

(C) II, III, and IV

(D) I, II, and IV

186. An investor purchased a corporate bond with a 6% coupon for 101. Depending on the number of years until maturity, this investor might expect a yield to maturity of

(A) 6.15%

(B) 6.10%

(C) 6.05%

(D) 5.75%

187. If a corporate bond was purchased at a price of $1,020 and the basis is 5, what is true of the nominal yield?

(A) It is 5%.

(B) It is greater than 5%.

(C) It is lower than 5%.

(D) It cannot be determined without knowing the number of years until maturity

188. A bond has increased in value by 50 basis points, which is equal to which TWO of the following?

I. 0.50%

II. 5%

III. $5

IV. $50

(A) I and III

(B) I and IV

(C) II and III

(D) II and IV

189. One point on a bond equals

(A) $10

(B) $1

(C) $100

(D) 1% of the current market value

190. Which of the following is rated by Moody's and Standard & Poor's?

(A) Default risk

(B) Market risk

(C) Systematic risk

(D) All of the above

191. Which of the following Moody's bond ratings are considered investment grade?

I. Aa

II. A

III. Baa

IV. Ba

(A) I and II

(B) I and III

(C) I, II, and III

(D) I, II, III, and IV

192. Which of the following would affect the liquidity of a bond?

I. The rating

II. The coupon rate

III. The maturity

IV. Call features

(A) I and II

(B) I, II, and III

(C) II, III, and IV

(D) I, II, III, and IV

193. One of your clients wants to purchase a corporate bond with a high degree of safety. You have recommended four different bonds with varying credit ratings. Place the following S&P bond ratings from highest to lowest:

I. A+

II. AA−

III. AA

IV. AAA

(A) IV, III, II, I

(B) IV, I, III, II

(C) I, IV, III, II

(D) I, II, III, IV

194. Place the following Moody's bond ratings from highest to lowest:

I. A1

II. Aa3

III. Aa2

IV. Aaa

(A) IV, III, II, I

(B) IV, I, III, II

(C) I, IV, III, II

(D) I, II, III, IV

195. Additional features added to bonds to make them more or less attractive to investors would include all of the following EXCEPT

(A) put

(B) maturity

(C) convertible

(D) call

196. A call feature on a bond

(A) allows the bondholder to force the issuer to call in the bonds prior to the maturity date only if interest rates drop

(B) allows the bondholder to force the issuer to call in the bonds prior to maturity if it's to the benefit of all bondholders

(C) allows the issuer to call in their bonds prior to the maturity date only if it's beneficial to the bondholders

(D) allows the issuer to call in their bonds prior to the maturity date if in their best interest

197. Which of the following is the MOST appealing to the issuer of a corporate bond?

(A) A high coupon rate

(B) A put feature

(C) A high call premium

(D) Little call protection

198. All of the following are true about callable bonds EXCEPT

(A) they usually offer higher yields than non-callable bonds

(B) any call features are stated on the indenture

(C) the investor decides when to exercise the call privilege

(D) an announcement of a call must be made before the actual call date

199. The call premium on a callable bond is

(A) the amount an investor must pay above par value when calling the bonds early

(B) the amount an issuer must pay above par value when calling its bonds early

(C) the amount of interest an issuer must pay on its callable bonds

(D) the difference in interest an issuer must pay on its callable bonds over its non-callable bonds

200. Which of the following BEST describes the call premium for debt securities?

(A) The amount that investors paid above par value to purchase the bond in the primary market

(B) The amount that investors paid above par value to purchase the bond in the secondary market

(C) The amount that investors must pay to the issuer for having the bond called early

(D) The amount that the issuer must pay to investors for calling its bonds early

201. Regarding callable and puttable bonds, which of the following are true?

I. The issuer would likely call their bonds if interest rates rise.

II. The issuer would likely call their bonds if interest rates fall.

III. The investor would likely put their bonds if interest rates rise.

IV. The investor would likely put their bonds if interest rates fall.

(A) II and IV

(B) I and III

(C) I and IV

(D) II and III

202. A convertible feature on ABDC corporate bonds

(A) allows ABDC bondholders the right to convert their bonds into ABDC preferred stock

(B) allows ABDC bondholders the right to convert their bonds into ABDC non-voting common stock

(C) allows ABDC bondholders the right to convert their bonds into ABDC common stock

(D) allows ABDC bondholders the right to convert their long-term bonds into ABDC bonds with a shorter maturity

203. If a bond is convertible into 50 shares of common stock, what is the conversion price?

(A) $20

(B) $25

(C) $40

(D) $50

204. A bond is convertible into 25 shares of common stock. The bond trades at 98, and the stock trades at $40. If the bond is called at 102, which of the following is the BEST alternative for an investor?

(A) Allow the bond to be called.

(B) Sell the bond in the market.

(C) Convert the bond and sell the stock.

(D) None of the above.

205. TUV Corp. has issued $10 million worth of convertible mortgage bonds, which are convertible for $40. The bonds are callable beginning in March 2020, while the maturity date is March 2030. The bond trades at 110, and the stock trades at $48. What is the conversion ratio of the bonds?

(A) 10

(B) 16.66

(C) 20

(D) 25

206. A bond is convertible into common stock for $25. If the stock trades at $28, what is the parity price of the bond?

(A) $990

(B) $1,020

(C) $1,040

(D) $1,120

207. Curly Fry Lighting Corporation bonds are convertible at $50. If DIM's common stock is trading in the market for $42 and the bonds are trading for 83, which of the following statements are TRUE?

I. The bonds are trading below parity.

II. The stock is trading below parity.

III. Converting the bonds would be profitable.

IV. Converting the bonds would not be profitable.

(A) I and III

(B) I and IV

(C) II and III

(D) II and IV

208. TUV convertible bonds are convertible into TUV common stock for $20. If the stock is trading at $24, what is the parity price of the bonds?

(A) $1,120

(B) $1,200

(C) $1,320

(D) $1,000

209–224 U.S. Government Securities

209. Debt securities issued by the U.S. Treasury

(A) are all issued in book-entry form

(B) all pay semiannual interest

(C) are sold in minimum denominations of $1,000

(D) all of the above

210. Which of the following are possible maturities for a Treasury bill?

I. 4 weeks

II. 8 weeks

III. 17 weeks

IV. 52 weeks

(A) I and II

(B) I, II, and III

(C) I, II, and IV

(D) I, II, III, and IV

211. Which of the following securities earns interest?

I. Treasury bills

II. Treasury bonds

III. Treasury stock

IV. Treasury STRIPS

(A) II only

(B) I, II, and IV

(C) II and III

(D) II and IV

212. Treasury bonds are

(A) issued at a maturity of 20 years or more

(B) issued at a maturity of 2 to 10 years

(C) issued at a maturity of 1 year or less

(D) issued at a maturity of 270 days or less

213. Place the following U.S. government securities in order of initial maturity from shortest term to longest term.

I. Treasury notes

II. Treasury bonds

III. Treasury bills

(A) I, II, III

(B) III, II, I

(C) III, I, II

(D) II, I, III

214. Treasury bills are issued in all of the following maturities EXCEPT

(A) 26 weeks

(B) 32 weeks

(C) 17 weeks

(D) 13 weeks

215. All of the following securities are directly backed by the U.S. government EXCEPT

(A) Treasury bills

(B) Treasury stock

(C) Treasury strips

(D) Treasury bonds

216. Mary Smith would like to start saving money for her son who will be going to college in 15 years. Which of the following U.S. government securities would best suit her needs?

(A) Treasury bills

(B) Treasury stock

(C) Treasury strips

(D) GNMAs

217. Interest on Treasury notes is stated as

(A) a percentage of the current market value

(B) a variable depending on current interest rates

(C) a percentage of the purchase price

(D) a percentage of par value

218. T-bonds

(A) pay interest semiannually and mature at par value

(B) pay interest monthly and mature at current market value

(C) are issued at a discount and mature at par value

(D) annually and mature at par value

219. Which of the following are debt securities that do not pay semiannual interest?

(A) T-notes

(B) Treasury STRIPS

(C) Corporate bonds

(D) T-bonds

220. These U.S. Treasury securities have interest payments that are tied to inflation or deflation.

(A) T-bills

(B) T-strips

(C) T-notes

(D) TIPS

221. All of the following debt securities make regular interest payments EXCEPT

(A) Treasury STRIPS

(B) Treasury notes

(C) Corporate bonds

(D) Treasury bonds

222. Which of the following U.S. government securities earns interest but doesn't pay interest?

(A) Treasury bills

(B) Treasury notes

(C) Treasury bonds

(D) TIPS

223. Which of the following debt securities are direct obligations of the U.S. government?

I. T-bills

II. GNMA

III. TIPS

IV. T-bonds

(A) I and IV

(B) I, II, and III

(C) II, III, and IV

(D) I, II, III, and IV

224. Which of the following are backed by the full faith and credit of the U.S. government?

(A) Ginnie Mae (GNMA)

(B) Freddie Mac (FHLMC)

(C) Fannie Mae (FNMA)

(D) All of the above

225–238 Money Market Instruments

225. When comparing money market securities with longer-term debt securities, holders of money market instruments would expect that they have securities

I. that are safer than longer-term debt securities

II. that are riskier than longer-term debt securities

III. that will provide a higher return than longer-term debt securities

IV. that will provide a lower return than shorter-term debt securities

(A) I and III

(B) I and IV

(C) II and III

(D) II and IV

226. Money market instruments are

(A) short-term debt

(B) long-term debt

(C) common stock

(D) preferred stock

227. Which of the following are money market instruments?

I. Banker's acceptances

II. T-notes

III. Commercial paper

IV. Treasury bills

(A) I and III

(B) I, II, and III

(C) I, III, and IV

(D) II, III, and IV

228. The risks of holding money market securities include which two of the following?

I. Money market instruments are typically illiquid.

II. The risk of potentially having to reinvest the money received at maturity at a lower rate.

III. Lower returns than longer-term maturities.

IV. They are consider safer than debt securities with long-term maturities.

(A) II and IV

(B) II and III

(C) I and III

(D) I and IV

229. Which of the following are capital market instruments?

(A) Common stocks

(B) Treasury bills

(C) Banker's acceptances (BAs)

(D) Repurchase agreements

230. Most money market instruments are

(A) debt securities with a fixed income and long-term maturity

(B) debt securities with a fixed income and short or intermediate-term maturity

(C) debt securities with a fixed income and short-term maturity

(D) debt securities with a variable rate and short- or intermediate-term maturity

231. A Federal Reserve member bank has deposits in excess of their reserve requirements. They lend this money to another member bank to help them meet their reserve requirements. These loans are

(A) banking funds

(B) depositors' funds

(C) certificates of deposit

(D) federal funds

232. Which of the following is TRUE about commercial paper?

I. It trades without accrued interest.

II. It is backed by the issuer's assets.

III. It is an exempt security.

IV. It matures in 270 days or less.

(A) I, III, and IV

(B) II and IV

(C) II, III, and IV

(D) I, II, and III

233. Corporate commercial paper has a maximum maturity of

(A) 30 days

(B) 45 days

(C) 90 days

(D) 270 days

234. TUBBB Corp. needs to raise money for seasonal inventory. Which of the following securities would they most likely issue?

(A) Commercial paper

(B) Bonds

(C) Common stock

(D) Preferred stock

235. Which of the following is true of negotiable CDs?

I. They are considered money market instruments and can be traded in the secondary market.

II. They are not considered money market instruments, and only non-negotiable CDs can trade in the secondary market.

III. They typically require a minimum investment of $100,000.

IV. They typically require a minimum investment of $1,000 when purchased from a bank.

(A) II and IV

(B) II and III

(C) I and III

(D) I and IV

236. What is the difference between regular CDs issued by a bank and negotiable CDs?

(A) Negotiable CDs can be traded in the secondary market whereas regular CDs cannot.

(B) Regular CDs can be trade in the secondary market whereas negotiable CDs cannot.

(C) Negotiable CDs have a fixed rate of return and regular CDs do not.

(D) Regular CDs have a fixed rate of return and negotiable CDs do not.

237. Which of the following money-market securities is a time draft used to facilitate the importing and exporting of products?

(A) Treasury bills

(B) Banker's acceptances

(C) Commercial paper

(D) Repurchase agreements

238. One of your new customers is currently looking to purchase a new home. As such, they would like to invest their money in securities with little risk. Which of the following securities would be suitable to meet their needs?

(A) High-yield bonds

(B) Treasury bills

(C) Treasury bonds

(D) An aggressive growth fund

Chapter 4

Municipal Bonds: Local Government Securities

Municipal bonds are ones issued by state governments, local governments, or U.S. territories. Municipalities may issue many types of municipal bonds, but the two main types are GO (general obligation) bonds and revenue bonds. Municipal bonds may be backed by taxes or by a revenue-producing facility.

After you become a licensed registered rep, you may not spend a lot of time selling municipal bonds, but you need to know about them for the Series 7 exam; you should expect to be tested heavily.

The Problems You'll Work On

When working through the questions in this chapter, be prepared to

- Compare the differences between GO bonds and revenue bonds.
- Compare other municipal bonds and notes.
- Understand the tax treatment of municipal bonds.
- Determine how new issues of municipal bonds come to market (primary market).
- Analyze municipal bonds and make recommendations.
- Remember rules relating to municipal bonds.

What to Watch Out For

This chapter includes a lot of municipal bond questions, so watch out for questions that require you to

- Recognize the difference between taxable and non-taxable municipal bonds.
- Understand an investor's needs when answering questions regarding recommendations.
- Pay attention to key words, like EXCEPT and NOT, that would change your answer choice.

239–268 GO and Revenue Bonds

239. All of the following are governed by MSRB rules EXCEPT

(A) issuers

(B) registered reps

(C) broker-dealers

(D) bank-dealers

240. Where did the tax-free reciprocal rule for municipal bonds and U.S. government securities originate from?

(A) The IRS

(B) FINRA

(C) The Supreme Court

(D) The SEC

241. One of your clients is interested in purchasing municipal GO bonds and is looking for guidance. You can inform him that

I. they are issued to fund revenue-producing facilities

II. they are backed by the taxing power of the municipality

III. they need approval of voters to be issued

IV. they are subject to a debt ceiling

(A) I and IV

(B) II, III, and IV

(C) II and III

(D) I, III, and IV

242. Which of the following municipal securities is backed by the full faith and credit of the issuer?

I. GO

II. Revenue

III. Double-barreled

IV. Moral obligation

(A) I and II

(B) I and III

(C) II and IV

(D) I, III, and IV

243. Municipal bonds can be issued by

I. local governments

II. states

III. the U.S. government

IV. corporations

(A) I only

(B) I and II

(C) I, II, and III

(D) I, II, III, and IV

244. Which of the following is NOT a source of funding for municipal revenue bonds?

(A) Airports

(B) Tolls

(C) Property taxes

(D) User fees

245. Municipal general obligation bonds are backed by

(A) property taxes

(B) traffic fines

(C) sales taxes

(D) all of the above

246. Municipal revenue bonds

I. are subject to voter approval

II. are not subject to voter approval

III. are subject to a debt ceiling

IV. are not subject to a debt ceiling

(A) I and III

(B) I and IV

(C) II and IV

(D) II and III

247. All of the following are possible sources of funding for municipal revenue bonds EXCEPT

(A) property taxes

(B) toll bridges

(C) sewer and water fees

(D) toll roads

248. Which of the following is NOT an important factor when evaluating a revenue bond?

(A) Feasibility study

(B) Property taxes

(C) Flow of funds

(D) Rate covenants

249. In which of the following instances would a municipal issuer require voter approval prior to bonds being issued?

I. Bonds being issued to build a public school

II. Bonds being issued to build a county jail

III. Bonds being issued to build a toll road

IV. Bonds being issued to build a new airport

(A) II and IV

(B) I and II

(C) III and IV

(D) I, III, and IV

250. All of the following are factors that would affect the marketability of municipal bonds EXCEPT

(A) the credit rating

(B) the dated date

(C) the maturity

(D) the issuer's name

251. Plano, Texas, is issuing $30 million worth of callable general obligation bonds. All of the following are TRUE about the call feature of these bonds EXCEPT

(A) the call feature makes the bonds less marketable

(B) callable bonds have a higher coupon rate than non-callable bonds

(C) the call feature makes the bonds more marketable

(D) callable bonds are issued with a certain degree of call protection

252. When helping a client compare municipal general obligation bonds from different issuers, you should compare

I. population trends

II. the home state

III. wealth of the community

IV. the diversity of industry within its tax base

(A) II and III

(B) II, III, and IV

(C) I and II

(D) I, II, III, and IV

253. Gary Goldbar is a wealthy investor who is in the highest income bracket. Gary is looking for an investment that would limit tax liability and put Gary on equal footing with investors in lower income-tax brackets. Which of the following securities would you MOST likely recommend?

(A) High-yield bonds
(B) Collateralized mortgage obligations (CMOs)
(C) Municipal bonds
(D) Hedge funds

254. One of your new clients is interested in purchasing municipal bonds for the first time. Which of the following information should you take into consideration prior to making a recommendation?

I. Your client's tax bracket
II. Your client's home state
III. The bond's rating
IV. The bond's maturity

(A) I and III
(B) I, II and III
(C) II, III, and IV
(D) I, II, III, and IV

255. Municipal bond insurance protects investors against

(A) market risk
(B) liquidity risk
(C) default risk
(D) inflation risk

256. All of the following could have overlapping debt EXCEPT

(A) a town
(B) a city
(C) a county
(D) a state

257. The largest source of backing for a local GO bond is

(A) property tax
(B) sales tax
(C) income tax
(D) traffic fines and parking tickets

258. All of the following are true about GO bonds EXCEPT

(A) they need voter approval to be issued
(B) they are subject to a debt ceiling
(C) they are issued to fund revenue-producing facilities
(D) they are backed by the taxing power of the municipality

259. Municipal revenue bonds may be issued to fund which of the following projects?

I. A toll road
II. A sports stadium
III. A public library
IV. An airport

(A) I, II, and III
(B) I, III, and IV
(C) I and IV
(D) I, II, and IV

260. Which of the following are true of municipal revenue bonds?

I. They are subject to a debt ceiling.
II. They are typically lower rated than general obligation bonds.
III. They do not require voter approval.
IV. They are backed by property taxes.

(A) I, II, and III
(B) II and III
(C) I and IV
(D) I, II, and IV

261. Due to an economic downturn a municipal bond backed by revenues of a facility did not make enough money over the previous few months to be able to make a debt service payment on the bonds. Which of the following is true?

(A) The municipal issuer will most likely default on the next interest payment.
(B) The interest payment will be covered by tax revenues.
(C) The bond issue will be called.
(D) The facility will be closed until the economy turns around.

262. All of the following statements regarding municipal revenue bonds are TRUE EXCEPT

(A) the maturity date of the issue will typically exceed the useful life of the facility backing the bonds
(B) they are not subject to a debt ceiling
(C) they may be issued by interstate authorities
(D) the principal and interest are paid from revenues received from the facility backing the bonds

263. Which of the following is TRUE of industrial development revenue bonds?

(A) They are backed by municipal taxes.
(B) They are backed by municipal revenues.
(C) They are backed by a corporation.
(D) None of the above.

264. Holders of which of the following municipal securities may be subject to alternative minimum tax?

(A) BANs
(B) Special assessment bonds
(C) GO bonds
(D) IDRs

265. Which of the following municipal securities might be included in the AMT calculation?

(A) GO bonds
(B) Special assessment bonds
(C) Special tax bonds
(D) Industrial development revenue bonds

266. Which of the following would NOT affect the credit rating of a general obligation bond?

(A) Rate covenants
(B) Per capita debt
(C) Assessed property values
(D) The tax collection history of the municipality

267. All of the following are important factors when examining the rating of a general obligation bond EXCEPT

(A) the debt ceiling
(B) overlapping debt
(C) debt per capita
(D) covenants

268. All of the following are important in analyzing a general obligation bond issued by a school district EXCEPT

(A) debt ceiling
(B) traffic fines
(C) insurance covenants
(D) property taxes

269–275 The Primary Market

269. Park City, Utah, decides to issue general obligation bonds to build an expansive children's park. Which of the following characteristics of the issuer should an investor consider when analyzing this issue of bonds?

I. Overall debt

II. Efficiency of the government

III. Rate covenants

IV. Flow of funds

(A) I and II

(B) II, III, and IV

(C) III and IV

(D) I, II, III, and IV

270. Which of the following is the BEST source of information about municipal bonds in the primary market?

(A) The *Blue List*

(B) *The Bond Buyer*

(C) Thomson Municipal News

(D) EMMA

271. Smithtown, New York, is auctioning a block of new bonds to underwriters. What document will Smithtown use to notify potential underwriters about the auction?

(A) The indenture

(B) Official statement

(C) Notice of sale

(D) Agreement among underwriters

272. When accepting bids for a municipal bond offering, what is the municipality looking for?

(A) A syndicate that could sell the issue at the highest price

(B) A syndicate that could sell the issue at the lowest price

(C) A syndicate that could sell the issue with the lowest cost to the municipality

(D) A syndicate that could help the issuer with day-to-day operations

273. An official notice of sale contains all of the following EXCEPT

(A) the bond rating

(B) interest and payment dates

(C) method and place of settlement

(D) the name of the bond counsel

274. Which of the following items can be found on the official notice of sale?

I. Call provisions

II. The name of the bond counsel providing the legal opinion

III. Maturity structure

IV. Type of bond

(A) II and IV

(B) I, II, and IV

(C) II and III

(D) I, II, III, and IV

275. Under MSRB rules, all syndicates must establish an allocation of orders, which states which orders are to be filled first. Place the typical allocation of orders in order from first to be filled to last to be filled.

I. Member

II. Designated

III. Syndicate

IV. Presale

(A) IV, III, II, I

(B) I, II, III, IV

(C) II, I, III, IV

(D) III, IV, I, II

276–286 Additional Municipal Bonds

276. A special tax bond

(A) is backed by charges on the benefitted property

(B) is backed by a private user

(C) is backed by excise taxes

(D) requires legislative approval

277. Smithtown, New York, is in the process of constructing new public sewers in one section of the town. Which of the following types of bonds would most likely have been issued to fund this project?

(A) A general obligation bond

(B) A special assessment bond

(C) A Build America Bond (BAB)

(D) A revenue bond

278. Which of the following is TRUE of special assessment bonds?

(A) They are backed by charges on the benefitted property.

(B) They are backed by excise taxes.

(C) They require legislative approval to be issued.

(D) They are backed by a revenue-producing facility.

279. A municipality issues revenue bonds. The revenues are not sufficient to meet the debt service payments. If the municipality is able to meet the debt service obligation of the revenue bonds by backing it with its taxing power, the debt is termed

(A) moral obligation bonds

(B) special situation bonds

(C) special tax bonds

(D) double-barreled bonds

280. A double-barreled bond is a combination of

I. revenue bonds

II. special tax bonds

III. Build America Bonds

IV. general obligation bonds

(A) I and II

(B) II and III

(C) II and IV

(D) I and IV

281. For clients looking for a safe investment, new housing authority bonds would be acceptable because

(A) they are backed by U.S. government subsidies

(B) they are backed by the taxing power of the municipal issuer

(C) they are backed by rental income, which remains constant

(D) they are typically backed by AMBAC insurance

282. Clint, one of your clients, is interested in investing in municipal bonds for the first time. Clint is primarily interested in safety. Which of the following should you recommend?

(A) Moral obligation bonds

(B) Public housing authority bonds

(C) Special assessment bonds

(D) Double-barreled bonds

283. Akron, Ohio, has issued revenue bonds to build a local stadium. The indenture of the bonds states that emergency funding from the Ohio State legislature would be pursued in the event that the debt service exceeds revenues. What type of bond is this?

(A) A moral obligation bond

(B) A double-barreled bond

(C) Debentures

(D) BABs

284. Which of the following types of municipal bonds would MOST likely be issued to build a bridge?

(A) BABs

(B) PHAs

(C) IDRs

(D) LRBs

285. Which of the following municipal bonds allows municipality to receive from the U.S. government tax credit payments of 35% of the amount of interest paid?

(A) IDRs

(B) Direct payment BABs

(C) Tax credit BABs

(D) Special assessment bonds

286. Which of the following municipal bonds pays interest that is federally taxable?

(A) General obligation (GO)

(B) Revenue

(C) Public Housing Authority (PHA)

(D) Build America Bonds (BABs)

287–296 Municipal Notes

287. RANs, BANs, TANs, and CLNs are issued by municipalities to

(A) provide short-term financing

(B) provide intermediate-term financing

(C) provide long-term financing

(D) provide flexible-term financing

288. All of the following are types of municipal notes EXCEPT

(A) PNs

(B) AONs

(C) TRANs

(D) CLNs

289. Suffolk County is experiencing a temporary cash flow shortage that is expected to last about three months. Which of the following would Suffolk County MOST likely issue to meet its current obligations?

(A) Construction loan notes

(B) Tax anticipation notes

(C) Revenue bonds

(D) general obligation bonds

290. The holders of grant anticipation notes (GANs) are paid from

(A) federal government funds

(B) a revenue producing facility owned by the municipality

(C) property taxes

(D) state funds

291. Which of the following are types of municipal notes?

I. PNs

II. TRANs

III. GANs

IV. RANs

(A) II and IV

(B) I, III, and IV

(C) III and IV

(D) I, II, III, and IV

292. MIG ratings are applied to

(A) municipal GO bonds

(B) municipal notes

(C) municipal revenue bonds

(D) Build America Bonds

293. Which of the following is the highest rating for a bond anticipation note?

(A) AAA

(B) Aaa

(C) MIG1

(D) MIG3

294. Which of the following is Moody's lowest investment grade rating for municipal notes?

(A) D

(B) SP1

(C) MIG1

(D) MIG3

295. All of the following municipal securities could have a rating of MIG3 EXCEPT

(A) PNs

(B) TRANs

(C) CLNs

(D) GOs

296. Municipal bond rating companies are mainly concerned with

(A) likelihood of default

(B) tax implications of the issue

(C) potential of market decline of the issue

(D) all of the above

297–302 Municipal Fund Securities

297. Qualified Tuition Plans (QTPs) must be sold by

(A) a prospectus

(B) a preliminary prospectus

(C) an official statement

(D) a statement of additional information

298. Which of the following IS NOT a type of municipal fund security?

(A) Section 529 plans

(B) ABLE account

(C) LGIPs

(D) LTGOs

299. Municipal fund securities include

(A) qualified tuition plans

(B) TANs

(C) growth funds

(D) RANs

300. This type of municipal fund security provides for educational savings accounts that are available to investors.

(A) TRAN

(B) ABLE

(C) LGIP

(D) 529

301. This type of municipal fund security is designed for people with provable disabilities and their families.

(A) BAN

(B) ABLE

(C) LGIP

(D) QTP

302. This type of municipal fund security provides a way for cities, counties, school districts, and so on to invest their excess funds on a short-term basis.

(A) BAN

(B) ABLE

(C) LGIP

(D) QTP

303–313 Taxes on Municipal Bonds

303. Which of the following is true regarding taxes on municipal bonds?

(A) The interest and any capital gains are federally tax free.

(B) The interest is federally taxable, but any capital gains are tax free.

(C) The interest is not taxable, but any capital gains are federally taxable.

(D) The interest and any capital gains are federally taxable.

304. All of the following is subject to federal taxation EXCEPT

I. interest on municipal bonds

II. interest on U.S. government bonds

III. capital gain on municipal bonds

IV. cash dividends on stocks

(A) I only

(B) I and III

(C) II, III, and IV

(D) II and III

305. Which of the following bonds generally have the lowest yields?

(A) AA rated corporate bonds

(B) GO bonds

(C) T-bonds

(D) Cannot be determined

306. Tito Sonnen lives in Oregon and is considering purchasing a bond. He has settled on either a 4% municipal bond offered by Oregon or a 6% corporate bond offered by Ground and Pound Corp., which has headquarters in Oregon. Tito needs some guidance and would like you to help him determine which bond will provide him with the greatest return. Which of the following information do you need before you can make the appropriate recommendation?

(A) Tito's place of employment

(B) Tito's tax bracket

(C) How long Tito has lived in Oregon

(D) Tito's other holdings

307. Which of the following investments would provide the BEST after-tax return for an individual in the 28% tax bracket?

(A) 4.25% treasury bond

(B) 5% AA rated corporate bond

(C) 4% GO bond

(D) 5.5% preferred stock

308. One of your clients who is in the 28% tax bracket is interested in two different debt securities. One of them is a 6% corporate bond, and the other is a 5% municipal general obligation bond. Which of the following is TRUE regarding his investment choices?

(A) The general obligation bond has a higher after-tax yield.

(B) The corporate bond has a higher after-tax yield.

(C) The corporate bond and municipal bond have an equivalent after-tax yield.

(D) There is not enough information given to determine the after-tax yield.

309. Mr. Jones is in the 31% tax bracket and owns a 6% corporate bond. What is the municipal equivalent yield?

(A) 3.96%

(B) 4.14%

(C) 5.11%

(D) 5.42%

310. You are in the process of convincing one of your clients to invest in triple tax-free municipal bonds. Which of the following U.S. territories issues municipal bonds that are triple tax-free?

I. U.S. Virgin Islands

II. Puerto Rico

III. Guam

IV. Hawaii

(A) I and IV

(B) I, II, and IV

(C) I, II, and III

(D) I, II, III, and IV

311. Which of the following factors should you determine before recommending a municipal bond to a client?

I. The client's state of residence

II. The client's tax bracket

III. The client's investment objectives

(A) I and II

(B) II and III

(C) I and III

(D) I, II, and III

312. Which of the following securities would provide the best after-tax return for an investor in the 24% tax bracket?

(A) 5% municipal general obligation (GO) bond

(B) 4.5% T-bond

(C) 6.25% corporate bond

(D) 6.10% corporate convertible bond

313. Gary Golden is a resident of Atlantic City, New Jersey. Gary purchased 20 New Jersey municipal bonds. What is the tax treatment of the interest that Gary earns on his New Jersey bonds?

(A) It is exempt from local taxes only.

(B) It is exempt from state taxes only.

(C) It is exempt from federal taxes only.

(D) It is exempt from federal, state, and local taxes.

314–335 Municipal Bond Rules

314. Which of the following must be included on a customer's confirmation of a municipal securities transaction?

I. The customer's name

II. The capacity of the broker-dealer

III. Par value

IV. Trade date and time of execution

(A) I and IV

(B) I, II and III

(C) I, II, and IV

(D) I, II, III, and IV

315. Municipal bonds settle the regular way in

(A) 1 business day after the trade date

(B) 2 business days after the trade date

(C) 3 business days after the trade date

(D) 3 calendar days after the trade date

316. Under MSRB rules, all of the following must be included on the confirmation of a trade EXCEPT

(A) the issuer's name

(B) the name of the broker-dealer

(C) the customer's signature

(D) the trade date

317. All municipal advertisements must be kept by the firm

(A) for a minimum of 2 years

(B) for a minimum of 3 years and easily accessible for 2 years

(C) for a minimum of 4 years and easily accessible for 3 years

(D) for a minimum of 6 years and easily accessible for 2 years

318. Advertisements relating to municipal GO bonds must be approved by

(A) the Fed

(B) the SEC

(C) the MSRB

(D) a municipal securities principal

319. Which of the following is considered a gift violation according to MSRB Rule G-20?

(A) Buying a $320 round-trip airline ticket for a client to come to the firm

(B) Spending $120 on business lunch with a client

(C) Buying a client season passes to the Yankees

(D) Sending a client a picture of yourself in an $80 frame

320. A municipal securities broker-dealer sells 100 GO bonds to a customer on a principal basis. How much of a markup may the broker-dealer charge?

(A) 5% of the selling price

(B) 8% of the selling price

(C) 8½% of the selling price

(D) Whatever is fair and reasonable

321. Which of the following would be found on the indenture of a revenue bond?

I. The legal opinion

II. The rating

III. Covenants

IV. Flow of funds

(A) I, II, and III

(B) I, III, and IV

(C) II, III, and IV

(D) I, II, III, and IV

322. The legal opinion for municipal bonds is prepared by the

(A) trustee

(B) municipal issuer

(C) syndicate manager

(D) bond counsel

323. A municipal bond counsel is responsible for all of the following EXCEPT

(A) making sure that the issue is valid and binding on the issuer

(B) making sure that the issue will be federally tax-free

(C) preparing the legal opinion

(D) guaranteeing timely payment of interest

324. In a municipal bond underwriting, an unqualified legal opinion means that the

(A) issue is without condition or restriction

(B) issuer has exceeded its debt limit

(C) attorney giving the opinion is not approved by the MSRB to give a legal opinion

(D) issue is low rated

325. Where would you tell a potential investor that they can find the most information about a municipal bond issue?

(A) The official notice of sale

(B) The final prospectus

(C) The bond indenture

(D) The official statement

326. A principal at a municipal securities firm must approve all of the following EXCEPT

(A) each new account

(B) each transaction

(C) advertisements sent out by the firm

(D) the preliminary official statement

327. Investors would be able to find information about a municipal issuer's financial condition by examining the

(A) official statement

(B) indenture

(C) notice of sale

(D) prospectus

328. Under MSRB rules, how often must broker-dealers and municipal securities dealers send out investment brochures to their customers stating that they are registered with the SEC and MSRB?

(A) Once, prior to the customer opening the account

(B) Once, within 60 days of the customer opening the account

(C) Once, any time prior to the first transaction

(D) Once a year

329. According to MSRB rules, which of the following are considered forms of advertising?

I. Market letter

II. Seminar text

III. Official statements

IV. Offering circulars

(A) I only

(B) I and II

(C) I, II, and III

(D) I, II, III, and IV

330. According to MSRB Rule G-37, what is the maximum contribution allowed for a municipal finance professional to a person running for local government office?

(A) $250 per year

(B) $250 per election

(C) $2,500 per year

(D) $2,500 per election

331. According to MSRB rules, municipal securities dealers have to keep which of the following records?

I. Blotters

II. Political contribution records

III. Customer complaints

IV. Account records for each customer account

(A) I only

(B) I and II

(C) I, II, and III

(D) I, II, III, and IV

332. Under MSRB rules, how long do customer complaints need to be held by a broker-dealer?

(A) 2 years

(B) 4 years

(C) 6 years

(D) For the life of the firm

333. Under MSRB rules, a broker-dealer should do due diligence to make sure any customer trades are executed at

(A) the highest available bid price or the lowest available ask price

(B) the highest available ask price or the lowest available bid price

(C) the average bid price or average ask price of all municipal securities dealers

(D) none of the above

334. Which TWO of the following statements are TRUE?

I. Municipal securities dealers can guarantee against loss.

II. Municipal securities dealers cannot guarantee against loss.

III. A municipal securities firm may share in the losses or gains in a customer's account.

IV. A municipal securities firm may not share in the losses or gains in a customer's account.

(A) I and III

(B) I and IV

(C) II and III

(D) II and IV

335. All of the following would violate the political contributions rule (MSRB Rule G-37) EXCEPT

(A) $100 contribution to a candidate for whom a municipal finance professional (MFP) may vote

(B) $100 contribution to a candidate for whom a municipal finance professional (MFP) may not vote

(C) $400 contribution to a candidate for whom a municipal finance professional (MFP) may vote

(D) $400 contribution to a candidate for whom a municipal finance professional (MFP) may not vote

Chapter 5

Delivering Diversification with Packaged Securities

Packaged securities include investment companies (mutual funds and closed-end funds), face-amount certificate companies, annuities, and so on. The idea is to provide investors a way to diversify their portfolios with a relatively small outlay of cash. Pretty much all investors have packaged securities in their portfolio. What's also nice about packaged securities for investors is that usually the funds are professionally managed, and the management fee is relatively small.

In this chapter, you should be aware of which funds are best for which investors according to their investment objectives.

The Problems You'll Work On

In this chapter, you'll work on questions that deal with the following:

- » Understanding the different types of funds and making appropriate investment recommendations
- » Knowing when investors are eligible for discounts and different methods of investing
- » Determining the sales charge and public offering price
- » Figuring out how funds are taxed and the rules
- » Comparing the differences between fixed and variable annuities
- » Looking at variable life insurance policies

What to Watch Out For

Keep the following tips in mind as you work through this chapter:

- When you're dealing with questions regarding investment recommendations, make sure you take the customer's investment objectives into consideration first.
- Know the difference between open- and closed-end funds.
- Make sure you have a good handle on variable annuities.
- Get a good grasp of what the question is asking and read all the answer choices before picking an answer.
- Pay attention to key words, like EXCEPT and NOT, that would change your answer choice.

336–340 Investment Company Rules

336. For an investment company to be considered diversified, what is the maximum percentage of outstanding shares that the investment company can own of another company?

(A) 1%

(B) 5%

(C) 10%

(D) 15%

337. Under the Investment Company Act of 1940, which of the following would be unlawful regarding the use of a mutual fund prospectus?

(A) Using a prospectus to help elicit a sale

(B) Sending a prospectus to someone who didn't ask for it

(C) Not reading over the prospectus yourself prior to sending it out to a potential customer

(D) Circling or highlighting a particular section of the prospectus

338. Mutual fund redemptions must be completed within

(A) 5 days

(B) 5 business days

(C) 7 days

(D) 7 business days

339. The custodian bank for a mutual fund

(A) provides security in the event of corporate bankruptcy of one of the securities held by the fund

(B) is responsible for the safekeeping of the fund's cash and securities

(C) provides loans for investors purchasing securities on margin

(D) redeems investor shares

340. Which of the following is true regarding Rule 17a-6?

(A) Affiliated persons of an investment company are not allowed to trade the fund's portfolio of securities and are not allowed to buy or redeem shares of the fund.

(B) Affiliated persons of an investment company are not allowed to trade the fund's portfolio of securities but are allowed to buy or redeem shares of the fund.

(C) Affiliated persons of an investment company are allowed to trade the fund's portfolio of securities but are not allowed to buy or redeem shares of the fund.

(D) Affiliated persons of an investment company are allowed to trade the fund's portfolio of securities and are allowed to buy or redeem shares of the fund.

341–384 Management Investment Companies

341. For mutual funds, what is the limit on the quantity of shares that can be sold to investors?

(A) There is no limit.

(B) The limit depends on the type of mutual fund.

(C) The limit is determined by the SEC.

(D) The limit is on a state-by-state basis determined by each state administrator.

342. Which of the following is FALSE of open-end investment companies?

(A) They offer shares to the public continuously.

(B) Their public offering price cannot be below the net asset value.

(C) They charge commissions to customers who purchase shares.

(D) They may not lend money to customers to purchase shares.

343. Which of the following is not true regarding mutual funds?

(A) They make it easier for smaller investors to have diversification.

(B) They offer automatic investment into their funds.

(C) Reinvested dividends and capital gains are taxed yearly.

(D) They may be purchased on margin.

344. While reading a newspaper an investor notices that the NAV of a fund increased by $0.80 while the POP decreased by $0.20. What type of fund does this have to be?

(A) Open-end

(B) Closed-end

(C) No-load

(D) Balanced

345. Blommerman closed-end fund has an NAV of $27.65 and a POP of $27.52. Purchasers of this fund would pay

(A) $27.52

(B) $27.52 plus a sales charge

(C) $27.52 plus a commission

(D) $27.65

346. You may tell one of your clients that closed-end investment companies

I. continuously issue new shares

II. make a one-time offering of new shares

III. may issue preferred stock

IV. may issue bonds

(A) II only

(B) I only

(C) I, III, and IV

(D) II, III, and IV

347. Which of the following is TRUE about closed-end funds?

I. They may only issue common stock.

II. They are generally listed on an exchange.

III. They have a fixed number of shares outstanding.

IV. They are redeemable.

(A) II and III

(B) I and IV

(C) I, III, and IV

(D) II, III, and IV

348. All of the following types of investment companies provide a way for investors to redeem their shares EXCEPT

(A) mutual funds

(B) closed-end funds

(C) unit investment trusts

(D) face amount certificate companies

349. Which of the following types of funds is least likely to provide current income for its investors?

(A) Asset allocation fund

(B) Balanced fund

(C) Growth fund

(D) Corporate bond fund

350. Which of the following are true regarding fixed unit investment trusts and participating unit investment trusts?

I. Fixed investment trusts invest in a portfolio of debt securities.

II. Participating trusts invest in a portfolio of mutual funds.

III. Fixed investment trusts invest in a portfolio of mutual funds.

IV. Participating trusts invest in a portfolio of debt securities

(A) I and II

(B) I and IV

(C) II and III

(D) II and IV

351. You have a client who has never invested in mutual funds and doesn't know where to start. You should inform them that the most important thing is a fund's

(A) sales charge

(B) 12b1 fees

(C) management fees

(D) investment objectives

352. All of the following are true about money market funds EXCEPT

(A) they offer a check writing feature as a way of redeeming shares

(B) investors are prohibited from redeeming the money market fund for a year

(C) they are no load

(D) they compute dividends daily and credit them monthly

353. An investor is looking to invest in a mutual fund that has a high rate of current income. Their best choice would be a(n)

(A) hedge fund

(B) growth fund

(C) aggressive growth fund

(D) income fund

354. This type of fund invests mainly in the stock of relatively new companies focusing on capital gains instead of current income.

(A) Income fund

(B) Aggressive growth fund

(C) Sector fund

(D) Specialized fund

355. Hedge funds are allowed to do certain things that mutual funds cannot. Which of the following are true?

(A) Hedge funds can purchase commodities and foreign currencies while mutual funds cannot.

(B) Hedge funds can purchase U.S. government securities while mutual funds cannot.

(C) Hedge funds can purchase foreign securities while mutual funds cannot.

(D) Hedge funds can purchase corporate debt securities while mutual funds cannot.

356. Which of the following is true regarding a highly leveraged hedge fund?

(A) They purchased a lot of call options.

(B) They purchased a lot of put options.

(C) They purchased a lot of securities on margin.

(D) All or any of the above.

357. Hedge funds

(A) attempt to achieve moderate returns by holding low-risk investments

(B) are available to all investors regardless of their financial position

(C) attempt to achieve high returns for their investors by taking riskier strategies and investing in higher-risk investments

(D) are traded on the NYSE

358. An individual primarily interested in current income would LEAST LIKELY buy which of the following funds?

(A) A municipal bond fund

(B) A sector fund investing in high-tech stocks

(C) A high-yield bond fund

(D) An income fund

359. A ___________ fund only invests in a specific industry.

(A) sector

(B) hedge

(C) balanced

(D) growth or aggressive growth

360. A fund that uses leverage, options, short sales, as well as other speculative investment strategies in an attempt to maximize gains is called a

(A) balanced fund

(B) growth fund

(C) aggressive growth fund

(D) hedge fund

361. Which of the following is true of private-equity funds?

I. They are exempt from SEC registration.

II. They must be registered with the SEC.

III. They may purchase private companies.

IV. They may not purchase private companies.

(A) I and III

(B) I and IV

(C) II and III

(D) II and IV

362. John Lavinsky purchased 500 shares of a municipal bond fund. Which of the following statements are TRUE?

I. Dividends are taxable.

II. Dividends are not taxable.

III. Capital gains distributions are taxable.

IV. Capital gains distributions are not taxable.

(A) I and IV

(B) I and III

(C) II and III

(D) II and IV

363. You have a client who has a high current income and is in the top federal income tax bracket. They are interested in purchasing a bond fund. The best suggestion would be

(A) a U.S. government bond fund

(B) a municipal bond fund

(C) a money market fund

(D) cannot be determined

364. You have a new 35-year-old client who is interested in investing in a mutual fund. They are looking to invest $400 per month and want a fund that will minimize risk as they get older. You should recommend a(n)

(A) aggressive growth fund

(B) life-cycle fund

(C) money-market fund

(D) tax-free municipal bond fund

365. The maximum time an investor has to meet the terms of the letter of intent (LOI) is

(A) 270 days

(B) 30 days

(C) 12 months

(D) 13 months

366. Can an investor redeem their shares while under the letter of intent?

(A) Yes, with no restrictions.
(B) No, not until after the letter of intent has expired.
(C) Yes, after holding the securities for at least 90 days.
(D) It varies from issuer to issuer.

367. Targeted-date funds are also known as

(A) fixed unit investment trusts
(B) life-cycle funds
(C) face-amount certificate companies
(D) a bond fund

368. Which of the following is TRUE about a Letter of Intent?

I. It remains in effect for 13 months.
II. It may be backdated for up to 90 days.
III. Shares may be held in escrow.

(A) I and II
(B) I and III
(C) II and III
(D) I, II, and III

369. A letter of intent may be backdated up to

(A) 30 days
(B) 60 days
(C) 90 days
(D) 120 days

370. What is the maximum sales charge for mutual funds?

(A) 5% of the NAV
(B) 8½% of the NAV
(C) 5% of the amount invested
(D) 8½% of the amount

371. What is the maximum sales charge for a mutual fund?

(A) 8%, which is built into the public offering price
(B) 8%, which is added to the public offering price
(C) 8½%, which is built into the public offering price
(D) 8½%, which is added to the public offering price

372. WXY growth fund has a net asset value of $21.40 and a public offering price of $22.60. What is the approximate sales charge percent?

(A) 5.15%
(B) 5.30%
(C) 5.60%
(D) 5.66%

373. Zippy income fund has a net asset value of $40.30 and a public offering price of $41.80. An investor is purchasing enough of this fund to receive a breakpoint and will pay only $41.55 per share. What is the approximate sales charge percent for this investor?

(A) 3%
(B) 3.1%
(C) 3.4%
(D) 3.6%

374. All of the following are true regarding breakpoints EXCEPT

(A) they must be disclosed in the mutual fund prospectus
(B) they are available to investment clubs
(C) they are available for individuals with a joint account
(D) they are discounts for large dollar purchases of a fund

375. The public offering price (POP) of Skunky balanced fund is $37.62 and the net asset value (NAV) is $36.21, what is the approximate sales charge percent?

(A) 5.01%

(B) 5.08%

(C) 5.22%

(D) 5.91%

376. What is the approximate public offering price (POP) of BullBear aggressive growth fund if the net asset value (NAV) is $27.24 and the sales charge is 3.5%?

(A) $27.89

(B) $28.17

(C) $28.23

(D) $28.77

377. What is the approximate public offering price of Dim Outlook municipal bond fund if the net asset value is $53.66 and the sales charge is 4%?

(A) $55.53

(B) $55.81

(C) $55.90

(D) $56.14

378. Alyssa H. purchased $1,000 worth of Zenith corporate bond fund. The public offering price was $56.40 at the time of purchase. This means that Alyssa was able to purchase 17 full shares and have $41.20 left over. What will happen to that $41.20?

(A) It will be used to purchase fractional shares.

(B) It will be held by Zenith and used for Alyssa's future purchases.

(C) It will be returned to Alyssa.

(D) Each fund will treat it differently.

379. FerdCo Communications Fund has a NAV of $14.20 and a POP of $15.02. FerdCo offers breakpoints for large dollar purchases. If FerdCo is only charging a 4% sales charge for purchases between $20,000 and $30,000, how many shares would Mr. Smith receive if purchasing $25,000 worth?

(A) 1,597.225 shares

(B) 1,662.882 shares

(C) 1,664.447 shares

(D) 1,690.331 shares

380. Which of the following investments is sold at its NAV?

(A) ETFs

(B) Mutual funds

(C) ETNs

(D) Closed-end funds

381. Which of the following classes of fund shares have a front-end sales charge?

(A) Class A

(B) Class B

(C) Class C

(D) Class D

382. Which of the following classes of fund shares are no load?

(A) Class A

(B) Class B

(C) Class C

(D) Class D

383. Which of the following is the most common way investors pay a sales charge on mutual funds?

(A) Front-end load

(B) Back-end load

(C) Level load

(D) Cannot be determined

384. Class C shares are most suitable for investors who are

(A) inexperienced

(B) expecting to redeem their shares in a short-period of time

(C) speculative looking for high risk, and high potential return

(D) expecting to leave the money in the mutual fund for a long period of time

385–406 Investment Company Options

385. Which of the following types of investment companies is most similar to a zero-coupon bond?

(A) Mutual fund

(B) Closed-end fund

(C) Unit investment trust

(D) Face amount certificate company

386. Which of the two of the following are true about unit investment trusts (UITs)?

I. They issue redeemable securities.

II. They issue non-redeemable securities.

III. They offer securities one time.

IV. They continuously offer new securities.

(A) I and III

(B) I and IV

(C) II and III

(D) II and IV

387. Which of the following is not an investment company?

(A) Unit investment trust

(B) Face amount certificate company

(C) Variable annuity

(D) Closed-end fund

388. This investment company does not charge a management fee.

(A) Face amount certificate company

(B) UIT

(C) A closed-end fund

(D) An income fund

389. Which of the following types of investment companies invests in a fixed portfolio of securities and charges no management fees?

(A) UIT

(B) REIT

(C) Face amount certificate company

(D) Mutual fund

390. An advantage to investing in a UIT as compared to a mutual fund is

(A) the initial investment is usually lower

(B) they are redeemable

(C) an investment manager who may be quicker to adjust to adverse market conditions

(D) lower operating costs

391. A tax-free fund invests in

(A) municipal bonds

(B) U.S. government bonds

(C) both (A) and (B)

(D) neither (A) nor (B)

392. One of your clients would like to purchase a mutual fund on margin. You should inform them that

(A) mutual funds cannot be purchased on margin

(B) to purchase on margin they must sign a letter of intent

(C) the minimum deposit to purchase mutual funds on margin is $25,000

(D) the minimum deposit to purchase mutual funds on margin is $100,000

393. John Lavinsky purchased 500 shares of a municipal bond fund. Which of the following statements are TRUE?

I. Dividends are taxable.

II. Dividends are not taxable.

III. Capital gains distributions are taxable.

IV. Capital gains distributions are not taxable.

(A) I and IV

(B) I and III

(C) II and III

(D) II and IV

394. When explaining the difference between exchange-traded funds and mutual funds, you can say that unlike mutual funds exchange-traded funds

I. can be sold short

II. can be purchased on margin

III. represent a basket of securities

IV. real-time pricing

(A) I, II, and III

(B) II and III

(C) II, III, and III

(D) I, II, and IV

395. Exchange traded funds

I. are purchased and sold at a price based on supply and demand

II. are purchased and sold at a price that reflects the current NAV

III. are purchased and sold based on forward pricing

IV. are purchased and sold that the current bid and ask prices

(A) I and III

(B) I and IV

(C) II and III

(D) II and IV

396. Which two of the following are true regarding ETFs and mutual funds?

I. ETFs can be purchased on margin.

II. Mutual funds can be purchased on margin.

III. ETFs have forward pricing.

IV. Mutual funds have forward pricing.

(A) I and III

(B) I and IV

(C) II and III

(D) II and IV

397. Out of the choices listed, which of the securities would most likely have the lowest expense ratio?

(A) Variable annuity

(B) ETF

(C) Growth fund

(D) Municipal bond fund

398. Which two of the following are true regarding exchange traded funds?

I. They can be traded throughout the day.

II. They can only be purchased or sold at the end of the trading day.

III. They have low expense ratios.

IV. They have high expense ratios.

(A) I and III

(B) I and IV

(C) II and III

(D) II and IV

399. An investor decides to redeem shares of a mutual fund. At what price will the trade be executed?

(A) The current bid price

(B) The current ask price

(C) The next computed bid price

(D) The next computed ask price

400. Alyssa Smith purchased shares of a mutual fund. Alyssa will be expected to pay the

(A) current bid price

(B) current ask price

(C) next computed bid price

(D) next computed ask price

401. This type of fund invests in more speculative common stocks.

(A) Growth fund

(B) Sector fund

(C) Balanced fund

(D) Income fund

402. This type of fund is looking for both growth and income.

(A) Global fund

(B) Balanced fund

(C) Money market fund

(D) Specialized fund

403. This type of fund provides a check-writing feature as a way of redeeming shares.

(A) International fund

(B) Balanced fund

(C) Money market fund

(D) Specialized fund

404. A(n) __________ fund would most likely have the most price volatility.

(A) international

(B) balanced

(C) income

(D) money market

405. Purchasers of outstanding exchange traded funds would pay

(A) the bid price plus a commission

(B) the NAV plus a commission

(C) the ask price plus a commission

(D) either (A) or (B)

406. One of your clients is bearish on the market. Which of the following investment choices would be appropriate for this client?

(A) Selling short an index fund

(B) An inverse exchange-traded fund

(C) A hedge fund

(D) Selling short a dual-purpose fund

407–431 Annuities

407. The investment return on a variable annuity is based on

(A) the performance of the securities held in the separate account

(B) the annuity's assumed interest rate (AIR)

(C) the performance of the insurance company's general account

(D) a calculation based on the consumer price index (CPI)

408. Which of the following securities are most likely to make payments to the investor on a monthly or quarterly basis for the entire life of the investor?

(A) Variable annuities and closed-end funds

(B) Variable annuities and face-amount certificate companies

(C) Fixed annuities and open-end funds

(D) Fixed annuities and variable annuities

409. Which of the following is true regarding the mortality guarantee on a variable annuity?

(A) Payments will continue for the life of the annuitant.

(B) The amount of the payment will not change for the life of the annuitant.

(C) Payments will continue for the expected life of the annuitant.

(D) The amount of the payment will not change for the expected life of the annuitant.

410. A fixed annuity is not considered a security because

(A) there is a fixed portfolio of securities held in the separate account

(B) it can't be traded

(C) the payout is guaranteed by the insurance company

(D) all of the above

411. Investors of variable annuities should be most concerned about

(A) the performance of the securities held in the insurance company's general account

(B) the credit rating of the insurance company's bonds

(C) the insurance company's profits or losses

(D) the performance of the securities held in the separate account

412. Variable annuities must be registered with

I. the SEC

II. the State Banking Commission

III. the State Insurance Commission

IV. the NYSE

(A) I and II

(B) II and IV

(C) I and III

(D) II, III, and IV

413. Which of the following is true regarding the early withdrawal penalty for an annuity?

(A) It applies to investors under the age of 59½.

(B) The penalty is 10% added to the investor's tax bracket.

(C) There may be a waiver of penalty for first-time home buyers or disability.

(D) All of the above.

414. Which of the following is exempt from the Investment Company Act of 1940?

(A) Mutual funds

(B) Closed-end funds

(C) Fixed annuities

(D) Variable annuities

415. All of the following securities are covered under the Investment Company Act of 1940 EXCEPT

(A) open-end funds

(B) fixed annuities

(C) closed-end funds

(D) variable annuities

416. All of the following are true of variable annuities EXCEPT

(A) the securities held in the separate account are professionally managed

(B) securities held in the separate account may be mutual funds

(C) investors are protected against capital loss

(D) they are more likely to keep pace with inflation than fixed annuities

417. One of your clients has a variable annuity contract with an AIR of 4.25%. Last month, the actual net return to the separate account was 5.75%. If your client is currently in the payout phase, how would this month's payment compare to the AIR?

(A) It will be the same.

(B) It will be higher.

(C) It will be lower.

(D) It cannot be determined until this month is over.

418. The investment risk in a variable annuity is assumed by

(A) the holder of the policy

(B) the insurance company

(C) 60% by the insurance company and 40% by the policyholder

(D) none of the above

419. The owner of a variable annuity dies during the accumulation phase. The death benefit will be paid to

(A) the IRS

(B) the account holder's estate

(C) the insurance company

(D) the designated beneficiary

420. Which of the following annuity options would hold accumulation units?

I. Single payment deferred annuity

II. Periodic payment deferred annuity

III. Immediate annuity

(A) II only

(B) I and II

(C) I and III

(D) I, II, and III

421. A 25-year-old investor has just received a very large inheritance and would like to purchase a variable annuity. Which of the following purchase options would be best for this investor?

(A) Immediate annuity with deferred payment

(B) Periodic payment deferred annuity

(C) Single payment immediate annuity

(D) Single payment deferred annuity

422. All of the following are ways a variable annuity can be purchased EXCEPT

(A) immediate annuity

(B) payment deferred immediate annuity

(C) single payment deferred annuity

(D) periodic payment deferred annuity

423. A 68-year-old investor owns a non-qualified variable annuity. They invested a total of $38,000. The annuity now has a value of $47,000. They decide to take a lump-sum withdrawal of $12,000. What is their tax liability if they are in the 28% tax bracket?

(A) $0

(B) $840

(C) $2,520

(D) $3,360

424. John Silverhouse has been investing in a variable annuity for 30 years and is about to retire. When receiving payouts from the variable annuity will John receive?

(A) A variable number of accumulation units based on the value of the annuity units

(B) A variable number of annuity units based on the value of the accumulation units

(C) A fixed number of accumulation units based on the value of the annuity units

(D) A fixed number of annuity units based on the value of the accumulation units

425. Which of the two following are true about accumulation and annuity units of a variable annuity?

I. The number of accumulation units remains the same during the surrender period.

II. The number of accumulation units varies during the surrender period.

III. The number of annuity units liquidated remains the same during the annuitization period.

IV. The number of annuity units liquidated varies during the annuitization period.

(A) I and III

(B) I and IV

(C) II and III

(D) II and IV

426. Which of the following payout options for variable annuities would provide the largest monthly payment to annuitants?

(A) Straight-life annuity

(B) Life with period certain

(C) Joint and survivor annuity

(D) Unit refund

427. One of your clients is interested in purchasing a variable annuity that would provide the largest monthly payment. Which of the following options would be most suitable for this client?

(A) Life income annuity

(B) Life with period certain annuity

(C) Joint and last survivor annuity

(D) Not enough information is given to answer this question.

428. Investors holding a variable annuity receive payments for life. This is called a

(A) life payment guarantee

(B) mortality guarantee

(C) deferred guarantee

(D) post-payment guarantee

429. A widowed mother would like to purchase an annuity that would cover the mother and a divorced daughter. Which of the following annuity purchase options would best suit their needs?

(A) Life with period certain

(B) Joint life with last survivor

(C) Straight life annuity

(D) Unit refund

430. An investor would like to purchase an annuity that will pay him for a minimum of 10 years or the balance of their life, whichever is later. Which of the following would meet this investor's needs?

(A) Life with period certain

(B) Joint life with last survivor

(C) Straight life annuity

(D) Unit refund

431. An investor is depositing $500 per month into a variable annuity. Which of the following is true?

(A) The investor is buying a fixed number of annuity units each month.

(B) The investor is buying a varying number of annuity units each month.

(C) The investor is buying a fixed number of accumulation units each month.

(D) The investor is buying a varying number of accumulation units each month.

432–436 Variable Life Insurance Products

432. Which TWO of the following are TRUE about variable life insurance policies?

I. The minimum death benefit is guaranteed.

II. The minimum death benefit is not guaranteed.

III. The minimum cash value is guaranteed.

IV. The minimum cash value is not guaranteed.

(A) I and III

(B) II and III

(C) I and IV

(D) II and IV

433. Which of the following life insurance products has a fixed premium?

(A) Variable life

(B) Variable universal life

(C) Both (A) and (B)

(D) Neither (A) nor (B)

434. The _______________ will affect the value of a variable life insurance policy.

(A) age of the policyholder

(B) insurance company's investments

(C) payout option chosen by the policyholder

(D) performance of the securities in the separate account

435. Which of the following are TRUE about variable universal life insurance policies?

I. The minimum death benefit is guaranteed.

II. The minimum death benefit is not guaranteed.

III. The minimum cash value is guaranteed.

IV. The minimum cash value is not guaranteed.

(A) I and III

(B) II and III

(C) I and IV

(D) II and IV

436. Reps selling variable life or variable universal life policies must have

(A) a securities license

(B) an insurance license

(C) both a securities license and an insurance license

(D) both a securities principal license and an insurance license

Chapter 6

Working with Direct Participation Programs and REITs

Direct participation programs (DPPs) are more commonly known as limited partnerships. DPPs raise money to invest in projects such as real estate, oil and gas, and equipment leasing. DPPs aren't for everyone because investors (limited partners) need to be prescreened by the registered representative and then accepted by the general partner.

DPPs are unique to other investments and even have their own tax category (passive). You should be prepared to answer questions about what makes these investments different.

Real estate investment trusts (REITs), unlike mutual funds that invest in a pool of securities, REITs invest in real estate. I'll give you several questions regarding REITs to round out the chapter.

The Problems You'll Work On

In this chapter, you should be ready to answer questions regarding

- The roles and responsibilities of the general partner and limited partners
- The different partnership paperwork
- The difference between partnership taxes and other investment taxes
- The three main types of partnerships
- The different types of REITs

What to Watch Out For

Be careful not to get tripped up by common mistakes, such as the following:

- Mixing up the roles of the general and limited partners
- Not reading each question thoroughly before choosing an answer
- Not understanding that the limited partnerships have their own unique tax category
- Thinking that everyone is eligible to (or should) invest in a direct participation program

437–457 DPPs, General, and Limited Partners

437. Which two of the following corporate characteristics are the easiest for a limited partnership to avoid?

I. Having perpetual life
II. Providing limited liability
III. Having centralized management
IV. Having free transferability

(A) I and III
(B) I and IV
(C) II and III
(D) II and IV

438. Marge is a 54-year-old investor from Utah who is looking to add some liquidity to her portfolio. All of the following investments would help Marge meet that goal EXCEPT

(A) an aggressive growth fund
(B) an oil and gas limited partnership
(C) blue-chip stocks
(D) Treasury bills

439. All of the following are true regarding limited partners EXCEPT

(A) they have access to unlimited financial information regarding the partnership
(B) they may participate in management decisions since they have a tremendous amount of risk
(C) they may vote to terminate a partnership
(D) they may invest in competing partnerships

440. Which of the following are fiduciarily responsible regarding a limited partnership?

(A) General partners
(B) Limited partners
(C) Both (A) and (B)
(D) Neither (A) nor (B)

441. Which of the following is true of limited partnerships?

(A) They have perpetual life.
(B) They must end on a predetermined date.
(C) They may end by vote.
(D) They must end on a predetermined date or end by vote.

442. Place in order from first to last how the remaining assets are distributed upon the dissolution of a limited partnership.

I. Limited partners
II. Secured creditors
III. General partners
IV. General creditors

(A) IV, II, I, III
(B) I, II, IV, III
(C) II, IV, I, III
(D) I, III, II, IV

443. Which of the following would be considered conflicts of interest for a general partner?

I. Borrowing money from the partnership
II. Providing a loan to the partnership at a lower rate than available at a bank
III. Managing a partnership that is direct competition with another one that he manages
IV. Charging a fee for managing the partnership

(A) I, III, and IV
(B) I and III
(C) II and III
(D) II, III, and IV

444. A decision to dissolve a limited partnership prior to the scheduled dissolution date requires

(A) a majority vote by the limited partners only

(B) a majority vote by the general partners only

(C) a majority vote by both the limited and general partners

(D) a majority vote by all shareholders

445. A general partner has

(A) an active role and unlimited liability

(B) an active role and limited liability

(C) an inactive role and unlimited liability

(D) an inactive role and limited liability

446. Limited partnerships must have at least

(A) one limited partner

(B) one general partner

(C) any combination of more than 10 limited and general partners

(D) both (A) and (B)

447. Which of the following is a benefit of investing in a direct participation program (DPP)?

(A) Professional management

(B) Pass-through of income and losses

(C) Limited liability

(D) All of the above

448. Which of the following is not an advantage of being a limited partner in a DPP?

(A) Pass through of income and losses

(B) Pass through of capital gains

(C) The ability to participate in management decisions

(D) Professional management

449. Which of the following would be associated with a limited partnership?

I. Pass through of gains and losses.

II. Certain programs may receive government tax credits.

III. Free transferability of limited partner interest.

IV. The limited partners are responsible for reporting gains and losses to the IRS.

(A) I, II, and IV

(B) I and III

(C) II and III

(D) II, III, and IV

450. Who assumes the most risk in an oil and gas limited partnership?

(A) Limited partners assume more risk.

(B) General partners assume more risk.

(C) Limited partners and general partners assume an equal amount of risk.

(D) It depends on how the partnership is set up.

451. Which of the following partnerships are limited partners allowed to claim non-recourse debt as a tax deduction?

(A) Equipment leasing

(B) Oil and gas wildcatting

(C) Oil and gas developmental

(D) Real estate

452. When a limited partnership is being dissolved, which of the following is the last to be paid?

(A) Secured creditors

(B) General partners

(C) General creditors

(D) Limited partners

453. An oil and gas DPP's tangible assets

I. will have salvage value at the dissolution of the partnership

II. will have no salvage value at the dissolution of the partnership

III. may be depreciated on an accelerated basis

IV. may be depreciated on a straight-line basis

(A) I and IV

(B) II and III

(C) I, III, and IV

(D) II, III, and IV

454. Which of the following is true of real estate DPPs?

I. Capital growth will come from rent received from the properties owned.

II. Capital growth will come from appreciation of the properties owned.

III. Income will come from rent received from the properties owned.

IV. Income will come from appreciation of the properties owned.

(A) I and IV

(B) II and III

(C) I and III

(D) II and IV

455. The general partner of an oil and gas developmental program is responsible for all of the following EXCEPT

(A) paying the partnership's expenses

(B) managing the partnership

(C) providing a bulk of the capital for the partnership

(D) accepting new limited partners

456. Out of the choices listed, which of the following is the biggest disadvantage of investing in DPPs?

(A) Flow through of gains and losses.

(B) Lack of liquidity.

(C) Capital appreciation.

(D) You're limited to investing in only a few different types of oil and gas programs.

457. Limited partners may

I. compete with the partnership

II. inspect the partnership books

III. vote to terminate the partnership

IV. make management decisions for the partnership

(A) I, II, and III

(B) I, III, and IV

(C) II, III, and IV

(D) I, II, and IV

458–464 Partnership Paperwork

458. Which of the following documents are required by a limited partnership?

I. Subscription agreement

II. Certificate of limited partnership

III. Registration form

IV. Partnership agreement

(A) I, II, and III

(B) II, III, and IV

(C) I, II, and IV

(D) I, II, III, and IV

459. Which of the following partnership documents includes the rights and responsibilities of the general and limited partners?

(A) Certificate of limited partnership
(B) Subscription agreement
(C) Partnership agreement
(D) Both (A) and (C)

460. Which of the following partnership documents needs to be filed with the SEC prior to making a public offering?

(A) Certificate of limited partnership
(B) Agreement of limited partnership
(C) Subscription agreement
(D) All of the above

461. Which of the following documents must a general partner sign to accept a new limited partner?

(A) A prospectus
(B) A certificate of limited partnership
(C) An agreement of limited partnership
(D) A subscription agreement

462. Which of the following investments would require written proof of the client's net worth?

(A) A variable annuity contract
(B) An aggressive growth fund
(C) A face amount certificate company
(D) An oil and gas limited partnership

463. Which of the following investments does NOT require written verification of an investor's financial status?

(A) Oil and gas partnerships
(B) Real estate limited partnerships
(C) Equipment leasing partnerships
(D) Real estate investment trusts

464. Which of the following paperwork is not required for a limited partnership?

(A) Agreement of limited partnership
(B) Bylaws
(C) Subscription agreement
(D) Certificate of limited partnership

465–470 Passive Gains and Losses

465. Which of the following does NOT describe the tax status of a limited partnership?

(A) Any gains generated are taxed as capital gains.
(B) Any income generated is taxed as ordinary income.
(C) The partnership is fully taxed by the IRS.
(D) The tax liability flows through to the limited and general partners.

466. A limited partner's cost basis in a real estate program could be increased by all of the following EXCEPT

(A) cash contributions
(B) cash distributions
(C) non-recourse debt
(D) property contributions

467. Losses from a real estate direct participation program can be used to offset which of the following?

I. Income from an oil and gas partnership
II. Earned income
III. Portfolio income
IV. Capital gains from a REIT

(A) I only
(B) IV only
(C) II and III
(D) I, II, III, and IV

468. All of the following are advantages of investing in a real estate limited partnership EXCEPT

(A) appreciation potential
(B) depreciation deductions
(C) depletion deductions
(D) cash flow

469. Which of the following is true regarding tax consequence of a limited partnership?

(A) Tax liability flows through to limited partners.
(B) Tax liability flows through to general partners.
(C) All tax liabilities are paid by the limited partnership.
(D) Both (A) and (B).

470. Which of the following deductions is allowed for oil and gas DPPs but not real estate DPPs?

(A) Depreciation deductions
(B) Depletion deductions
(C) Both (A) and (B)
(D) Neither (A) nor (B)

471–491 Types of DPPs

471. Which of the following IS NOT a type of direct participation program?

(A) REIT
(B) Real estate
(C) Equipment leasing
(D) Oil and gas

472. Mary Gold is interested in investing $25,000 in a real estate limited partnership. Mary's main investment objective is capital growth potential. If all of the rest of Mary's money is tied up in non-liquid investments, which of the following types of partnerships should you recommend?

(A) Raw land
(B) New construction
(C) Existing properties
(D) You should not recommend a limited partnership.

473. An investor in an undeveloped land limited partnership is mostly concerned with

(A) depletion
(B) depreciation
(C) appreciation
(D) cash flow

474. All of the following are types for real estate DPPs (direct participation programs) EXCEPT

(A) income
(B) existing properties
(C) new construction
(D) raw land

475. Which of the following are intangible drilling costs relating to an oil and gas DPP?

(A) Wages
(B) Fuel
(C) Insurance
(D) All of the above

476. Partners in an equipment leasing program would be allowed to make all of the following deductions EXCEPT

(A) Depreciation
(B) Depletion
(C) Interest expenses
(D) General operating expenses

477. Which of the following oil and gas partnerships drills in unproven areas only?

(A) Exploratory

(B) Developmental

(C) Income

(D) Combination

478. Which of the following securities is least liquid?

(A) Limited partnerships

(B) Municipal bonds

(C) Corporate bond funds

(D) ADRs

479. Tangible drilling costs associated with oil and gas DPPs

(A) can be depreciated yearly and have no salvage value at the end of the program

(B) can be depreciated yearly but have salvage value at the end of the program

(C) cannot be depreciated yearly and have no salvage value at the end of the program

(D) cannot be depreciated yearly but have salvage value at the end of the program

480. Which of the following is NOT a benefit of investing in a long-term equipment leasing program?

(A) A steady stream of income

(B) Depreciation deductions

(C) Capital appreciation potential

(D) Operating expenses to help offset revenues

481. Real estate limited partnerships that receive tax credits

I. have income from historic rehabilitation

II. have income from raw land

III. have income from government assisted housing

IV. have income from all income producing properties

(A) I only

(B) I and III

(C) II and IV

(D) I, III, and IV

482. Which of the following types of partnerships has the highest IDCs?

(A) Exploratory

(B) Raw land

(C) Existing property

(D) Income

483. Oil and gas program depletion deductions are based on the amount of oil

(A) stored

(B) extracted

(C) lost

(D) sold

484. Which of the following partnerships could claim depletion deductions?

I. Real estate

II. Oil and gas

III. Equipment leasing

(A) I only

(B) II only

(C) I and III

(D) II and III

485. General partners of real estate DPPs have

I. limited liability
II. unlimited liability
III. an active role in the partnership
IV. a passive role in the partnership

(A) I and III
(B) I and IV
(C) II and III
(D) II and IV

486. Rank the following oil and gas limited partnerships from safest to riskiest.

I. Income
II. Developmental
III. Exploratory

(A) I, II, III
(B) II, I, III
(C) III, I, II
(D) III, II, I

487. John Wegner is a limited partner in a real estate DPP that invests in public housing. John receives passive income that exceeds the passive deductions by a significant amount and would like to shelter more of their passive income. Which of the following recommendations would be appropriate for John?

(A) Oil and gas exploratory program
(B) Oil and gas developmental program
(C) Oil and gas income program
(D) Real estate program that invests in existing properties

488. Depletion deductions may be claimed for

(A) equipment leasing programs
(B) raw land real-estate programs
(C) exploratory oil and gas programs
(D) income oil and gas programs

489. Frack-for-Life Oil and Gas partnership drills only in proven areas. This is considered a(n)

(A) exploratory program
(B) developmental program
(C) income program
(D) combination program

490. One of your risk-averse clients is interested in investing in an oil and gas limited partnership. Which of the following types of partnerships should you recommend?

(A) A wildcatting program
(B) A developmental program
(C) An income program
(D) A combination program

491. Tito Rousey wants a diversified oil and gas investment portfolio. Which of the following oil and gas partnerships offers the MOST diversification?

(A) An exploratory program
(B) An income program
(C) A combination program
(D) A developmental program

492–502 REITs

492. Which of the following real-estate investment trusts have income that at least partially is derived from rent collected?

I. Equity REITs
II. Mortgage REITs
III. Hybrid REITs

(A) I and III
(B) II and III
(C) I and II
(D) I, II, and III

493. All of the following are types of REITs EXCEPT

(A) equity

(B) mortgage

(C) double-barreled

(D) hybrid

494. A REIT must distribute at least ________ of its income to shareholders to avoid being taxed as a corporation.

(A) 25%

(B) 75%

(C) 90%

(D) 95%

495. REITs are organized as

(A) corporations

(B) partnerships

(C) mutual funds

(D) trusts

496. Proof of financial status for investors is required for all of the following EXCEPT

(A) equipment leasing programs

(B) real estate investment trusts

(C) oil and gas exploratory programs

(D) oil and gas income programs

497. Which of the following is NOT TRUE of real estate investment trusts (REITs)?

(A) They are registered as investment companies under the Investment Company Act of 1940.

(B) Unlike DPPs they can only pass through gains and not losses.

(C) There is very limited trading of REITs in the secondary market.

(D) REITs are equity securities.

498. All of the following securities are exempt from SEC registration EXCEPT

(A) TIPS

(B) General obligation bonds

(C) Special assessment bonds

(D) Publicly traded REITs

499. Which of the following is true of hybrid REITs?

(A) They may generate income from rent.

(B) They may generate income from capital gains.

(C) They may generate income from mortgage interest.

(D) All of the above.

500. Which of the following REITs are exempt from SEC registration?

(A) Registered non-listed REITSs

(B) Listed REITs

(C) Private REITs

(D) None of the above

501. A PNLR is a

(A) registered non-listed REITS

(B) listed REIT

(C) private REIT

(D) none of the above

502. Equity REITs generate their income from

(A) rental income and mortgage interest

(B) rental income and capital gains from properties sold

(C) mortgage interest and capital gains from properties sold

(D) rental income, mortgage interest, and capital gains from properties sold

Chapter 7

Options: Understanding the Basics of Puts and Calls

Options are also known as derivatives because they derive their value from the value of an underlying security. Options give the holder the right to buy or sell the underlying security at a fixed price for a fixed period of time. Options give holders a leveraged position because they have an interest in a large amount of securities for a relatively small outlay of cash. Options are risky investments and aren't for everyone because of the likelihood of losing all the money invested.

Options are more heavily tested areas on the Series 7 exam than on the SIE. Although you may have heard horror stories about how tough options are, using an options chart makes life much easier. You can expect at least as many questions where you don't need an options chart as ones that you do, so don't spend all your time just practicing calculations.

The Problems You'll Work On

To work the problems in this chapter, you need to

» Be familiar with the option basics, such as what is a put and what is a call.

» Figure out questions related to simple option strategies.

» Understand option markets and remember option rules.

» Recognize the best option positions for someone who already owns the stock.

» Calculate maximum gains, losses, and break-even points for investors.

What to Watch Out For

Here are a couple things to watch out for when working with option questions:

» Don't focus entirely on the calculations; you're likely going to get more questions that don't require an options chart than do.

» When using an options chart, make sure you put the numbers on the correct side of the chart.

503–535 Option Basics

503. Unless otherwise stated, a stock option contract represents

(A) 1 share of the underlying security

(B) 10 shares of the underlying security

(C) 100 shares of the underlying security

(D) 1,000 shares of the underlying security

504. An ABC call option premium increased by .65. What is the dollar amount of the increase?

(A) $0.65

(B) $6.50

(C) $65

(D) $650

505. Standard option contracts are issued with an expiration of

(A) 6 months

(B) 9 months

(C) 12 months

(D) 39 months

506. Bullish option strategies include

I. buying calls

II. buying puts

III. writing in-the-money calls

IV. writing in-the-money puts

(A) I and III

(B) I and IV

(C) II and III

(D) II and IV

507. If holding which of the following positions would an investor deliver the stock if exercised?

(A) Long a call or short a call

(B) Long a call or short a put

(C) Long a put or short a call

(D) Long a put or short a put

508. An investor owns 100 shares of DIM common stock. Which of the following would provide this investor a full hedge for this position?

(A) Long a DIM call

(B) Long a DIM put

(C) Short a DIM call

(D) Short a DIM put

509. Bearish option positions are

(A) writers of puts and writers of calls

(B) buyers of puts and buyers of calls

(C) writers of puts and buyers of calls

(D) buyers of puts and writers of calls

510. The buyer of a call option has the

(A) right to buy stock at a fixed price

(B) right to sell stock at a fixed price

(C) obligation to buy stock at a fixed price

(D) obligation to sell stock at a fixed price

511. The breakeven point is a price at which

(A) the buyer would have a profit if the option was exercised

(B) the seller would have a profit if the option was exercised

(C) both the buyer and seller would have a profit if the option is exercised

(D) neither the buyer nor seller would have a profit if the option is exercised

512. An investor who sells an ABC call option with no other positions on the underlying security

I. is bearish on ABC stock

II. is bullish on ABC stock

III. has the obligation to sell stock if the option is exercised

IV. has the obligation to buy stock if the option is exercised

(A) I and III

(B) I and IV

(C) II and III

(D) II and IV

513. One of your clients is convinced that DWN common stock will decline in value over the next few months. Which investment strategy would you recommend to your client that would allow him to take advantage of the expected decline with the smallest cash investment?

(A) Buying a DWN call option

(B) Buying a DWN put option

(C) Shorting DWN stock

(D) Buying a DWN straddle

514. An investor who writes a put has the

(A) right to buy stock at a fixed price

(B) right to sell stock at a fixed price

(C) obligation to buy stock at a fixed price if exercised

(D) obligation to sell stock at a fixed price if exercised

515. Which of the following option contracts are in-the-money when UPP is trading at 43.50?

I. Short UPP 35 call

II. Short UPP 40 put

III. Long UPP 40 call

IV. Long UPP 50 put

(A) I, III, and IV

(B) II and IV

(C) III and IV

(D) I, II, and III

516. Buyers of DEF call options

(A) have the right to buy 100 shares of DEF stock at a fixed price

(B) have the right to sell 100 shares of DEF stock at a fixed price

(C) have the obligation to buy 100 shares of DEF stock at a fixed price if exercised

(D) have the obligation to sell 100 shares of DEF stock at a fixed price if exercised

517. If an investor wants to write a call option, all of the following positions would cover this investor EXCEPT

(A) owning put options on the same stock with a higher strike price

(B) owning call options on the same stock with a lower strike price

(C) having an escrow receipt for the same stock

(D) owning the underlying stock

518. If an SPX index call option is exercised, which of the following is true?

(A) The writer must deliver the underlying index.

(B) The writer must deliver cash equal to the in-the-money amount.

(C) The writer must purchase the underlying index.

(D) Any of the above.

519. A customer purchased an option for a premium of 3.5. This relates to a purchase price of

(A) $3.50

(B) $35.00

(C) $350.00

(D) $3,500.00

520. Which of the following are true regarding the seller of a covered call?

I. Unlimited profit potential

II. Limited profit potential

III. Unlimited loss potential

IV. Limited loss potential

(A) I and III

(B) I and IV

(C) II and III

(D) II and IV

521. Sellers of LMN put options

(A) have the right to buy 100 shares of LMN stock at a fixed price

(B) have the right to sell 100 shares of LMN stock at a fixed price

(C) have the obligation to sell 100 shares of LMN stock at a fixed price if exercised

(D) have the obligation to buy 100 shares of LMN stock at a fixed price if exercised

522. Which of the following would provide protection for an investor who is short ABC common stock?

(A) Short an ABC call option

(B) Short an ABC put option

(C) Long an ABC call option

(D) Long an ABC put option

523. An investor is long 1 GHI Oct 30 call. If GHI has a current market value of 33, which of the following is TRUE?

(A) The option is out-of-the-money.

(B) The option is at-the-money.

(C) The option is in-the-money.

(D) The call has a negative intrinsic value.

524. Which option is out-of-the-money if ABC is at $40?

(A) ABC May 45 put

(B) ABC May 35 call

(C) ABC May 50 call

(D) ABC May 55 put

525. Which option is out-of-the-money if LMN is at $60?

(A) LMN May 65 put

(B) LMN Aug 45 call

(C) LMN Nov 80 call

(D) LMN Dec 70 put

526. An investor is short 1 XYZ Oct 50 call at 3. Which of the following is true of this investor?

(A) The investor can exercise the option to purchase XYZ at $50 per share.

(B) The investor has received $300 for the call contract.

(C) The investor has the right to purchase 300 shares of stock under the contract.

(D) All of the above.

527. A put option never goes in the money and expires unexercised. Which two of the following are true regarding that option?

I. The seller loses the premium paid.

II. The seller keeps the premium received.

III. The buyer loses the premium paid.

IV. The buyer keeps the premium paid.

(A) I and III

(B) I and IV

(C) II and III

(D) II and IV

528. Which of the following would affect the premium of an option?

I. Volatility of the underlying security

II. The amount of time until the option expires

III. The intrinsic value

(A) I and II

(B) II and III

(C) I and III

(D) I, II, and III

529. An October 40 call option is two days away from expiration. The current market value of the underlying stock is 52. What is the most likely premium?

(A) .754

(B) 2

(C) 12.25

(D) 16

530. What is the intrinsic value of an ABC 50 call option with a premium of 4 when the current market value is 40?

(A) −$6

(B) −$10

(C) $0

(D) $6

531. An investor has purchased a put option. At what point will the option have intrinsic value?

(A) When the underlying stock is below the exercise price

(B) When the underlying stock is above the exercise price

(C) When the underlying stock is below the exercise price less the premium paid

(D) When the underlying stock is above the exercise price plus the premium paid

532. A QRS Dec 50 call is trading for 9 when QRS is at $55. What is the time value of this option?

(A) 0

(B) 4

(C) 5

(D) 9

533. A LMN Dec 45 put is trading for 3.5 when LMN is at $47.50. What is the time value of this option?

(A) 0

(B) 1

(C) 2.5

(D) 3.5

534. An investor owns an option that has no intrinsic value at expiration. Which of the following is the investor most likely to do?

(A) Exercise the option.

(B) Let the option expire.

(C) Sell the option.

(D) Wait for automatic exercise.

535. The holder of a call option

(A) may generate income from the premium paid for the option

(B) has a position that will help him limit losses on stock owned

(C) may purchase stock at a predetermined price

(D) will profit if the price of the underlying stock declines

536–573 Standard Option Math

536. Which TWO of the following options are TRUE of an investor who writes a call option?

I. The maximum potential gain is the premium.

II. The maximum potential loss is the premium.

III. The break-even point is the premium added to the strike price.

IV. The break-even point is the premium subtracted from the strike price.

(A) I and III

(B) I and IV

(C) II and III

(D) II and IV

537. The breakeven point on a call option is

(A) the stock price plus the premium

(B) the stock price minus the premium

(C) the exercise price plus the premium

(D) the exercise price minus the premium

538. John Smith purchased 5 HIJ Oct 50 calls at 3.25 each. At expiration, the calls are not in the money, and they expire unexercised. How much did John lose as a result?

(A) $325

(B) $1,625

(C) $2,500

(D) $5,325

539. An investor would face an unlimited maximum loss potential if

I. writing 3 XYZ Dec 25 puts
II. shorting 200 shares of XYZ
III. writing 4 XYZ Dec 30 naked calls
IV. writing 2 XYZ Dec 30 covered calls

(A) I and II
(B) I and III
(C) II and III
(D) II and IV

540. An investor who is long a call option will realize a profit if exercising the option when the underlying stock price is

(A) above the exercise price plus the premium paid
(B) below the exercise price
(C) below the exercise price minus the premium paid
(D) above the exercise price

541. Mr. Couture is long 1 MMA Feb 40 call at 1.75. If MMA is currently trading at $39.50, what is Mr. Couture's breakeven point?

(A) $37.75
(B) $38.25
(C) $41.25
(D) $41.75

542. The breakeven point on a put option is

(A) the stock price plus the premium
(B) the stock price minus the premium
(C) the exercise price plus the premium
(D) the exercise price minus the premium

543. An investor writes an RST Dec 60 call for 7. What is this investor's maximum potential gain?

(A) $700
(B) $5,300
(C) $6,700
(D) Unlimited

544. What is the breakeven point for an investor who writes a Sep 40 call for 3?

(A) 37
(B) 40
(C) 43
(D) 34

545. When selling an uncovered put, an investor would realize a profit in all of the following situations EXCEPT

(A) the price of the underlying stock increases in value above the strike price of the option
(B) the premium of the put option decreases
(C) the option expires unexercised
(D) the option is exercised when the price of the underlying stock is below the strike price minus the premium

546. Use the following exhibit to answer this question

	BID	OFFER
ZAM Dec45 call	5	5.25
ZAM Dec45 put	4	4.25
ZAM Dec50 call	1	1.25
ZAM Dec50 put	7	7.25

What is the maximum potential gain for an investor who sells an RST Dec 50 put?

(A) $150
(B) $415
(C) $4,585
(D) Unlimited

547. Mr. Drudge writes a naked put option on WIM common stock. What is the maximum loss per share that Mr. Drudge can incur?

(A) Strike price minus the premium
(B) Strike price plus the premium
(C) The entire premium received
(D) Unlimited

548. An investor wrote 10 uncovered puts on DWN common stock. What is the maximum potential loss?

(A) Unlimited

(B) The premium received

(C) (Strike price – the premium) × 100 shares × 10 options

(D) (Strike price + the premium) × 100 shares × 10 options

549. An investor buys an XYZ May 60 call for a premium of 5. What is the maximum potential gain?

(A) $500

(B) $5,500

(C) $6,500

(D) Unlimited

550. An investor buys an LMNO May 35 call for a premium of 3.5. What is the maximum potential loss?

(A) $350

(B) $3,150

(C) $3,850

(D) Unlimited

551. An investor buys an OPQ June 30 call for a premium of 6.5. What is the investor's breakeven point?

(A) 23.5

(B) 30

(C) 36.5

(D) 40

552. An investor shorts a DEF Aug 60 call for 7. What is the maximum potential gain for this investor?

(A) $700

(B) $5,300

(C) $6,700

(D) Unlimited

553. An investor writes an EFG Dec 65 call for 7. What is the maximum potential loss for this investor?

(A) $700

(B) $5,800

(C) $7,200

(D) Unlimited

554. Ayla K. sold an FGH July 45 call for a premium of 4.5. What is Ayla's breakeven point?

(A) 40.5

(B) 45

(C) 49.5

(D) 54.5

555. The breakeven point for an investor who is short a put is

(A) the market price minus the premium

(B) the market price plus the premium

(C) the strike price minus the premium

(D) the strike price plus the premium

556. Declan Goldbar buys an ABC March 50 put for 6. What is Declan's maximum potential gain?

(A) $600

(B) $4,400

(C) $5,600

(D) Unlimited

557. An investor purchases an LMN Oct 60 put for 4. What is this investor's breakeven point?

(A) 56

(B) 60

(C) 64

(D) 68

558. An investor purchases an XYZ Oct 65 put for 6. What is this investor's maximum potential loss per share?

(A) $6
(B) $59
(C) $71
(D) Unlimited

559. An investor sells 1 HIJ Jun 40 put at 6. What is the breakeven point?

(A) 34
(B) 40
(C) 46
(D) Cannot be determined

560. An investor is sold 1 WXYZ Jan 35 put at 3.5 when WXYZ was trading at $36.10. What is the investor's breakeven point as a result of this transaction?

(A) 31.5
(B) 32.6
(C) 38.5
(D) 39.6

561. With no previous positions in an account, Mr. Jones writes an XYZ May 75 put for 6.62 while XYZ trades at 63.25. If XYZ later closes at 60.88, what is Mr. Jones's breakeven point?

(A) 54.25
(B) 56.63
(C) 68.38
(D) 81.63

562. An investor writes a JKL October 40 put for 8. What is this investor's maximum potential gain?

(A) $800
(B) $3,200
(C) $4,800
(D) Unlimited

563. An investor writes a GHI May 45 put for 3. What is this investor's maximum potential loss?

(A) $300
(B) $4,200
(C) $4,800
(D) Unlimited

564. An investor writes a LMN May 40 put for 8. What is this investor's breakeven point?

(A) 48
(B) 32
(C) 40
(D) 56

565. Melissa previously wrote 10 MKR Aug 45 puts for 6 each when the market price of MKR was 46. MKR is currently trading at 41, and the options are one week away from expiration. Melissa would like to buy her way out of that position. If she does, how would the second option order ticket be marked?

(A) Opening sale
(B) Opening purchase
(C) Closing sale
(D) Closing purchase

566. One of your customers wishes to liquidate a long option. How would you mark the option order ticket?

(A) Opening purchase
(B) Opening sale
(C) Closing purchase
(D) Closing sale

567. An investor with no other position in RST writes 1 RST Dec 40 put at 3.25. If the put option is exercised when RST is trading at 37.50 and the investor immediately sells the stock in the market, what is their gain or loss excluding commissions?

(A) $75 loss

(B) $75 gain

(C) $575 loss

(D) $575 gain

568. An investor sells a TUV Sep 70 put for 5 and sells a TUV Sep 80 call for 4. If the investor closes the put for 4 and the call for 3, what is the gain or loss?

(A) $200 loss

(B) $200 gain

(C) $400 loss

(D) No gain or loss

569. An investor buys an ABC April 60 call option for a premium of 4. ABC goes up to $75 just prior to expiration. The investor exercises the option and sells the stock in the market. What is the gain or loss?

(A) $1,100 gain

(B) $1,100 loss

(C) $1,900 gain

(D) $1,900 loss

570. Alyssa H. writes an HIJ May 40 call for 9. HIJ increases to $45 just prior to expiration, and the call is exercised. After Alyssa buys the stock in the market to meet the obligation, what is the gain or loss?

(A) $400 gain

(B) $400 loss

(C) $900 gain

(D) $900 loss

571. An investor buys a TTT December 60 put for 7. TTT drops to 50 just prior to expiration. The investor buys the stock in the market and exercises the put. What is the gain or loss?

(A) $1,700 gain

(B) $1,700 loss

(C) $300 gain

(D) $300 loss

572. An investor buys an HIJ August 90 call for 9. If the investor closes the option for 6, what is the gain or loss?

(A) $300 gain

(B) $300 loss

(C) $600 gain

(D) $600 loss

573. Melissa Rice purchased 100 shares of HHH common stock at $50 per share. Two weeks later, Melissa sold 1 HHH Oct 55 call at 6. Melissa held that position for three months before selling the HHH stock at $52 per share and closing the HHH Oct 55 call at 4. What is Melissa's gain or loss on the transactions?

(A) $400 gain

(B) $400 loss

(C) $600 gain

(D) no gain or loss

574–602 Option Paperwork and Rules

574. Which of the following is TRUE regarding option contracts?

I. The OCC sets the contract size.

II. The OCC sets the strike prices.

III. The OCC sets the premiums.

IV. The OCC sets the expiration dates.

(A) I and III

(B) I, II, and III

(C) II and III

(D) I, II, III, and IV

575. An investor purchases a TUV Oct 45 call for a premium of 3. What is the aggregate exercise price?

(A) $45

(B) $48

(C) $4,500

(D) $4,800

576. A FINRA member who has been admitted to membership in the OCC is a

(A) a broker-dealer

(B) ROP

(C) CROP

(D) clearing member

577. An investor owns 100 shares of WXY common stock at $45. Which of the following would create a delta neutral position for this investor?

(A) Buying a WXY 45 call option

(B) Buying a WXY 50 put option

(C) Buying a WXY 45 put option

(D) Either (A) or (C)

578. An investor is short 10 HIJ Feb 20 put options. Which of the following transactions would bring this investor into a net delta position?

(A) Purchasing 100 shares of HIJ

(B) Purchasing 1,000 shares of HIJ

(C) Selling short 100 shares of HIJ

(D) Selling short 1,000 shares of HIJ

579. Position limits are

(A) the number of option contracts that a person can hold on the same side of the market

(B) the number of call option contracts (both short and long positions) an investor can hold at one time

(C) the number of put option contracts (both short and long positions) an investor can hold at one time

(D) both (B) and (C)

580. What happens to open option orders on the ex-dividend date of the underlying security?

(A) The strike price is raised to reflect the dividend.

(B) The strike price remains the same.

(C) The strike price is lowered to reflect the dividend.

(D) It depends on the particular security.

581. Option confirmations must include which of the following?

I. The type of option

II. The underlying security or index

III. Whether it is a purchase or sale

IV. Whether it's an opening or closing transaction

(A) I, II, and III

(B) II, III, and IV

(C) I and IV

(D) I, II, III, and IV

582. Who is the issuer and guarantor of all listed options?

(A) OAA

(B) OCC

(C) ODD

(D) FINRA

583. Place the following in order from first to last:

I. Have a ROP approve the account.

II. Send out an ODD.

III. Have the customer sign and return the OAA.

IV. Execute the options trade.

(A) I, II, III, IV

(B) II, I, IV, III

(C) III, I, II, IV

(D) IV, III, II, I

584. The individual responsible for approving all options accounts at a firm is

(A) a registered options principal

(B) a general securities principal

(C) an office manager

(D) the compliance officer

585. New options investors must sign an Options Account Agreement

(A) at or prior to approval of the new account

(B) at or prior to the investor's first option transaction

(C) within 15 days after approval of the account

(D) whenever the investor sees fit

586. If an investor sells a covered call on stock owned in an account, which of the following is true?

(A) The premium increases the cost basis.

(B) The premium decreases the cost basis.

(C) The investor has unlimited risk.

(D) The trade must be executed in a margin account.

587. When is the last time an investor can exercise an option contract?

(A) 4:00 p.m. EST on the third Friday of the expiration month

(B) 5:30 p.m. EST on the third Friday of the expiration month

(C) 11:59 p.m. EST on the third Friday of the expiration month

(D) 11:59 p.m. CST on the third Friday of the expiration month

588. The OCC uses which of the following methods when assigning exercise notices?

(A) First in, first out

(B) Random selection

(C) To the member firm holding the largest position

(D) Any of the above

589. Options of the same series have the

I. same stock

II. same expiration date

III. same strike price

IV. same type

(A) I only

(B) I and III

(C) I, II, and III

(D) I, II, III, and IV

590. Declan K. is opening a new options account at a broker-dealer. Declan K. must return the signed options account agreement

(A) prior to the account being approved

(B) within 15 days after approval of the account

(C) any time prior to the first transaction

(D) sometime prior to receiving the risk disclosure document

591. The last time an investor can trade an option is

(A) 3:00 p.m. EST on the business day of expiration

(B) 4:00 p.m. EST on the business day of expiration

(C) 5:30 p.m. EST on the business day of expiration

(D) 11:59 p.m. EST on the business day of expiration

592. Which of the following is the riskiest option strategy?

(A) Buying calls

(B) Buying puts

(C) Selling uncovered calls

(D) Selling uncovered puts

593. An investor must receive an options disclosure document

(A) at or prior to approval of the account

(B) within 15 days after the first transaction

(C) only if requested

(D) at some point in-between the first and second transaction

594. Listed options expire

(A) 3:00 p.m. EST on the business day of expiration

(B) 4:00 p.m. EST on the business day of expiration

(C) 5:30 p.m. EST on the business day of expiration

(D) 11:59 p.m. EST on the business day of expiration

595. The OCC is responsible for setting all of the following EXCEPT

(A) the exercise price

(B) the amount of shares per option

(C) the expiration date

(D) the premium

596. Which of the following choices contain options of the same class?

I. ABC Nov 50 call / ABC Nov 60 put

II. XYZ Dec 65 put / XYZ Oct 50 put

III. RST Jan 70 call / RST Mar 60 call

IV. HIJ May 80 put/ HIX May 90 put

(A) I and III

(B) I and IV

(C) II and III

(D) II and IV

597. When the firm chooses a customer to have an option exercised, the firm may use all of the following methods EXCEPT

(A) randomly

(B) first in first out

(C) based on size

(D) any method fair and reasonable

598. Option trades settle in ______________ business day(s) after the trade date.

(A) one

(B) two

(C) three

(D) four

599. If a customer doesn't sign and return the option's account agreement

(A) all existing option positions must be closed

(B) the customer cannot establish any new options positions

(C) all existing option positions must be closed, and no new positions can be established

(D) the customer's account is frozen for 90 days

600. A new customer would like to start trading options. The first entity to determine if the customer is able to handle the risk of investing in options is

(A) the registered options principal

(B) the registered rep

(C) the Options Clearing Corporation

(D) any of the above

601. A broker-dealer is assigned an exercise notice by the OCC. The broker-dealer may choose the customer to assign the exercise notice in any of the following ways EXCEPT

(A) the customer holding the position for the longest period of time

(B) any method fair and reasonable

(C) random selection

(D) the customer with the largest position

602. An investor who is long a call option exercises the option to purchase the stock. When does that trade settle?

(A) T + 1

(B) T + 2

(C) T + 3

(D) In 3 calendar days

Chapter **8**

Customer Accounts: Doing the Right Thing

Certainly, a large portion of your job as a registered rep will be opening accounts. As such, you'll need to understand how those accounts should be labeled, what is needed on the account paperwork, margin accounts, and so on.

I've given you a decent amount of questions so that you will feel well prepared when taking the actual exam.

The Problems You'll Work On

In this chapter, you'll need to have a good handle on the following:

- » The new account paperwork
- » Selecting the appropriate type of account
- » Gathering the right information to be able to make proper recommendations
- » Short and long margin accounts
- » Margin account calculations
- » Telephone Consumer Protection Act of 1991

What to Watch Out For

The following tips can help you determine the correct answers:

- » If you're not sure of the correct answer, eliminate what you can.
- » Don't get your rules confused.
- » Make sure you're getting the numbers right when dealing with margin accounts.
- » Watch for words such as EXCEPT, NOT, and so on, which could change your answer.

603–622 Opening Accounts

603. Which of the following must be verified when opening an account for new client?

I. Citizenship

II. Whether or not their name appears on the SDN list

III. Whether they work at another broker-dealer or not

IV. Whether they have any accounts at another broker-dealer

(A) I and IV

(B) II and III

(C) I, II, and III

(D) I, II, III, and IV

604. All of the following information must be obtained from a new individual customer EXCEPT

(A) the individual's Social Security number

(B) the individual's date of birth

(C) the individual's educational background

(D) the individual's residential address

605. A client's nonfinancial considerations are typically as important as their financial considerations. Nonfinancial considerations include

(A) the client's age

(B) the client's marital status

(C) the client's employment status

(D) all of the above

606. You are in the process of opening a new customer account. Which of the following information do you need?

I. The customer's Social Security number or tax ID

II. The customer's investment experience

III. The customer's occupation and employer

IV. The customer's legal name and address

(A) I and IV

(B) I, II, and IV

(C) I, III, and IV

(D) I, II, III, and IV

607. Which of the following needs to be filled out on a new account form?

I. The customer's name and address

II. The customer's date of birth

III. The type of account

IV. The customer's investment objectives

(A) I and II

(B) I, II, and III

(C) I, II, and IV

(D) I, II, III, and IV

608. As part of the USA Patriot Act of 2001, all financial institutions must maintain

(A) customer identification programs

(B) a fidelity bond

(C) SIPC coverage

(D) all of the above

609. Under the USA Patriot Act, all banks and brokerage firms must maintain ______________ to help prevent money laundering and the financing of terrorist operations.

(A) CIPs

(B) SDNs

(C) OFACs

(D) FinCEN

610. Which signatures are not required on a new account form?

(A) The customer's

(B) The registered rep's

(C) The principal's

(D) All are required

611. Changes inwhich of the following non-financial information might change an investor's investment objectives?

I. The investor growing older

II. Getting married or divorced

III. Investment experience

IV. Family responsibility

(A) II and IV

(B) I, II, and III

(C) I, II, and IV

(D) I, II, III, and IV

612. As a registered representative, you need to keep track of each client's investment objectives. Which of the following changes may affect a client's investment objectives?

I. Aging

II. Getting divorced

III. Having a child

IV. Winning $5 million in the lottery

(A) I and III

(B) II and III

(C) I, III, and IV

(D) I, II, III, and IV

613. Whose signature is required on a new account form?

I. The customer's

II. The registered rep's

III. A principal's

(A) I and II

(B) I and III

(C) II and III

(D) I, II, and III

614. Which of the following is the MOST important consideration when making investment recommendations to a client?

(A) The client's age

(B) The client's marital status

(C) The client's financial needs

(D) The client's investment objectives

615. Your client has an investment objective of total return. They currently have 100% of their portfolio invested in common stocks and common stock mutual funds. What would you suggest they add to their portfolio to help them meet their investment objective?

(A) Blue chip stocks

(B) Preferred stocks

(C) Aggressive growth mutual funds

(D) Corporate bonds

616. Which of the following must occur before a registered representative makes an investment recommendation to their client?

(A) The registered representative must determine the client's suitability.

(B) The registered representative must receive written approval from a principal.

(C) The registered representative must obtain a written power of attorney from the client.

(D) All of the above.

617. Which of the following investments would be proper for investors interested in capital growth?

(A) T-bonds

(B) Municipal bonds

(C) The stock of new corporations

(D) REITs

618. If a client is interested in investing in liquid securities, which TWO of the following would you NOT recommend:

I. Municipal bonds

II. Direct participation programs

III. Mutual funds

IV. Blue chip stocks

(A) I and II

(B) III and IV

(C) II and III

(D) I and IV

619. One of your wealthy clients is in the highest tax bracket and has a portfolio with a nice mixture of corporate bonds and stocks. What would be the BEST recommendation to help the client round out their portfolio?

(A) U.S. Treasury securities

(B) Municipal bonds

(C) REITs

(D) CMOs

620. Which of the following would be the BEST recommendations for an investor who has an investment objective of speculation?

I. Sector funds

II. Blue chip stocks

III. Zero-coupon bonds

IV. Technology stocks

(A) I and II

(B) II and III

(C) I and IV

(D) I, II, and IV

621. Chael Weidman wants to open an account at MMA Broker-Dealer. Chael does not want their name to appear on the account. How would MMA Broker-Dealer handle this request?

(A) MMA would open a numbered account for Chael.

(B) MMA would set up a street-named account for Chael if they are an accredited investor.

(C) MMA would refuse to open the account until Chael agrees to have the account in their name.

(D) MMA would provide a fictitious name for Chael from its book of approved names.

622. You have a new client who would like to open a numbered account. To open that account, what must occur?

(A) The client must sign a written statement attesting to ownership of the account.

(B) The client would need to receive permission from FINRA.

(C) The client would need to receive permission from the SEC.

(D) Choices (B) and (C).

623–640 Selecting the Appropriate Type of Account

623. A registered representative may open which of the following accounts?

I. A minor's account by a custodian

II. A corporate account by a designated officer

III. A partnership account by a designated partner

IV. An account in the name of Mr. Rice for Mrs. Rice

(A) I and IV

(B) II and III

(C) I, II, and III

(D) I, II, III, and IV

624. Which of the following people CANNOT open a joint account?

(A) A parent and a minor daughter

(B) Two close friends

(C) A husband and wife

(D) Three business partners

625. Mr. and Mrs. Faber opened a joint account several years ago as a JTWROS. Mr. Faber was involved in a sky-diving accident and didn't survive. Upon receiving confirmation of Mr. Faber's passing, what must be done with the account?

(A) The entire account would be transferred to Mrs. Faber.

(B) Mr. Faber's portion of the account would be transferred to his estate.

(C) The account is divided up depending on percentage invested.

(D) Any one of the above is acceptable.

626. What type of joint account is typically set up for unrelated individuals where the estate is the beneficiary?

(A) Joint tenants with rights of survivorship

(B) Tenancy in common

(C) Discretionary account

(D) Custodial account

627. Your clients, a husband and wife, open a joint account as tenants in common. If one spouse dies, what must be done with the account?

(A) The entire account is transferred to the survivor.

(B) The deceased party's portion of the account is transferred to their estate.

(C) The account is divided up on percentage invested.

(D) None of the above.

628. Three unmarried business partners have set up a joint tenants with rights of survivorship account. All of the following is true of the account EXCEPT

(A) all of the partners typically would have trading authority

(B) if one partner dies, that partner's portion in account is passed on to the remaining partners

(C) if one partner dies, that partner's portion in account is passed on to their estate

(D) the information from all three partners would be on the account form

629. Most married couples set up this type of account.

(A) A partnership account

(B) Joint with tenants in common

(C) Joint tenants with rights of survivorship

(D) Custodial account

630. Which of the following occurs under the Uniform Gifts to Minors Act when a minor reaches the age of majority?

(A) The account must be changed to an UTMA account.

(B) The account is transferred to the donor.

(C) The account is closed, and the former minor receives a check from the broker-dealer equal to the market value of the securities in the account.

(D) The account is transferred to the former minor.

631. What happens when one partner in an account set up as joint with tenants in common dies?

(A) That partner's portion of the account is transferred to their estate.

(B) That partner's portion of the account is transferred to the remaining partners in the account.

(C) That partner's portion of the account is transferred to their spouse.

(D) Any of the above.

632. Pam Platinum would like to open an UGMA account for a 10-year-old daughter. Pam is also interested in being the custodian for the account. Which of the following governs investments purchased for UGMA accounts?

I. The legal list

II. The FINRA list of approved investments for minors' accounts

III. The prudent man rule

(A) I and II

(B) I and III

(C) II and III

(D) I, II, and III

633. You may open up a joint account for each of the following couples EXCEPT

(A) a parent and a minor daughter

(B) three unrelated individuals

(C) a husband and wife

(D) an individual and their 71-year-old mother

634. Which of the following accounts may a client open up without a written power of attorney?

(A) An account for a spouse

(B) An account for a minor daughter

(C) An account for a business partner

(D) None of the above

635. In order for a corporation to open a cash account, it would need to send a brokerage firm a copy of a

(A) corporate charter

(B) corporate resolution

(C) corporate charter and corporate resolution

(D) neither the corporate charter nor corporate resolution

636. Regarding UGMA accounts, which TWO of the following are TRUE?

I. The minor is responsible for taxes.

II. The custodian is responsible for taxes.

III. There may be more than one custodian per UGMA account.

IV. There may be only one custodian per UGMA account.

(A) I and III

(B) I and IV

(C) II and III

(D) II and IV

637. Which of the following is NOT TRUE about UGMA accounts?

(A) Taxes are the responsibility of the minor.

(B) Certificates are endorsed by the minor.

(C) The custodian cannot give anyone else power of attorney over the account.

(D) The custodian cannot be compensated for services.

638. An UGMA account is a(n)

(A) joint account

(B) individual account

(C) custodial account

(D) trust account

639. Power of attorney is required for

I. discretionary accounts

II. custodial accounts

III. joint accounts

IV. fiduciary accounts

(A) I only

(B) I and II

(C) I, II, and IV

(D) I, II, III, and IV

640. A corporate customer would like to open a cash account for their company. To open the account, you would need a copy of the

(A) corporate charter

(B) corporate resolution

(C) corporate charter and corporate resolution

(D) none of the above

641–664 Margin Accounts

641. A customer's signature is required to open a

(A) cash account

(B) margin account

(C) both a cash and margin account

(D) neither a cash nor margin account

642. Who sets the Regulation T margin requirement?

(A) FINRA

(B) NYSE

(C) The Federal Reserve Board

(D) The Securities and Exchange Commission

643. AylDec Corporation would like to open a margin account at Guess Right Broker-Dealer. To open the account, Guess Right would need

I. to fill out a new account form

II. a copy of the corporate resolution from AylDec

III. a copy of the corporate charter from AylDec

IV. a signed copy of the margin agreement

(A) II and IV

(B) I and IV

(C) I, II, and IV

(D) I, II, III, and IV

644. You are opening a long margin account for one of your customers. You should inform them that they will have to sign

I. a credit agreement

II. a risk disclosure document

III. a hypothecation agreement

IV. a loan consent form

(A) I and II

(B) I, II, and IV

(C) I, III, and IV

(D) II, III, and IV

645. Which of the following margin documents discloses the interest rate to be charged on the debit balance?

(A) The credit agreement

(B) The hypothecation agreement

(C) The loan consent form

(D) The margin interest rate form

646. One of your clients opens a long margin account and fills out the required paperwork. Which of the following are TRUE regarding this account?

I. The securities in the account will be held in street name.

II. Your client will be required to pay interest on the debit balance.

III. A decrease in market value would lower the debit balance.

IV. A portion of the securities may be pledged as collateral for a loan.

(A) II and III

(B) I and IV

(C) II, III, and IV

(D) I, II, and IV

647. A margin loan consent form

(A) allows the broker-dealer to provide a loan to the customer

(B) allows the broker-dealer to loan a customer's margined securities to other investors

(C) allows the broker-dealer to borrow money from a bank for margin accounts

(D) is required for both cash and margin accounts

648. Which of the following documents must be sent to a margin customer prior to the signing of the margin agreement?

(A) Credit agreement

(B) Hypothecation agreement

(C) Loan consent form

(D) Risk disclosure document

649. Which of the following regulations of the Federal Reserve Board regulates how much credit a bank can allow a customer for the purposes of purchasing securities on margin?

(A) Regulation T

(B) Regulation G

(C) Regulation U

(D) Regulation B

650. Which of the following transactions must be executed in a margin account?

(A) The short sale of a corporate stock

(B) Buying put options

(C) Shorting call options

(D) Buying Industrial Development Revenue Bonds

651. A partnership would like to trade on margin. They may do so

(A) without restriction

(B) under no circumstances

(C) only if permitted in their partnership documentation

(D) only with approval from the SEC

652. Margined securities will be held

(A) in the name of the customer but using a number instead of the customer's name

(B) in the name of the broker-dealer

(C) in the name of both the customer and broker-dealer

(D) in the name of the bank rehypothecating the loan

653. Minimum maintenance is

(A) 25% on a long margin account and 25% on a short margin account

(B) 30% on a long margin account and 30% on a short margin account

(C) 30% on a long margin account and 25% on a short margin account

(D) 25% on a long margin account and 30% on a short margin account

654. Which of the following securities can be purchased on margin by depositing the Regulation T margin requirement?

I. Exchange-listed stocks

II. Exchange-listed bonds

III. Mutual funds

IV. IPOs

(A) I and II

(B) III and IV

(C) I and III

(D) III only

655. What is the minimum equity requirement for a pattern day trader?

(A) $5,000

(B) $10,000

(C) $25,000

(D) $50,000

656. In an initial transaction in a margin account, Alyssa Hudson purchases 100 shares of Hopeful Corporation common stock at $12 per share. How much must Alyssa deposit to meet the margin requirement?

(A) $600

(B) $1,200

(C) $2,000

(D) Cannot be determined

657. In an initial transaction in a margin account, a customer purchases 100 shares of RRR at $18 per share. What is the margin call?

(A) $900

(B) $1,800

(C) $2,000

(D) $2,900

658. An investor opens a margin account by purchasing 1,000 shares of ABC at $15 per share and shorting 1,000 shares of DEF at $12 per share. What is the investor's margin call as a result of these transactions?

(A) $1,500

(B) $3,000

(C) $13,500

(D) $27,000

659. One of your customers wants to open a margin account by selling short 100 shares of GHI at $15. What is the margin call?

(A) $750

(B) $1,500

(C) $2,000

(D) $3,000

660. All of the following securities can be purchased on margin EXCEPT

(A) open-end funds

(B) ADRs

(C) warrants

(D) closed-end funds

661. In the initial transaction in a margin account, a customer purchases 100 shares at $32. What is the margin call?

(A) $1,600

(B) $800

(C) $3,200

(D) $2,000

662. Which of the following is true regarding Regulation T and minimum maintenance?

(A) They are set by the Fed and can only be increased or decreased by the Fed.

(B) The Fed sets Regulation T and maintenance, but they may be increased by the broker-dealer.

(C) The Fed sets the maximum Regulation T and maintenance, but they may be lowered by the broker-dealer.

(D) The Fed sets Regulation T, but the maintenance requirement is set by the broker-dealer.

663. An investor opens a margin account by selling short $5,000 worth of securities. What is the margin call?

(A) $1,500

(B) $2,000

(C) $2,500

(D) $5,000

664. A customer sells short 1,000 shares of Sketchy Corporation common stock at $3.80 per share. What is the margin call?

(A) $1,900

(B) $2,000

(C) $3,800

(D) $5,000

665–667 Telephone Act of 1991

665. According to the Telephone Act of 1991, which of the following is TRUE?

(A) You may not make calls to potential customers before 8 a.m. or after 9 p.m.

(B) You may not make calls to potential customers before 8 a.m. or after 9 p.m. local time of the customer.

(C) You may not make calls to potential customers before 9 a.m. or after 8 p.m.

(D) You may not make calls to potential customers before 9 a.m. or after 8 p.m. local time of the customer.

666. While cold-calling, a registered rep finds that one of the people called is not interested in investing with their firm now or any time in the future. What should the registered rep do with that information according to the Telephone Consumer Protection Act of 1991 (TCPA)?

(A) A principal of the firm should call the individual to find out what the problem is.

(B) The rep must stop making cold calls for a period of no less than 30 days.

(C) All correspondence with the individual must be made via email.

(D) Nobody from the rep's firm may contact the individual.

667. Which of the following are exempt from the call time requirements of the TCPA?

(A) Tax-exempt non-profit organizations

(B) Existing customers

(C) Calling potential customers

(D) Both (A) and (B)

Chapter 9

Securities Analysis: Doing a Little Market Research

Instead of just randomly recommending securities to customers or potential customers, you're expected to know why you're recommending those securities. Typically, most brokerage firms have their own analysts who are responsible for doing the research and recommending which securities the registered reps should promote. The two main types are fundamental analysts, who examine the specifics of corporations, and technical analysts, who follow the market to determine the best time to buy or sell. As a registered rep, you'll also be responsible for examining your customers' portfolios to help them keep in line with their investment objectives.

The Problems You'll Work On

The questions in this chapter test your ability in the following areas:

- Making appropriate recommendations based on your customers and their individual needs
- Understanding a customer's investment objectives so you can accurately help manage his portfolio
- Grasping the concepts of fiscal policy, money supply, the Fed, and how governmental intervention is likely to affect the market
- Comprehending certain definitions and economic indicators
- Recognizing the roles of fundamental analysts and technical analysts
- Understanding the different types of issues and their risks and rewards
- Remembering the different indexes

What to Watch Out For

Simple things can trip you up; here's what you need to watch out for as you work through this chapter:

- Really make sure you understand an investor's investment objectives and needs.
- Always be aware of the key words, such as EXCEPT and NOT, that can change an answer.
- Eliminate answers that you know are wrong to increase your chances of selecting the right one.
- Perform math calculations carefully to avoid careless errors.

668–686 Systematic and Nonsystematic Risk

668. Which of the following securities is subject to the LEAST market risk?

(A) GNMA

(B) AAA rated GO bonds

(C) AAA rated corporate bonds

(D) Bond anticipation notes

669. One of your clients is interested in purchasing the common stock from several companies based in Europe. As their registered representative, you should explain to them the risks of investing in these securities. The risks include

I. political risk

II. market risk

III. currency risk

IV. interest rate risk

(A) I and III

(B) I, III, and IV

(C) I, II, and III

(D) I, II, III, and IV

670. One of your customers wants to invest in a retirement plan that protects against purchasing power risk, Which of the following would be the most suitable investment?

(A) Corporate bonds

(B) Preferred stock

(C) Variable annuities

(D) Fixed annuities

671. Zero coupon bonds have no ____________ risk.

(A) reinvestment

(B) purchasing power

(C) market

(D) interest

672. Investors who have international investments are subject to ________________ risk.

(A) political

(B) currency

(C) regulatory

(D) all of the above

673. Which of the following is the risk of not being able to sell a security quickly if needed?

(A) Reinvestment risk

(B) Credit risk

(C) Liquidity risk

(D) Call risk

674. Which of the following securities faces the most inflationary risk?

(A) T-bonds

(B) Utility stocks

(C) Money market securities

(D) Blue-chip stocks

675. A client owns a large amount of Treasury bonds and long-term investment grade corporate bonds. Their main risk concern should be

(A) credit risk

(B) inflationary risk

(C) systematic risk

(D) timing risk

676. If the FDA increases pollution standards that are more costly for oil companies, investors who own shares of oil company stock would most likely see the value of their shares decline due to

(A) purchasing power risk

(B) reinvestment risk

(C) credit risk

(D) regulatory risk

677. Which TWO of the following statements are TRUE regarding portfolio diversification?

I. Diversification reduces systematic risk.

II. Diversification doesn't reduce systematic risk.

III. Diversification reduces non-systematic risk.

IV. Diversification doesn't reduce non-systematic risk.

(A) I and III

(B) I and IV

(C) II and III

(D) II and IV

678. An investor is interested in purchasing debt securities for the first time. If their biggest concern is credit risk, which of the following bonds should they NOT purchase?

I. Income bonds

II. High-yield bonds

III. AA-rated corporate bonds

IV. AAA-rated industrial development revenue bonds

(A) I only

(B) I and II

(C) II and III

(D) II, III, and IV

679. A client would like to make sure their portfolio is diversified. Which of the following are ways that a portfolio can be diversified?

I. Buying different types of securities (equity, debt, options, DPPs, and packaged)

II. Buying securities from different industries

III. Buying bonds with different ratings

IV. Buying securities from different areas of the country or world

(A) I only

(B) I and III

(C) II, III, and IV

(D) I, II, III, and IV

680. Which of the following debt securities has no reinvestment risk?

(A) Municipal GO bonds

(B) Equipment trusts

(C) Industrial development revenue bonds

(D) Treasury STRIPS

681. Which TWO of the following would make a corporate bond LEAST subject to liquidity risk?

I. Bonds with a high credit rating

II. Bonds with a low credit rating

III. Bonds with a long-term maturity

IV. Bonds with a short-term maturity

(A) I and III

(B) I and IV

(C) II and III

(D) II and IV

682. One of your new clients has a long-term investment objective of aggressive growth. However, they are planning on purchasing a fixer-upper home within the next year. Which of the following investments would you determine to be MOST suitable for their portfolio?

(A) Treasury bills

(B) High-yield bond fund

(C) Aggressive growth fund

(D) An oil and gas wildcatting program

683. A customer of yours has preservation of capital as their primary investment objective. Which of the following securities would you recommend to help them meet their objective?

I. AAA-rated corporate bonds

II. An exploratory direct participation program

III. Blue chip stocks

IV. U.S. government bonds

(A) I, II, and III

(B) I, III, and IV

(C) II and IV

(D) II, III, and IV

684. One of your clients is interested in purchasing municipal securities for the first time. You would like to help them purchase a diversified portfolio of municipal securities. All of the following factors are important in municipal diversification EXCEPT

(A) type

(B) rating

(C) amount

(D) geographical

685. A client new to investing has $10,000 to invest and wants to build a diversified portfolio. Which of the following is the BEST investment recommendation?

(A) Purchasing several different mutual funds

(B) Purchasing three different types of bonds and several different blue chip stocks

(C) Purchasing T-bonds and gradually adding stocks to the portfolio with the interest received

(D) Waiting until the client has more money to invest because you can't build a diversified portfolio with $10,000

686. Which of the following is a way an investor can diversify investments?

(A) Geographically

(B) Investing in stocks from different sectors

(C) Purchasing bonds with different maturity dates

(D) All of the above

687–709 Fundamental and Technical Analysis

687. A fundamental analyst examines all of the following EXCEPT

(A) earnings per share

(B) balance sheets

(C) income statements

(D) trend lines

688. A fundamental analyst examines which of the following features of a corporation?

(A) Earnings trends

(B) Support and resistance

(C) Breadth of the market

(D) None of the above

689. The lower portion of a security's trading range is called

(A) the resistance

(B) the support

(C) a trading channel

(D) the bottom

690. All of the following can be found on a corporation's balance sheet EXCEPT

(A) fixed assets

(B) long-term liabilities

(C) retained earnings

(D) net income

691. Use the balance sheet below to answer the question:

Assets		Liabilities	
Cash	$10	Accts Payable	$10
Securities	$10	Bonds Due This Year	$10
Accts Receivable	$20	Bonds Due in 10 Years	$30
Inventory	$20		
Machinery	$10		
Land	$10		

All numbers in the chart above are in millions

What is the working capital?

(A) $10 million

(B) $20 million

(C) $30 million

(D) $40 million

692. If a corporation issues bonds at par value, which two of the following are true?

I. Net worth increases

II. Net worth remains the same

III. Working capital increases

IV. Working capital remains the same

(A) I and III

(B) I and IV

(C) II and III

(D) II and IV

693. Analysts who believe in the Dow Theory would examine all of the following Dow Jones Indexes to indicate economic trends EXCEPT

(A) industrial

(B) utility

(C) transportation

(D) none of the above are exceptions

694. Fixed assets on a corporation's balance sheet include

(A) equipment

(B) patents

(C) trademarks

(D) inventory

695. Current liabilities of a corporation include all of the following EXCEPT

(A) accounts payable

(B) outstanding corporate bonds

(C) wages

(D) declared dividends

696. Which of the following are intangible assets?

(A) Trademarks and patents

(B) Patents and equipment

(C) Equipment and land

(D) Trademarks and treasury stock

697. Which of the following would a technical analyst use to determine whether a security is a good investment?

(A) The price earnings ratio

(B) Balance sheets

(C) Income statements

(D) Trend lines

698. Where would Treasury stock be placed on a corporation's balance sheet?

(A) In the assets section

(B) In the current assets section

(C) In the stockholder's equity section

(D) In the intangible assets section

699. When assessing ABC Corporation's stock, a technical analyst will consider all of the following EXCEPT

(A) the market price

(B) the trading volume

(C) the earnings

(D) market momentum

700. Which of the following Dow Jones stock indexes includes 20 listed common stocks?

(A) Utilities

(B) Industrial

(C) Composite

(D) Transportation

701. If a corporation pays a cash dividend, how is its balance sheet affected?

I. Assets decrease

II. Liabilities decrease

III. Net worth decreases

IV. Net worth remains the same

(A) I and III

(B) II and III

(C) I, II, and III

(D) I, II, and IV

702. Which of the following is the balance sheet equation?

(A) Assets = liabilities + shareholder's equity

(B) Assets + liabilities = shareholder's equity

(C) Shareholder's equity + assets = liabilities

(D) None of the above

703. Which of the following is an index of mutual funds?

(A) Wilshire

(B) Russell 2000

(C) S&P 500

(D) Lipper

704. Which of the following indexes is the most widely used to indicate the performance of the market?

(A) DJIA

(B) S&P 500

(C) NYSE Composite

(D) Wilshire

705. According to the Dow theory, the reversal of a bearish trend would be confirmed by

(A) advance/decline ratio

(B) the amount of short interest

(C) an increase in the DJIA and the DJTA

(D) an increase in investors buying call options

706. Looking at the stages of the business cycle, if the economy is expanding, what stages would you expect to follow placed in order from next to last?

I. Trough

II. Peak

III. Contraction

(A) I, II, III

(B) II, III, I

(C) III, II, I

(D) I, III, II

707. Bearish strategies include

I. selling stocks short

II. buying put options

III. buying inverse ETFs

IV. selling uncovered put options

(A) I, II, and III

(B) I and IV

(C) II, III, and IV

(D) I, III, and IV

708. Rising corporate inventories are most likely to occur during which period of the business cycle?

(A) Expansion

(B) Peak

(C) Trough

(D) Contraction

709. Which of the following are considered fiscal policies implemented by the U.S. government?

(A) Changing reserve requirements and buying or selling U.S. government securities

(B) Increasing or decreasing government spending and changing tax rates

(C) Changing reserve requirements and changing tax rates

(D) Increasing or decreasing government spending and buying or selling U.S. government securities

710–734 Money Supply and Monetary Policy

710. All of the following would indicate that the money supply is tightening EXCEPT an increase in the

(A) prime rate

(B) call loan rate

(C) money available for bank loans

(D) yields on Treasury bills

711. Which of the following is responsible for conducting the U.S. monetary policy?

(A) The Federal Reserve Board

(B) The Securities and Exchange Commission

(C) The Internal Revenue Service

(D) All of the above

712. All of the following are likely outcomes if the Fed tightens the money supply EXCEPT

(A) the lowering of inflation

(B) an increase in the value of the U.S. dollar

(C) the lowering of outstanding bond prices

(D) increased consumer spending

713. All of the following are likely outcomes if the Fed eases the money supply EXCEPT

(A) the lowering of interest rates

(B) higher inflation

(C) a weakening of the U.S. dollar

(D) an increase in foreign imports

714. If the U.S. dollar is strong in relation to foreign currencies, which two of the following will likely happen?

I. An increase in U.S. exports

II. An increase in U.S. imports

III. An increase in the balance of payments deficit

IV. An increase in the balance of payments surplus

(A) I and III

(B) I and IV

(C) II and III

(D) II and IV

715. Which of the following is a way the Fed can use to tighten the money supply?

(A) Selling U.S. Treasury securities to banks

(B) Increasing the discount rate

(C) Increasing reserve requirements

(D) All of the above

716. Which TWO of the following actions may the Fed take to ease the money supply?

I. Purchase T-bills

II. Sell T-bills

III. Increase reserve requirements

IV. Decrease reserve requirements

(A) I and III

(B) I and IV

(C) II and III

(D) II and IV

717. Which of the following is the tool MOST commonly used by the Fed to control the money supply?

(A) Open market operations
(B) Changing the federal funds rate
(C) Changing the discount rate
(D) Changing reserve requirements

718. The Federal Reserve Board is responsible for all of the following EXCEPT

(A) open market operations
(B) setting the prime rate
(C) setting the discount rate
(D) setting minimum margin requirements

719. Which of the following outstanding bonds will likely decrease MOST in price if the Fed increases the discount rate?

(A) T-bills
(B) T-notes
(C) T-bonds
(D) Cannot be determined

720. Which of the following actions may the Fed take to tighten the money supply?

I. Increase reserve requirements.
II. Lower reserve requirements.
III. Raise the discount rate.
IV. Lower the discount rate.

(A) I and III
(B) I and IV
(C) II and III
(D) II and IV

721. The discount rate is

(A) the interest rate that banks charge their best customers for loans
(B) the interest rate that the Fed charges banks for loans
(C) the interest rate charged in margin accounts
(D) the interest rate that banks charge each other for overnight loans

722. If the Fed increases the discount rate, all of the following would occur EXCEPT

(A) bond yields increase
(B) stock prices decrease
(C) the federal funds rate increases
(D) inflation increases

723. Which type of company is most adversely affected by increasing interest rates?

(A) A brewery
(B) Household appliances
(C) Utilities
(D) Tobacco

724. The Fed Funds rate is

(A) the interest rate that banks charge each other for overnight loans
(B) the interest rate that the banks charge their best customers for loans
(C) the interest rate that the Fed charges banks for loans
(D) the interest rate charged in margin accounts

725. The Federal Reserve Board (Fed or FRB) is responsible for which of the following?

(A) Setting Regulation T
(B) Setting reserve requirements
(C) Easing the money supply
(D) All of the above

726. Which of the following actions may the Federal Reserve take to ease the money supply?

I. Increase reserve requirements.
II. Lower reserve requirements.
III. Buy U.S. government securities.
IV. Sell U.S. government securities.

(A) I and III
(B) I and IV
(C) II and III
(D) II and IV

727. If the Fed increases the discount rate, all of the following would likely occur EXCEPT

(A) inflation increases

(B) yields on bonds increase

(C) stock prices decrease

(D) the call loan rate increases

728. If the federal government believes the economy is running too hot, what can they do to slow the economy?

(A) Give out stimulus checks.

(B) Increase government spending.

(C) Purchase U.S. government securities from banks.

(D) Increase taxes.

729. Which of the following would cause an increase in the balance of trade deficit?

I. An increase in imports of foreign goods

II. An increase in exports of U.S. goods

III. Overseas investors buying land in the United States

IV. U.S. investors buying ADRs

(A) II and III

(B) I and IV

(C) I, III, and IV

(D) II, III, and IV

730. The Federal Reserve Board would likely be inclined to increase the money supply in which of the following conditions?

(A) Rising home prices

(B) Declining GDP

(C) Decreasing interest rates

(D) Decreasing bond yields

731. The U.S. dollar has been on a steady decline to foreign currencies. If this continues, which of the following are likely to occur?

(A) U.S. exports are likely to fall.

(B) The Euro will buy fewer U.S. dollars.

(C) U.S. products will cost more for foreign consumers.

(D) U.S. exports will increase.

732. Which of the following interest rates is considered the most volatile?

(A) The prime rate

(B) The rate on one-year T-bills

(C) The Fed Funds rate

(D) The discount rate

733. Which of the following will likely happen if the U.S. dollar weakens against foreign currencies?

(A) An increase in U.S. exports and a surplus in the balance of payments

(B) An increase in U.S. exports and a deficit in the balance of payments

(C) An increase in U.S. imports and a deficit in the balance of payments

(D) An increase in U.S. imports and a surplus in the balance of payments

734. The U.S. dollar has been steadily falling against the euro. If the pattern continues, which of the following statements would be TRUE?

I. The amount of U.S. exports would likely increase.

II. The amount of U.S. exports would likely decrease.

III. This would most likely happen during a tight-money period.

IV. This would most likely happen during an easy-money period.

(A) I and III

(B) I and IV

(C) II and III

(D) II and IV

735–744 Economic Indicators

735. All of the following are leading indicators EXCEPT

(A) the prime rate
(B) M2 money supply
(C) the discount rate
(D) stock prices

736. Which of the following is a leading economic indicator?

(A) Industrial production
(B) The unemployment rate
(C) Building permits
(D) GDP

737. Which of the following is a lagging economic indicator?

(A) Personal income
(B) Industrial production
(C) Prime rate
(D) Fed Funds rate

738. Which of the following is a coincidental economic indicator?

(A) Personal income
(B) M2 money supply
(C) Corporate profits
(D) Unemployment rate

739. A recession occurs when there is a negative gross domestic product (GDP), increases in unemployment, falling retail sales, and a lowering of income and manufacturing for a period of

(A) 60 days
(B) 1 year
(C) 1 quarter
(D) 2 consecutive quarters

740. Which of the following is the best measure of a nation's economic activity by its citizens?

(A) GDP
(B) GNP
(C) CPI
(D) DJIA

741. During a period in which inflation is historically low and we have just entered a recession, the Federal Reserve will likely take which of the following actions?

(A) Buy U.S. government securities in the open market.
(B) Increase reserve requirements.
(C) Increase Regulation T.
(D) Lower the tax rate.

742. Which of the following measures the inflation rate?

(A) GDP
(B) GNP
(C) CPI
(D) DJIA

743. Which of the following is not a leading indicator?

(A) Unemployment claims
(B) Personal income
(C) Reserve requirements
(D) The money supply

744. Which of the following is measured in constant dollars?

(A) The Fed Funds rate
(B) The M2 money supply
(C) The prime rate
(D) The GDP

745–752 Cyclical, Defensive, and Growth Investments

745. Which of the following types of companies would be most adversely affected by rising interest rates?

(A) Alcohol

(B) Household appliances

(C) Utilities

(D) Pharmaceutical

746. During periods of economic downturns, which of the following types of companies would be most adversely affected?

(A) Food

(B) Household appliances

(C) Clothing

(D) Pharmaceutical

747. Which of the following types of companies are countercyclical?

(A) Discount retailers

(B) Alcohol

(C) Clothing

(D) Tobacco

748. Growth companies include

(A) clothing

(B) cosmetic

(C) technology

(D) tobacco

749. In relation to how economic factors affect securities, which of the following is a true statement?

(A) Clothing manufacturers are growth companies.

(B) Alcohol companies are defensive.

(C) Tourism companies are countercyclical.

(D) Fast food companies are cyclical.

750. GLD stock tends to move in the opposite direction of the economy. GLD would be termed

(A) defensive stock

(B) blue chip stock

(C) cyclical stock

(D) countercyclical stock

751. A client wants to strengthen their portfolio by adding some defensive stocks. Which of the following stocks would be defensive?

I. Appliance company

II. Automotive

III. Pharmaceutical

IV. Alcohol

(A) I and II

(B) III and IV

(C) I, III, and IV

(D) I and III

752. Which of the following are defensive industries?

I. Household appliances

II. Food

III. Pharmaceutical

IV. Tobacco

(A) II, III, and IV

(B) I, II, and III

(C) III and IV

(D) II and III

753–755 Economic Theories

753. The economic theory that says that less government spending and lower taxes will result in economic growth is

(A) the monetary theory

(B) demand-side theory

(C) supply-side theory

(D) Keynesian theory

754. This economic theory promotes government spending, borrowing money, and raising taxes as a way to stimulate the economy.

(A) The monetary theory

(B) Keynesian theory

(C) Supply-side theory

(D) None of the above

755. This economic theory that supports controlling the money supply in order to stimulate economic growth is called

(A) the FRB

(B) the Keynesian theory

(C) supply-side theory

(D) the monetarist theory

Chapter 10

Securities Markets: Taking Orders and Executing Trades

As a registered rep, you'll need to know the intricacies of orders and trades and, if needed, be able to explain them to customers or potential customers. This chapter covers questions about the different securities markets, primary and secondary markets, the roles of broker-dealers, types of orders, reporting systems, and so on.

The Problems You'll Work On

In this chapter, you should be prepared to answer questions on

- » The different securities markets
- » The difference between the primary and secondary markets
- » The roles of brokers and dealers
- » The different types of orders
- » The rules and reasons for short sales
- » Some of the rules of the Securities Exchange Act of 1934

What to Watch Out For

As you work through the problems in this chapter, keep the following in mind:

- » Make sure you know the difference between the role of a broker and a dealer.
- » Read each question and answer choice completely before answering each question.
- » Watch out for key words, such as EXCEPT and NOT, that can change the answer you're looking for.
- » Focus on the last sentence of each question to make sure you know what's being asked.

756–763 Primary and Secondary Market

756. All of the following trades occur in the secondary market EXCEPT

(A) a syndicate selling new issues of municipal GO bonds to the public

(B) a designated market maker purchasing common stock for their own account

(C) a corporation selling its shares of treasury stock to the public using the services of a broker-dealer

(D) a trade between an insurance company and a bank without using the services of a broker-dealer

757. The first time a corporation ever sells securities is called a(n)

(A) primary offering

(B) first market trade

(C) opening transaction

(D) initial public offering

758. A corporation was authorized to sell 50 million shares to the public. In the initial public offering, they only sold 30 million shares. One year later, they now want to sell another 5 million shares. The 5 million shares being sold would be a

(A) primary offering

(B) first market trade

(C) secondary offering

(D) second market trade

759. Which of the following describe the secondary market?

I. The trading for OTC issues

II. The trading of listed securities

III. The trading of outstanding issues

IV. The underwriting of new issues

(A) I and III

(B) II and IV

(C) I, II, and III

(D) I, II, and IV

760. Which TWO of the following are true regarding primary and secondary distributions?

I. Primary distributions are involved in the sale of new shares by the issuing corporation.

II. Primary distributions are involved in the sale of previously issued and outstanding shares.

III. Secondary distributions are involved in the sale of new shares by the issuing corporation.

IV. Secondary distributions are involved in the sale of previously issued and outstanding shares.

(A) I and III

(B) I and IV

(C) II and III

(D) II and IV

761. The second market is

(A) listed securities trading OTC

(B) listed securities trading on an exchange

(C) institutional trading without using the services of a broker-dealer

(D) unlisted securities trading OTC

762. Which of the following BEST describes a third market trade?

(A) Listed securities trading on an exchange

(B) Unlisted securities trading OTC

(C) Listed securities trading OTC

(D) Institutional trading without using the services of a broker-dealer

763. A trade of securities between ABC Bank and DEF Insurance Company without using the services of a broker-dealer would be a

(A) first market trade

(B) second market trade

(C) third market trade

(D) fourth market trade

764–774 Making the Trade

764. Who is responsible for maintaining a fair and orderly market on the NYSE trading floor?

(A) Floor brokers

(B) Designated market makers

(C) Two-dollar brokers

(D) Order book officials

765. The New York Stock Exchange (NYSE) is an

(A) auction market

(B) negotiated market

(C) free market

(D) unregulated market

766. Which of the following are TRUE regarding listed and unlisted securities?

(A) Listed securities can only be traded on an exchange, and unlisted securities can be traded on an exchange and over the counter.

(B) Listed securities can only be traded on an exchange, and unlisted securities can only be traded over the counter.

(C) Listed securities can be traded on an exchange and over the counter; unlisted securities can only be traded over the counter.

(D) Listed securities can only be traded over the counter, and unlisted securities can only be traded on an exchange.

767. All of the following are stock exchanges EXCEPT

(A) CBOE

(B) NYSE

(C) Nasdaq BX

(D) OTCBB

768. Corporations too small to be placed on the OTCBB may still sell their securities in the

(A) pink market

(B) green market

(C) blue list

(D) yellow sheets

769. A designated market maker (DMM) executes trades as a

(A) broker

(B) dealer

(C) broker or dealer

(D) market maker

770. Which TWO of the following are true regarding commission and markups or markdowns?

I. The markup or markdown must be disclosed on a dealer transaction.

II. The markup or markdown need not be disclosed on a dealer transaction.

III. The commission must be disclosed on a broker transaction.

IV. The commission need not be disclosed on a broker transaction.

(A) I and III

(B) I and IV

(C) II and III

(D) II and IV

771. The over-the-counter market is best described as

(A) an auction market

(B) a negotiated market

(C) unregulated market

(D) Choices (A) and (C)

772. In the over-the-counter market, the term spread means

(A) the difference between bid and asked prices of a security

(B) the difference between the opening and closing prices of a security

(C) the difference between the par value and market value of a security

(D) the difference between the price a dealer paid to have a security in inventory and the market price

773. A member of a stock exchange who is responsible for making sure that there is liquidity for a particular security and is willing to purchase and sell during all times the market is open is called a

(A) broker

(B) registrar

(C) transfer agent

(D) market maker

774. When can a firm act as a broker and dealer for the same trade?

(A) Whenever deemed necessary

(B) For trades in excess of $50,000 only

(C) For trades in excess of $100,000 only

(D) Under no circumstances

775–781 Broker-Dealer

775. A broker-dealer charges a commission for a customer's stock purchase. The broker-dealer is acting as a(n)

(A) agent

(B) underwriter

(C) market maker

(D) principal

776. Which two of the following are TRUE?

I. Dealers charge a markup or markdown for trades.

II. Dealers charge a commission for trades.

III. Brokers charge a markup or markdown for trades.

IV. Brokers charge a commission for trades.

(A) I and III

(B) I and IV

(C) II and III

(D) II and IV

777. When a broker-dealer makes a market in a particular security, they are acting as a(n)

(A) agent

(B) broker

(C) principal

(D) syndicate member

778. An accredited investor is dealing with a few different broker-dealers. They would like to be able to have all of the statements combined into one. They can use the services of a(n)

(A) introducing broker

(B) clearing broker

(C) prime broker

(D) market maker

779. Which of the following would not only handle orders to buy and sell, but also maintain custody of a customer's securities and cash?

(A) Introducing broker

(B) Clearing broker

(C) A two dollar broker

(D) A designated market maker

780. Which of the following types of firms does not execute trades for customers?

(A) Introducing brokers
(B) Clearing brokers
(C) Prime brokers
(D) None of the above

781. Which TWO of the following are TRUE relating to a firm that sells securities out of its own inventory?

I. It is acting as a broker.
II. It is acting as a dealer.
III. It charges a commission.
IV. It charges a markup.

(A) I and III
(B) I and IV
(C) II and III
(D) II and IV

782–810 Executing Customer Orders

782. Short sellers are

(A) bullish
(B) bearish
(C) bullish/neutral
(D) bearish/neutral

783. All of the following are reasons why an investor might sell a security short EXCEPT

(A) to take advantage of a bullish market
(B) to take advantage of an arbitrage situation
(C) for speculation
(D) for hedging an existing position

784. A market order to sell is

(A) price specific to purchase at the lowest ask price
(B) price specific to purchase at the highest bid price
(C) not price specific to purchase at the lowest ask price
(D) not price specific to purchase at the highest bid price

785. A market order to buy is

(A) price specific to purchase at the lowest ask price
(B) price specific to purchase at the highest bid price
(C) not price specific to purchase at the lowest ask price
(D) not price specific to purchase at the highest bid price

786. Which TWO of the following are TRUE of short sellers?

I. They are taking a bullish position.
II. They are taking a bearish position.
III. They have a maximum gain potential that is unlimited.
IV. They have a maximum loss potential that is unlimited.

(A) I and III
(B) I and IV
(C) II and III
(D) II and IV

787. All of the following securities are typically sold short EXCEPT

(A) over-the-counter common stock
(B) preferred stock
(C) exchange-listed stock
(D) municipal bonds

788. All of the following are TRUE of short sales EXCEPT

(A) they must be executed in margin accounts

(B) securities listed on an exchange may be sold short

(C) short sellers have unlimited risk

(D) OTCBB stocks may be sold short

789. Which of the following orders becomes a market order as soon as the underlying security passes a specific price?

(A) Limit

(B) Stop limit

(C) Market

(D) Stop

790. Why would an investor place a stop order?

I. To protect the profit on a long position

II. To protect the profit on a short position

III. To limit the loss on a long position

IV. To limit the loss on a short position

(A) I and II

(B) II and IV

(C) III and IV

(D) All of the above

791. One of your clients has an unrealized gain from selling short FFF common stock. If your client wants to protect their profit, you should recommend that they enter a

(A) buy stop order on FFF

(B) buy limit order on FFF

(C) sell stop order on FFF

(D) sell limit order on FFF

792. Sell stop orders are entered

(A) below the current market price

(B) at the current market price

(C) above the current market price

(D) either at or above the current market price

793. Darla Diamond purchases 1,000 STU at $42. After STU increases to $47, Darla would like to protect the profit on her investment. Out of the following choices, which of the following orders should you recommend?

(A) Sell limit at $50

(B) Sell limit at $45

(C) Sell stop at $46

(D) Sell stop at $48

794. Melissa R. owns 1,000 shares of JKL common stock at $42. Melissa is concerned that the price of JKL will drop below $40, but if it does, she wants to make sure she gets at least $39.75 per share. What type of order should Melissa place?

(A) A sell stop order to sell 1,000 shares of JKL at $39.75

(B) A sell limit order to sell 1,000 shares of JKL at $39.75

(C) An order to sell $1,000 shares of JKL at $40 stop, $39.75 limit

(D) An order to sell $1,000 shares of JKL at $39.75 stop, $40 limit

795. Regulation SHO covers

(A) margin requirements for municipal and U.S. government securities

(B) the short sale of securities

(C) margin requirements for commodities

(D) portfolio margining rules

796. Which of the following orders guarantee the order is executed at a specific price or better?

(A) Buy limits and sell stops

(B) Buy limits and sell limits

(C) Sell limits and buy stops

(D) Buy stops and sell stops

797. A customer places an order to buy 100 shares of RST at 50. Which TWO of the following are TRUE of this order?

I. It is a limit order.

II. It is a market order.

III. It is good for the day.

IV. It is good until canceled.

(A) I and III

(B) I and IV

(C) II and III

(D) II and IV

798. A customer places an open order to sell 1,000 shares of MKR common stock at $35 stop. Which of the following are TRUE of this order?

I. The order will stay in place until cancelled.

II. The order is good for the day.

III. If the order is triggered, the stock will be sold at the next bid price.

IV. If the order is triggered, the stock will be sold at $35 per share or better.

(A) I and III

(B) I and IV

(C) II and III

(D) II and IV

799. A not held order gives a broker discretion as to

(A) which security is traded

(B) the time at which a security is traded

(C) whether to purchase, sell, or sell short a security

(D) all of the above

800. Which TWO of the following are TRUE of fill-or-kill orders?

I. They must be executed entirely.

II. They allow for partial execution.

III. They must be executed in one attempt immediately.

IV. They may be executed in several attempts.

(A) I and III

(B) I and IV

(C) II and III

(D) II and IV

801. Which TWO of the following are TRUE regarding immediate-or-cancel orders?

I. They must be executed entirely.

II. They allow for partial execution.

III. They must be executed in one attempt immediately.

IV. They may be executed in several attempts.

(A) I and III

(B) I and IV

(C) II and III

(D) II and IV

802. All-or-none orders

(A) must be executed in their entirety immediately, or the order is canceled

(B) must be executed in their entirety, or the order is canceled

(C) must be at least partially executed immediately, or the order is canceled

(D) must be at least partially executed, or the order is canceled

803. If an at-the-open order is not executed at the opening price, what happens to the order?

(A) It is cancelled.

(B) It becomes a market order.

(C) It becomes a day order.

(D) It becomes a limit order.

804. A DNR is used for what type of orders?

(A) Market and stop

(B) Stop and limit

(C) Stop and at-the-open

(D) Limit and at-the-close

805. A registered representative placed a discretionary order for a customer. Which of the following is TRUE regarding that order?

I. They must be approved by a principal.

II. The order ticket must be marked as discretionary.

III. They require prior verbal approval from a customer before being entered.

IV. They require a written power of attorney from the customer.

(A) I, II, and III

(B) II, III, and IV

(C) I, II, and IV

(D) I, II, III, and IV

806. A customer calls up their registered representative and says that they want to purchase 100 shares of DDD common stock. Which of the following is TRUE of that order?

(A) It is a limit order.

(B) It must be marked as unsolicited.

(C) It is a stop order.

(D) Because the customer placed the order, a principal's approval is not necessary.

807. Mrs. Rice purchased 100 shares of MKR stock at $42 per share. Six months later, with MKR trading at $47, Mrs. Rice would like to sell stock if it goes up to $50 or drops to $45. What type of order should be placed?

(A) A limit order

(B) A stop order

(C) An alternative order

(D) A stop-limit order

808. Which of the following customer orders are discretionary?

I. Buy 1,000 shares of a growth company.

II. Buy or sell 500 shares of LMN.

III. Buy or sell as many shares of TUV as you think I can handle.

(A) I and II

(B) II and III

(C) I and III

(D) I, II, and III

809. Which TWO of the following are FALSE regarding unsolicited orders?

I. They cannot be accepted without prior approval from a principal.

II. They can be accepted without prior approval from a principal.

III. They must be limited in size.

IV. They are not limited in size.

(A) I and III

(B) I and IV

(C) II and III

(D) II and IV

810. The ______________ provides reliability to the global financial system.

(A) CBOE

(B) FINRA

(C) IRS

(D) DTCC

811–815 Types of Investors

811. Which of the following would be considered accredited investors?

I. Banks

II. An individual investor with a net worth of $2,000,000 excluding their primary residence

III. A corporation with a net worth of $10,000,000

IV. Insurance companies

(A) II and IV

(B) I, II, and III

(C) II and III

(D) I, II, III, and IV

812. One spouse is a pilot, and the other spouse is a pediatrician. They have a combined income that exceeded $400,000 per year for the last several years and is only expected to get better this year. They would be considered

(A) a qualified institutional buyer

(B) a joint couple

(C) an accredited investor

(D) market makers

813. Institutional investors include all of the following EXCEPT

(A) joint investors

(B) insurance companies

(C) hedge funds

(D) commercial banks

814. Which of the following would be considered institutional investors?

I. Commercial banks

II. Pension funds

III. Real Estate Investment Trusts

IV. Endowment funds

(A) II and IV

(B) I, II, and III

(C) II and III

(D) I, II, III, and IV

815. Which of the following is TRUE of retail investors?

(A) They are considered nonprofessional investors.

(B) They trade for their own accounts.

(C) They often trade in much smaller amounts than institutional investors.

(D) All of the above.

Chapter **11**

Making Sure the IRS Gets Its Share: Taxes and Retirement Plans

Taxes are a part of life. Investors face additional taxes that aren't imposed on your average consumer, including capital gains and dividends. In addition, this chapter covers different retirement plans and how they're taxed. The Series 7 exam tests your ability to understand the tax categories, what happens when you purchase a bond at a discount or premium, qualified versus non-qualified retirement plans, health savings accounts (HSAs), and so on.

The Problems You'll Work On

The types of problems in this chapter require you to

- Understand the different tax categories and types of income.
- Calculate interest income and taxes on dividends.
- Handle capital gains and losses.
- Compute accretion and amortization.
- Be familiar with wash sale rules, gift taxes, and estate taxes.
- Recognize qualified and non-qualified plans.
- Compare traditional IRAs and Roth IRAs.

What to Watch Out For

Don't let common mistakes trip you up; be careful that you

- Read each question and answer choice completely before choosing an answer.
- Eliminate false answers when the correct one doesn't reveal itself right away.
- Watch out for key words such as EXCEPT, NOT, and so on, that can change the answer choice you're looking for.
- Remember the difference between progressive and regressive (flat) taxes.

816–822 Tax Categories and Types of Income

816. All of the following taxes are progressive EXCEPT

(A) personal income
(B) gift
(C) estate
(D) sales

817. Which of the following taxes are regressive?

I. Income
II. Gas
III. Alcohol
IV. Sales

(A) I and III
(B) II and IV
(C) II, III, and IV
(D) I, II, and III

818. Property tax is a

I. flat tax
II. graduated tax
III. regressive tax
IV. progressive tax

(A) I and III
(B) I and IV
(C) II and III
(D) II and IV

819. Earned income includes all of the following EXCEPT

(A) capital gains
(B) salary
(C) bonuses
(D) income received from active participation in a business

820. Portfolio income includes

I. income from an oil and gas DPP
II. income from stock dividends
III. interest from corporate bonds
IV. capital gains from the sale of municipal bonds

(A) I, II, and III
(B) II, III, and IV
(C) II and III
(D) I, II, III, and IV

821. Income received from a limited partnership is considered

(A) capital gains
(B) dividend income
(C) earned income
(D) passive income

822. Earning income includes

(A) wages
(B) bonuses
(C) commissions
(D) all of the above

823–843 Taxes on Investments

823. Which of the following are taxable to investors?

I. Stock splits
II. Stock dividends
III. Cash dividends
IV. Corporate bond interest

(A) I and II
(B) III and IV
(C) I and III
(D) II, III, and IV

824. Losses from a limited partnership can be written off against

I. passive income
II. interest income
III. capital gains
IV. earned income

(A) I only
(B) II and III
(C) I, II, and III
(D) I, II, III, and IV

825. An investor purchased a municipal bond fund, and the fund paid this investor a dividend based on the interest they received. That dividend is

(A) taxable on all levels
(B) exempt from state tax
(C) exempt from federal tax
(D) exempt from both federal and state tax

826. One of your clients who lives in Utah purchased an Atlantic City, New Jersey, municipal revenue bond. The interest is

I. subject to state tax
II. exempt from state tax
III. subject to federal tax
IV. exempt from federal tax

(A) I and III
(B) I and IV
(C) II and III
(D) II and IV

827. Interest on U.S. government T-bonds is subject to

(A) state tax but not federal tax
(B) federal tax but not state tax
(C) neither state tax nor federal tax
(D) both state and federal tax

828. Which of the following is NOT a type of investment income?

(A) ADR dividends
(B) Interest from T-bonds
(C) Dividends from a balanced fund
(D) Running a business

829. Dirk Diamond purchased 100 shares of UPP preferred stock, paying a yearly dividend of $6 per share. Dirk originally purchased the stock one year ago and three months prior to the first dividend being paid. Exactly one year later to the day, Dirk sold the stock for a profit of $320. Which TWO of the following are TRUE relating to the tax treatment of Dirk's transactions?

I. The dividends will be taxed at the qualified dividend rate.
II. The dividends will be taxed as passive income.
III. The sale will be treated as a short-term capital gain.
IV. The sale will be treated as a long-term capital gain.

(A) I and III
(B) I and IV
(C) II and III
(D) II and IV

830. Which of the following is taxable for an investor for the year on which it occurs?

(A) Interest received from corporate bonds, interest received from T-bonds, and cash dividends
(B) Interest received from corporate bonds, stock dividends, and cash dividends
(C) Interest received from T-bonds, stock dividends, and cash dividends
(D) Interest received from corporate bonds, stock dividends, and stock splits

831. Which of the following is TRUE of an investor who receives a stock dividend?

(A) The dividend will be taxable at their current tax bracket.

(B) Their cost basis on the stock owned will be reduced.

(C) If they've held the stock for more than a year, the dividend may be taxable at a lower percentage.

(D) The share price on the stock owned will be increased to reflect the dividend.

832. Jake Jones and his wife, Melinda, received cash dividends in their brokerage accounts as follows:

Jake: $2,000

Melinda: $1,000

Joint: $1,500

How much of these dividends are subject to taxation if they file their taxes jointly?

(A) $0

(B) $1,500

(C) $3,000

(D) $4,500

833. An investor buys 1,000 shares of a stock at $40. If the stock increases in value to $60, how would the result be categorized?

(A) As a profit

(B) Ordinary income

(C) Appreciation

(D) Capital gain

834. Short-term capital gains would be realized on a security sold at a profit if held for

(A) more than six months but less than a year

(B) less than one year

(C) one year or less

(D) more than one year but no more than two years

835. A customer purchased 100 shares of ABC stock at $40 per share on March 24. On March 24 of the following year, the customer sold the stock at $46 per share. Which TWO of the following are TRUE regarding these transactions?

I. They would be taxed as a short-term capital gain.

II. They would be taxed as a long-term capital gain.

III. The gain would be taxed at the customer's tax bracket.

IV. The gain would be taxed at either 0%, 15%, or 20% depending on the customer's adjusted gross income.

(A) I and III

(B) I and IV

(C) II and III

(D) II and IV

836. A client would like to sell short ABC common stock but is unfamiliar with the tax treatment of short sales. You should inform them that

(A) all gains are taxed as ordinary income

(B) all gains or losses are taxed as passive income or losses

(C) all gains or losses are considered short term

(D) all gains or losses are considered long term

837. A security purchased on September 30 would become long term on

(A) September 30 of the following year

(B) September 31 of the following year

(C) October 1 of the following year

(D) December 31 of the current year

838. One of your clients has the following investments for the current year:

Capital gains: $14,500

Capital losses: $21,000

What is the tax status for this investor?

(A) They have a $6,500 loss for the current year.

(B) They have a $3,000 loss for the current year and $3,000 carried over to the following year.

(C) They have a $3,000 loss for the current year and $3,500 carried over to the following year.

(D) They have a $6,500 loss for the current year and $3,000 carried over to the following year.

839. An investor sold DEF common stock at a loss. Which of the following securities may the investor buy back immediately without violating the wash sale rule?

(A) DEF convertible bonds

(B) DEF call options

(C) DEF warrants

(D) DEF preferred stock

840. If Marty sells LMN common stock at a loss on July 3 for 30 days, he can't buy which of the following securities without being subject to the wash sale rule?

I. LMN common stock

II. LMN warrants

III. LMN call options

IV. LMN preferred stock

(A) I only

(B) I and IV

(C) I, II, and III

(D) I, II, III, and IV

841. According to the wash sale rule, if a customer sold a security at a loss, which of the following is TRUE?

(A) The customer cannot purchase call options on the same security for 30 days before or after the sale and be able to claim the loss.

(B) The customer cannot purchase bonds by the same issuer for 30 days before and after the sale and be able to claim the loss.

(C) The customer cannot sell short the same security within 30 days before or after the sale and be able to claim the loss.

(D) The customer cannot purchase mutual funds holding the same security for 30 days before and after the sale and be able to claim the loss.

842. If an investor sells a security at a loss and wants to claim the tax deduction, the investor cannot buy back the same security nor anything convertible into the same security for at least

(A) 20 days

(B) 30 days

(C) 45 days

(D) 60 days

843. Mrs. Jones purchased 100 shares of ABC common stock at 48. Six months later Mrs. Jones sold the stock when ABC was trading at $40. Two weeks later Mrs. Jones repurchased ABC when it was trading at $42 and decides to take the loss on the original purchase and sale. Which of the following is true?

(A) The loss will not be allowed because it is a violation of the wash sale rule.

(B) The loss will not be allowed because it is a violation of the matching orders rule.

(C) The investor will be able to claim an $800 loss.

(D) The cost basis will be adjusted to $42.

844–876 Retirement Plans

844. Which of the following would LEAST likely purchase revenue bonds?

(A) Individual investors

(B) Banks

(C) Retirement plans

(D) Mutual funds

845. Which of the following securities would be LEAST suitable for a pension fund to purchase?

(A) Common stocks

(B) Preferred stocks

(C) Corporate bonds

(D) Municipal bonds

846. All of the following business retirement plans are regulated by ERISA EXCEPT

(A) money purchase plans

(B) ESOPs

(C) payroll deduction plans

(D) 401(k)

847. ERISA regulations cover

(A) private pension plans

(B) public pension plans

(C) private and public pension plans

(D) none of the above

848. Which TWO of the following statements regarding qualified retirement plans are TRUE?

I. Distributions are 100% taxable at the holder's tax bracket.

II. Distributions are partially taxable at the holder's tax bracket.

III. Contributions are made with pretax dollars.

IV. Contributions are made with after-tax dollars.

(A) I and III

(B) I and IV

(C) II and III

(D) II and IV

849. All of the following are types of tax-qualified retirement plans EXCEPT

(A) 401(k)

(B) profit-sharing

(C) IRA

(D) deferred compensation

850. All of the following are types of nonqualified retirement plans EXCEPT

(A) deferred compensation

(B) payroll deduction

(C) 401(k)

(D) 457

851. What is the maximum yearly traditional IRA contribution limit to for a 45-year old investor who is not covered by another retirement plan?

(A) $6,000

(B) $6,500

(C) $7,000

(D) $7,500

852. Traditional and Roth IRAs allow an additional catch-up contribution of

(A) $500 per year for investors aged 50 and older

(B) $500 per year for investors aged 55 and older

(C) $1,000 per year for investors aged 50 and older

(D) $1,000 per year for investors aged 55 and older

853. For investors under the age of 50 that own both traditional and Roth IRAs, the maximum annual contribution is

(A) $6,000 combined

(B) $6,500 combined

(C) $12,000 combined

(D) $13,000 combined

854. Which TWO of the following statements are TRUE regarding traditional 401(k) plans?

I. They are defined contribution plans.

II. They are defined benefit plans

III. Contributions are made with pretax dollars.

IV. Contributions are made with after-tax dollars.

(A) I and III

(B) I and IV

(C) II and III

(D) II and IV

855. An individual investor who lives at home with their parents is covered by an employer pension plan. However, they would like more coverage at retirement and decide to put the maximum allowable contribution into an IRA. If their salary is $52,000 per year, which of the following is TRUE?

(A) Contributions to the IRA are fully deductible.

(B) Contributions to the IRA are partially deductible.

(C) Contributions to the IRA are not deductible.

(D) Cannot be determined.

856. What is the last day an investor can deposit money into a traditional IRA and be able to claim it as a write-off on the current year's taxes?

(A) December 31 of the current year

(B) January 31 of the following year

(C) April 1 of the following year

(D) April 15 of the following year

857. Which of the following are TRUE regarding Roth IRAs and Roth 401(k)s?

(A) Withdrawals from both are tax-free provided that investors have held the accounts for at least five years and have reached the age of 59½.

(B) There are no contribution limits.

(C) Contributions made to both are made pre-tax.

(D) All of the above.

858. An investor received an eligible rollover from a traditional IRA and intends to roll it over into their 403(b) plan. How long do they have to roll it over into the 403(b) plan without the money being taxed as a distribution?

(A) Within 5 business days

(B) Within 30 calendar days

(C) Within 60 calendar days

(D) Up to one year

859. An investor has been contributing to a 401(k) set up at their place of work. They would like to start contributing to an IRA also. Which of the following is TRUE?

(A) They would not be able to contribute to an IRA since they already have another retirement plan.

(B) Contributions to the IRA would be taxable.

(C) Contributions to the IRA may be taxable.

(D) Contributions to the IRA will not be taxable.

860. When an investor starts receiving payments at retirement from a 403(b) plan, they are

(A) not taxable

(B) 100% taxable at the investor's tax bracket

(C) partially taxable at the investor's tax bracket

(D) either fully taxable or partially taxable depending on the investor's tax bracket

861. Which of the following types of retirement plans is a salary reduction plan set up for public school employees?

(A) SEP-IRAs

(B) 401(k)s

(C) 403(b)s

(D) Keogh plans

862. Which TWO of the following are TRUE?

I. Qualified dividends from Roth 401(k)s are excluded from federal income tax.

II. Qualified dividends from Roth 401(k)s are not excluded from federal income tax.

III. Qualified dividends from Roth IRAs are excluded from federal income tax.

IV. Qualified dividends from Roth IRAs are not excluded from federal income tax.

(A) I and III

(B) I and IV

(C) II and III

(D) II and IV

863. When must an individual begin withdrawing money from most retirement plans?

(A) At age 59½

(B) At age 70½

(C) On April 15 of the year after the investor turns age 72

(D) On April 1 of the year after the investor turns age 73

864. If an investor withdraws money from a pension plan, how long does the investor have to roll over money into another retirement plan or IRA?

(A) 20 days

(B) 30 days

(C) 60 days

(D) 6 months

865. If a 77-year-old investor doesn't take money out of their Roth IRA this year, what are the consequences?

(A) No consequences

(B) 6% penalty on the amount that was supposed to be withdrawn

(C) 10% penalty on the amount that was supposed to be withdrawn

(D) 50% penalty on the amount that was supposed to be withdrawn

866. ERISA (Employee Retirement Income Security Act) regulations cover

(A) private pension plans

(B) public pension plans

(C) both private and public pension plans

(D) neither private nor public pension plans

867. An investor deposits $30,000 into an IRA over a period of several years. When the investor is ready to withdraw from the account, the value of the IRA is $50,000. If the investor withdraws $30,000 from the account, which of the following is true?

(A) The withdrawal is tax free.

(B) $20,000 of the withdrawal is taxed as ordinary income.

(C) The $30,000 withdrawn is taxed as ordinary income.

(D) The $30,000 withdrawn is taxed as a capital gain.

868. An investor may start taking withdrawals from an IRA beginning at age __________ without facing a penalty.

(A) 50

(B) 59½

(C) 65

(D) 73

869. Which of the following is TRUE regarding the vesting of SEP IRAs?

(A) All employees are fully vested immediately.

(B) All employees are 50% vested for the first 3 years and fully vested after that.

(C) All employees are 50% vested for the first 5 years and fully vested after that.

(D) All employees are 50% vested for the first 3 years, 75% vested between 3 and 5 years, and fully vested after that.

870. What happens if an investor contributes more to an IRA one year than they're supposed to?

(A) There is a 6% penalty on the amount over contributed.

(B) There is a 10% penalty on the amount over contributed.

(C) There is a 50% penalty on the amount over contributed.

(D) The amount over contributed will be deducted from the amount they can contribute the following year.

871. An investor had some gambling losses and needs to withdraw money from their IRA to be able to pay rent this month. If they are only 52 years old, what happens to the withdrawal?

(A) Since the investor is over age 50, the withdrawal is taxed at their current tax bracket.

(B) The withdrawal is taxed at their tax bracket plus a 6% penalty.

(C) The withdrawal is taxed at their tax bracket plus a 10% penalty.

(D) The withdrawal is taxed at their tax bracket plus a 50% penalty.

872. The maximum contribution allowed for a SEP IRA is

(A) 6% of an employee's pay

(B) 10% of an employee's pay

(C) 20% of an employee's pay

(D) 25% of an employee's pay

873. If a 75-year-old investor doesn't take their required minimum distribution this year, what are the consequences?

(A) They will have to double the amount to be taken the following year.

(B) They receive a 6% penalty on the amount that was supposed to be withdrawn.

(C) They receive a 10% penalty on the amount that was supposed to be withdrawn.

(D) They receive a 50% penalty on the amount that was supposed to be withdrawn.

874. Which of the following are TRUE regarding defined contribution plans?

(A) The contribution amount is fixed, and the benefit amount is fixed.

(B) The contribution amount is fixed, and the benefit amount is variable.

(C) The contribution amount is variable, and the benefit amount is fixed.

(D) The contribution amount is variable, and the benefit amount is variable.

875. Which of the following plans require a minimum distribution to take place by April 1 after the investor turns age 73?

(A) 401(k), traditional IRA, Roth IRA

(B) 403(b), traditional IRA, Roth IRA

(C) 403(b), 401(k), Roth IRA

(D) 403(b), 401(k), traditional IRA

876. Which of the following is TRUE regarding SEP IRAs?

(A) Contributions can be made by employees only.

(B) Contributions can be made by the employer only.

(C) Contributions can be made by both the employee and employer.

(D) Contributions can't be made by the employee nor employer.

Chapter 12

Rules and Regulations: No Fooling Around

The Series 7 exam is riddled with rules and regulations. And believe it or not, they're not just in this chapter. Unfortunately, this chapter, more than any other one, requires you to remember specifics. But don't fear: A lot of the rules make sense, and the correct answer usually stands out like a sore thumb.

The number of questions in this category increased greatly when the USA Patriot Act was enacted. Due to the act, each firm must have and follow customer identification programs (CIPs) and anti-money laundering rules.

The Problems You'll Work On

In this chapter, you'll work on problems that deal with rules and regulations, including

- Understanding the different self-regulatory organizations and agent registration
- Getting into anti-money laundering rules
- Remembering the specifics for order tickets, trade confirmations, and account statements
- Figuring out the payment and delivery dates for different trades
- Handling customer complaints and the legal remedies
- Recognizing violations
- Acknowledging the roles of the FDIC and SIPC

What to Watch Out For

The following tips can help you determine the correct answers for questions in this chapter:

- » Eliminate wrong answers when the correct one doesn't "pop out" at you right away.
- » Double-check that you're not confusing your rules before picking an answer.
- » Focus on the last sentence of the question to help guide you to the correct answer.
- » As always, watch for key words which can change your answer, such as: EXCEPT, NOT, and so on.

877–892 Securities Regulatory Organizations

877. The U.S. Securities and Exchange Commission regulates trading of which of the following securities?

I. Stock options

II. Commodity futures

III. Common stock

IV. Corporate bonds

(A) I, III, and IV

(B) III and IV

(C) II and III

(D) I, II, III, and IV

878. Which of the following securities acts created the Securities and Exchange Commission?

(A) The Securities Act of 1933

(B) The Securities and Exchange Act of 1934

(C) The Trust Indenture Act of 1939

(D) The Investment Company Act of 1940

879. What is the primary purpose of self-regulatory organizations such as FINRA?

(A) To register and create a market for new securities

(B) To prosecute people for insider trading activities

(C) To help promote fair and equitable practices among its members

(D) To insure investors in the event of broker-dealer bankruptcy

880. Which of the following is NOT TRUE of the Securities Exchange Act of 1934?

(A) It regulates the extension of credit.

(B) It regulates trades of securities in the primary market.

(C) It regulates trades of securities in the OTC market.

(D) It regulates trades of securities in the exchange market.

881. All of the following are mandated or regulated under the Securities Exchange Act of 1934 EXCEPT

(A) the creation of the SEC

(B) market manipulation

(C) margin rules

(D) the full and fair disclosure required on new offerings

882. All of the following are SROs EXCEPT

(A) FINRA

(B) MSRB

(C) SEC

(D) NYSE

883. All of the following enforce MSRB rules EXCEPT

(A) FINRA

(B) SEC

(C) FED

(D) MSRB

884. The Trust Indenture Act (TIA) covers sales of

(A) corporate bonds

(B) corporate stock

(C) limited partnerships

(D) options

885. Open-end (mutual) funds would be covered under the

(A) Securities Exchange Act of 1934

(B) Trust Indenture Act of 1939

(C) Investment Advisers Act of 1940

(D) Investment Company Act of 1940

886. Who is responsible for registering securities and registered representatives on the state level?

(A) The SEC

(B) FINRA

(C) The state administrators

(D) MSRB

887. Which of the following are TRUE of investment advisers?

I. They receive a fee for giving investment advice.

II. They charge a commission for giving investment advice.

III. If they have less than $25 million, they don't have to register with the SEC.

IV. All investment advisers have to register with the SEC.

(A) I and III

(B) I and IV

(C) II and III

(D) II and IV

888. All of the following are excluded from the definition of investment adviser according to the Investment Advisers Act of 1940 EXCEPT

(A) lawyers

(B) teachers

(C) engineers

(D) economists

889. Which self-regulatory organization (SRO) is responsible for the operation and regulation of the over-the-counter market and exchanges, such as the New York Stock Exchange?

(A) SEC

(B) CBOE

(C) MSRB

(D) FINRA

890. The ________________ was/were established to manage U.S. revenue.

(A) Department of the Treasury

(B) Federal Reserve Board

(C) 12 Federal Reserve member banks

(D) None of the above

891. FINRA and the NYSE have the authority to do which of the following?

I. Incarcerate

II. Fine

III. Expel

IV. Censure

(A) II and III

(B) II, III, and IV

(C) I and II

(D) I and IV

892. Which of the following regulatory organizations has the authority to punish registered representatives for rule violations?

I. SEC

II. FINRA

III. NYSE

IV. MSRB

(A) I only

(B) I and II

(C) I, II, and III

(D) I, II, III, and IV

893–904 FINRA Registration and Reporting Requirements

893. Which of the following will prohibit an individual from becoming an employee or officer of a brokerage firm?

I. The individual has been convicted of a felony within the last ten years.

II. The individual has been charged with a misdemeanor marijuana violation within the last ten years.

III. The individual has been charged with a DUI within the last ten years.

IV. The individual has been convicted of securities-related fraud within the last ten years.

(A) I, II, and III

(B) II, III, and IV

(C) I and IV

(D) I, II, III, and IV

894. A person will be statutorily disqualified from membership from FINRA under which of the following circumstances?

I. If they had a felony conviction within the last 15 years.

II. If they have been barred from membership in an SRO.

III. If they have made false statements on their application.

(A) I and III

(B) II and III

(C) I and II

(D) I, II, and III

895. A registered representative would like to register with a new firm and fills out a U-4 form. Which of the following is true of the information on the form?

I. It includes the registered rep's residential history.

II. It includes a 10-year employment history of the registered rep.

III. It includes an arbitration disclosure.

IV. It must be reviewed by a principal of the firm.

(A) II and IV

(B) II, III, and IV

(C) I, II, and IV

(D) I, II, III, and IV

896. A registered rep feels that their firm cheated them out of a commission on a large sale of common stock. Can the registered rep take this firm to court?

(A) No, they must go through arbitration.

(B) It depends on their length of employment.

(C) Yes, but only with approval from a principal of the firm.

(D) Yes, without restriction.

897. Mike Goldbar was a Series 7 registered representative for most of his working life. Mike had to leave the business for a while due to a family issue. Mike will be required to take his exams all over again if he has been unaffiliated with a broker/dealer for more than

(A) nine months

(B) one year

(C) two years

(D) one year longer than his length of employment prior to leaving the firm

898. A registered representative has not completed their regulatory element training within the prescribed period of time. What are the consequences?

(A) Their license will be suspended until they meet the requirements.

(B) Their license will be suspended for no less than 60 days after they meet the requirements.

(C) Their license will be suspended for no less than 60 days after they meet the requirement, and they'll face a fine of $1,000 for a first offense.

(D) Their license will be suspended until they meet the requirements and pay a first-time fine of $1,000.

899. While trying to build their book, a registered rep decides they want to bartend on weekends. Which of the following is true?

(A) They need to get verbal permission from a principal of the firm.

(B) They must notify their firm.

(C) They need to get written permission from a manager of the firm.

(D) They can only do so with written permission from FINRA.

900. Which of the following employees of a broker-dealer would be required to be fingerprinted?

(A) Registered representatives

(B) Individuals handling cash or certificates

(C) Principals

(D) All of the above

901. Which TWO of the following are TRUE about an associated person who would like to open an account at another firm?

I. It requires written permission from the associated person's firm.

II. It requires verbal permission from the associated person's firm.

III. Duplicate confirmations and statements must be sent to the associated person's firm.

IV. Duplicate confirmations and statements must be sent to the associated person's firm if requested.

(A) I and III

(B) I and IV

(C) II and III

(D) II and IV

902. Regarding continuing education, which of the following is TRUE?

(A) Member firms must have annual meetings, and registered persons must take the regulatory element every two years.

(B) Member firms must have semiannual meetings, and registered persons must take the regulatory element every three years.

(C) Member firms must have annual meetings, and registered persons must take the regulatory element within 120 days of their two-year anniversary and every three years after that.

(D) Member firms must have semiannual meetings, and registered persons must take the regulatory element within 120 days of their two-year anniversary and every three years after that.

903. Which of the following is true when a registered representative leaves a member firm?

(A) The firm files a U-4 form, and the registered representative has up to one year to get registered with another firm or their license will expire.

(B) The firm files a U-4 form, and the registered representative has up to two years to get registered with another firm or their license will expire.

(C) The firm files a U-5 form, and the registered representative has up to one year to get registered with another firm or their license will expire.

(D) The firm files a U-5 form, and the registered representative has up to two years to get registered with another firm or their license will expire.

904. Which of the following individuals are exempt from FINRA registration?

I. A person whose functions are solely clerical

II. A person who solely and exclusively is involved in transactions of municipal securities

III. A person who solely and exclusively is involved in transactions of commodities

IV. A person who solely and exclusively is involved in transactions of options

(A) I, II, and III

(B) I and III

(C) I, II, and IV

(D) I, II, III, and IV

905–957 Trading After the Account Is Open

905. All order tickets must be signed by

(A) a principal

(B) the customer

(C) the state administrator

(D) a compliance officer

906. Which of the following information is required on an order ticket?

I. The registered rep' s identification number

II. A description of the securities

III. The time of the order

IV. Whether the order was solicited or unsolicited

(A) I and II

(B) I, II, and III

(C) I, II and IV

(D) I, II, III, and IV

907. All of the following information would be found on an order ticket EXCEPT

(A) the name of the brokerage firm

(B) the customer's name

(C) the quantity of securities

(D) the investor's occupation

908. One of your clients is nearing retirement age, and their main investment objective is risk aversion. However, your client is dead set on purchasing a low-priced stock that you deem too risky considering their age and investment objectives. You should

(A) refuse the order

(B) take the order and mark it as "unsolicited"

(C) not take the order until the new account form is adjusted

(D) not take the order without a principal's approval

909. Which of the following items are required on an order ticket?

I. The time of the order

II. A description of the security

III. Whether the rep has discretionary authority over the account

IV. The registered rep's identification number

(A) I, III, and IV

(B) I and III

(C) I, II, and IV

(D) I, II, III, and IV

910. Gina wants to buy 1,000 shares of Biff Spanky Corporation at $1.20 per share. As Gina's agent, you inform Gina that the investment doesn't fit into their investment profile and is probably too risky. If Gina still insists on buying Biff Spanky Corporation, you should

(A) refuse the order

(B) refuse the order unless Gina changes their investment profile

(C) take the order but mark it as "unsolicited"

(D) hand the phone to your principal to see if they can talk some sense into Gina

911. A customer wishes to purchase a security that does not fit their investment objectives. After making them aware of that fact, they decide that they want to go ahead with the purchase anyway. What should you do?

(A) Refuse the order.

(B) Change the customer's investment objectives.

(C) Talk it over with a principal prior to taking the order.

(D) Take the order and mark the order ticket "unsolicited."

912. Principals must approve trades made by registered representatives

(A) at or prior to execution

(B) at or prior to completion of the transaction

(C) the same day as execution of the order

(D) none of the above

913. When may a registered representative open a joint account with a client?

I. Under no circumstances

II. If obtaining approval from a principal

III. If obtaining a signed proportionate sharing agreement from the client

(A) I only

(B) II only

(C) III only

(D) II and III

914. A customer purchases 1,000 shares of XYZ common stock on Friday, October 3. What is the settlement date?

(A) Monday, October 6

(B) Tuesday, October 7

(C) Wednesday, October 8

(D) Thursday, October 9

915. What is the settlement date for a corporate bond transaction?

(A) One business day after the trade date

(B) Two business days after the trade date

(C) Three business days after the trade date

(D) Ten business days after the trade date

916. Which of the following are TRUE regarding a regular-way purchase of municipal bonds?

I. The settlement is in one business day after the trade date.

II. The settlement is in two business days after the trade date.

III. The payment is due in one business day after the trade date.

IV. The payment is due in two business days after the trade date.

(A) I and III

(B) I and IV

(C) II and III

(D) II and IV

917. A corporation announces a dividend with record date Thursday, September 18. When is the last day an investor can buy the stock "regular way" and receive the dividend?

(A) Monday, September 15

(B) Tuesday, September 16

(C) Wednesday, September 17

(D) Monday, September 22

918. Treasury bonds settle in

(A) one business day after the trade date

(B) two business days after the trade date

(C) three business days after the trade date

(D) ten business days after the trade date

919. Issued transactions settle

(A) in one business day after the trade date

(B) in two business days after the trade date

(C) in three business days after the trade date

(D) on a date to be assigned

920. What is the regular way settlement for option transactions?

(A) T+1

(B) T+2

(C) T+3

(D) T+4

921. Which of the following are TRUE regarding securities transactions in cash?

I. Payment is due the same day as the trade date regardless of the type of security.

II. Payment is due the next business day after the trade date regardless of the type of security.

III. Settlement is the same day as the trade date regardless of the type of security.

IV. Settlement is the next business day after the trade date regardless of the type of security.

(A) I and III

(B) I and IV

(C) II and III

(D) II and IV

922. All brokerage firms are required to have safeguards in place to protect customers' non-public information. The SEC regulation that outlines brokerage firm requirements to safeguard customers' information is

(A) Regulation T

(B) Regulation G

(C) Regulation S-P

(D) Regulation A

923. Prior to an initial recommendation to a client, a customer relationship survey must be provided to that client. This falls under

(A) Regulation S-P

(B) Regulation BI

(C) Regulation M

(D) Regulation T

924. Diamond Broker-Dealer sent a client a confirmation of their latest trade of Mineshaft Corp. common stock. Which of the following items should be on the confirmation?

I. The trade date and the settlement date

II. Whether Diamond Broker-Dealer acted as an agent or principal

III. The name of the security and how many shares were traded

IV. The amount of commission paid if Diamond Broker-Dealer acted as an agent

(A) I and III

(B) I, II, and III

(C) I, III, and IV

(D) I, II, III, and IV

925. Broker-dealers, investment companies, and investment advisers must have written policies designed to protect customers' records and information. This falls under

(A) Regulation S-P

(B) Regulation D

(C) Regulation M

(D) Regulation BI

926. For member-to-customer transactions, the member firm must send a trade confirmation

(A) at or prior to the completion of the transaction

(B) no later than one business day after the trade date

(C) no later than two business days after the trade date

(D) no later than three business days after the trade date

927. All of the following must be included on a customer's trade confirmation EXCEPT

(A) the commission, if the trade was executed on an agency basis

(B) the price of the security

(C) the customer's signature

(D) the customer's account number

928. A client's confirmation must include

I. the markup or markdown for a principal transaction

II. the commission for an agency transaction

III. a description of the security

IV. the registered representative's identification number

(A) I and III

(B) I, II, and III

(C) II, III, and IV

(D) I, II, III, and IV

929. The certificate sent out to customers at the completion of the trade, which supplies all the details of the trade, is called a(n)

(A) proxy

(B) order ticket

(C) confirmation

(D) account statement

930. Under MSRB rules, a client's confirmation must include

(A) the markup or markdown

(B) the location of the bond resolution

(C) the settlement date

(D) whether the trade was executed on a dealer or agency basis

931. All accounts for specified adults must have a

(A) named "Trusted Contact Person"

(B) named "Beneficiary"

(C) signed "Proportionate Sharing Agreement"

(D) named "Associated Person"

932. If a member believes that the financial exploitation of a specified adult has taken place, what action may they take?

(A) Contact FINRA to find out what action to take.

(B) Contact the SEC to find out what action to take.

(C) Place a temporary hold on the disbursement of funds or securities from the account.

(D) Freeze the account for 90 days.

933. The term "specified adult" refers to investors

(A) aged 65 or older

(B) individuals aged 18 or older with a mental impairment that render them unable to protect their own interests

(C) individuals aged 18 or older with a physical impairment that render them unable to protect their own interests

(D) all of the above

934. Dim Outlook Securities has procedures allowing their registered representatives to borrow money from and lend money to certain customers. Under what circumstance may a registered representative of Dim Outlook borrow money from or lend money to a customer?

I. The customer is an immediate family member of the registered representative.

II. The customer and the registered representative have a business relationship outside of the broker-customer relationship.

III. The customer is a bank.

(A) I and II

(B) I and III

(C) II and III

(D) I, II, and III

935. Declan Smith has an account at Ayla Broker-Dealer. Declan has not traded any securities at Ayla Broker-Dealer for more than three years. How often is Ayla Broker-Dealer required to send an account statement to Declan?

(A) Monthly

(B) Quarterly

(C) Semiannually

(D) Annually

936. If your client, Sara Silver, requests a statement of a brokerage firm's financial condition, what document(s) must the brokerage firm send to Sara immediately?

(A) The most recent income statement

(B) The most recent balance sheet

(C) Both Choices (A) and (B)

(D) Neither Choice (A) nor (B)

937. MKR Corp. has decided to pay its common shareholders a dividend. Place the following dividend dates in order from first to last.

I. The payment date

II. The declaration date

III. The ex-date

IV. The record date

(A) II, III, IV, I

(B) I, II, III, IV

(C) IV, II, II, I

(D) III, II, I, IV

938. The ex-date is

(A) the date on which the corporation ceases paying a dividend

(B) the date on and after the date the seller is entitled to the dividend

(C) the third business day before the record date

(D) the day the stock price is increased by the amount of the dividend

939. The ex-dividend date is ________ business day(s) before the record date.

(A) one

(B) two

(C) three

(D) five

940. The SEC and FINRA require that customer account statements be sent out at least

(A) every time a trade takes place

(B) monthly

(C) semiannually

(D) quarterly

941. Mutual funds must send out financial statements to shareholders at least

(A) monthly

(B) quarterly

(C) semiannually

(D) annually

942. Zimbot Corp. has just announced a 30-cent dividend to shareholders of record. If the record date is Friday, October 8, when is the first day an investor can purchase the stock and not receive the dividend?

(A) Wednesday, October 6

(B) Thursday, October 7

(C) Friday, October 8

(D) Monday, October 11

943. Miesha Silva has written a letter of complaint regarding a recent purchase of blue chip stocks to their broker-dealer. Upon receipt of the complaint, the broker-dealer must

(A) return the commission charged

(B) accept the complaint and write down any action taken

(C) guarantee to make Miesha whole

(D) repurchase the stocks at a price that is at or slightly above Miesha's purchase price

944. Nothing but Net Broker-Dealer doesn't require their customers to sign an arbitration agreement. One of their customers believes money was stolen from their account and decides to take Nothing but Net to litigate it through code of procedure. Who has the first jurisdiction over the complaint?

(A) The SEC complaint review board

(B) The Supreme Court

(C) The FINRA board of governors

(D) The DBCC

945. Which of the following are TRUE regarding arbitration and mediation?

(A) Arbitration and mediation decisions are both appealable.

(B) Arbitration and mediation decisions are both binding and non-appealable.

(C) Arbitration decisions are binding and non-appealable, but mediation decisions are appealable.

(D) Mediation decisions are binding and non-appealable, but arbitration decisions are appealable.

946. FINRA divides communication into which of these three categories?

(A) Commercial, institutional, and retail

(B) Institutional, retail, and correspondence

(C) Written, verbal, and text

(D) Industrial, commercial, and retail

947. Retail communications must be

(A) approved by a principal of the firm

(B) filed with FINRA at least 10 business days prior to first use

(C) made available to more than 25 retail investors within a 30-day period

(D) all of the above

948. Which of the following disputes must be resolved using arbitration?

I. A dispute between a FINRA member and a registered representative

II. A dispute between a FINRA member and a customer

III. A dispute between two FINRA members

IV. A dispute between a FINRA member and a bank

(A) I, III, and IV

(B) I and III

(C) II and IV

(D) IV only

949. All of the following is TRUE about arbitration EXCEPT

(A) members may take non-members to arbitration

(B) non-members may take members to arbitration

(C) members may take other members to arbitration

(D) decisions are binding and non-appealable

950. In which of the following procedures for handling complaints is the decision binding and cannot be appealed?

(A) Code of procedure

(B) Mediation

(C) Arbitration

(D) Both (B) and (C)

951. Simplified arbitration is used to resolve disputes for up to

(A) $10,000

(B) $25,000

(C) $50,000

(D) $100,000

952. A broker-dealer must keep corporate or partnership documents for

(A) two years

(B) three years

(C) six years

(D) a lifetime

953. Which of the following records must be maintained by brokerage firms for six years?

I. Ledgers

II. Closed accounts

III. U-4 forms of terminated employees

IV. Blotters

(A) I and III

(B) II, III, and IV

(C) I, II, and III

(D) I, II, and IV

954. Under FINRA rules, which of the following records must be kept by a brokerage firm for a minimum of six years?

I. Customer account statements

II. U-5 forms

III. Records of all trades executed

IV. Sales literature

(A) I, II, and III

(B) II, III, and IV

(C) I and III

(D) I, II, and IV

955. Under FINRA rules, all of the following brokerage firm records must be kept for a minimum of three years EXCEPT

(A) ledgers

(B) trade confirmations

(C) order tickets

(D) U-4 forms of former employees

956. Broker-dealer records must be kept easily accessible for at least

(A) six months

(B) two years

(C) three years

(D) six years

957. Under FINRA rules, a brokerage firm must keep trade confirmations, order tickets, and advertisements for a minimum of

(A) two years

(B) three years

(C) four years

(D) six years

958–993 Additional Rules

958. The 5% markup policy applies to which of the following?

(A) IPOs

(B) The sale of mutual fund shares

(C) Regulation D offerings

(D) The over-the-counter sale of outstanding non-exempt securities

959. The 5% markup policy applies to which of the following types of secondary market transactions?

(A) Riskless or simultaneous transactions

(B) Common stock sold from a dealer's inventory

(C) Proceeds transactions on non-exempt securities

(D) All of the above

960. All of the following may be factors used in determining the markup charged to a customer EXCEPT

(A) dealer cost

(B) the market price of the security

(C) the size of the trade

(D) expenses of executing the trade

961. The 5% markup policy applies to which of the following over-the-counter transactions?

(A) Securities sold with a prospectus

(B) Municipal bond transactions

(C) Sales of outstanding shares of corporate stock

(D) Mutual fund purchases

962. All of the following are important factors when determining the markup or commission on a municipal bond trade EXCEPT

(A) the fact that you and the firm you work for are entitled to make a profit

(B) the difficulty of the trad

(C) the 5% policy

(D) the market value of the securities at the time of the trade

963. Municipal finance professionals may make campaign contributions to a municipal candidate they're allowed to vote for up to ____________ per election.

(A) $100

(B) $250

(C) $500

(D) $1,000

964. The 5% markup policy applies to

(A) riskless or simultaneous transactions

(B) markups and markdowns on stock sold from and purchased for a firm's inventory

(C) commissions charged when executing trades for a customer

(D) all of the above

965. The prohibited action of mixing a customer's securities with the account of the broker-dealer is called

(A) free riding

(B) hypothecation

(C) commingling

(D) conjoining

966. Which of the following are violations?

(A) Commingling of funds

(B) Interpositioning

(C) Signatures of convenience

(D) All of the above

967. A client purchases a security and sells it shortly after without ever making a payment. This is a violation called

(A) matching orders

(B) freeriding

(C) commingling

(D) interpositioning

968. Matching orders is

(A) combining fully paid securities and margined securities to use as collateral

(B) the illegal manipulation of a security

(C) bringing in a third party to execute a trade

(D) buying securities with no intention of paying for the trade

969. All of the following are acceptable contributions from a registered rep to a client EXCEPT

(A) a baby shower gift of $80

(B) a gift of theatre tickets for a client and daughter for a total of $250

(C) a gift of football game tickets for $300 where the rep will attend with the client

(D) a gift card for $75 for use in a department store

970. Which of the following is selling dividends?

(A) A registered representative encouraging investors to withdraw reinvested mutual fund dividends to purchase more securities so that the registered representative will make more commission

(B) A registered representative encouraging clients to sell stock just prior to a dividend being paid so that the stock will be easier to sell

(C) A registered representative encouraging clients to buy equity securities just prior to a dividend being paid so that they will receive the dividend

(D) A registered representative providing a plan for investors on how to invest dividends received

971. All of the following are considered violations EXCEPT

(A) frontrunning

(B) hypothecation

(C) signatures of convenience

(D) interpositioning

972. When FINRA is considering the possibility that a brokerage account is being churned, all of the following are considered EXCEPT

(A) the profit or loss

(B) the amount of trades

(C) the client's investment objectives

(D) the amount of money in the client's account

973. Which of the following is a violation that includes a form of market manipulation?

(A) Commingling

(B) Frontrunning

(C) Pump and dump

(D) Interpositioning

974. Mr. Smith buys 1,000 shares of HIJ common stock at $22 per share. Several months later, HIJ is trading at $20.40–$20.55, and the registered representative offers to purchase back the shares for their own account at $22 per share. This procedure is

(A) permitted by FINRA under certain circumstances

(B) permitted with the written permission of a principal

(C) a violation of the Code of Procedure

(D) prohibited

975. All brokerage firms are required to have customer identification programs and to check the names of any new customers against

(A) the SDN list maintained by OFAC

(B) the SDN list maintained by the Department of Treasury

(C) the SDN list maintained by the Secret Service

(D) the SDN list maintained by FINRA

976. An investor making several large cash deposits into their brokerage account may indicate that they are engaged in

(A) money laundering

(B) insider trading

(C) front-running

(D) a takeover

977. All of the following are stages of money laundering EXCEPT

(A) placement

(B) intermediation

(C) layering

(D) integration

978. Which of the following transactions require the filing of Form 112 with FinCEN?

(A) A check deposit of $35,000

(B) A credit card transaction of $20,000

(C) A cash deposit of $15,000

(D) All of the above

979. Which of the following establishes the U.S. Treasury Department as the regulator for anti-money-laundering programs?

(A) The Bank Secrecy Act

(B) OFAC

(C) SDN

(D) None of the above

980. Which of the following transactions are considered structured?

I. Mr. and Mrs. Jones each transfer $9,500 to their joint account on the same day.

II. Mr. Smith wiring $9,000 to an account on three separate occasions during the same week.

III. Mrs. Jones and Mr. Smith each wiring $9,000 to each of their own accounts at the same time.

(A) I and II

(B) I and III

(C) II and III

(D) I, II, and III

981. A customer is about to open a new account. Which of the following indicates that your new customer may be interested in laundering money?

(A) A concern with U.S. government reporting requirements

(B) A reluctance to inform you of their business activity

(C) A first trade that is inconsistent with their investment objectives

(D) All of the above

982. You are in the process of opening a new account. Which of the following indications of money laundering should you be concerned with?

I. Irrational transactions that are inconsistent with the potential client's investment objectives

II. A reluctance to provide information about business activities

III. The potential customer's concern about U.S. government reporting requirements

IV. A suspect ID

(A) I only

(B) I and III

(C) II and IV

(D) I, II, III, and IV

983. One of your customers has made three cash deposits into their account over the last few weeks of $9,900 each. This is called

(A) structuring

(B) layering

(C) integration

(D) placement

984. Judging by a client's trading pattern, you have a very strong suspicion that they are trading on inside information. You should

(A) contact a principal immediately

(B) contact the SEC and send it supporting documentation

(C) contact FINRA and send it supporting documentation

(D) all of the above

985. A client is the CEO of ABC Corporation, which is going under some significant changes. The CEO shares some information with their registered regarding those changes. Which of the following could be considered inside information?

I. Changes in the management of ABC

II. Undisclosed financial difficulties with ABC

III. ABC's declaration of a 10% stock dividend

IV. The downgrading of their bonds by Moody's

(A) II and IV

(B) I, II, and IV

(C) II and III

(D) I and II

986. Which of the following investors are contemporaneous traders who can sue insiders in court for insider trading violations?

I. Buyers who purchased stock at the time that insiders were buying

II. Buyers who purchased stock at the time insiders were selling the stock

III. Sellers who sold stock at the time insiders were buying the stock

IV. Sellers who sold stock at the time insiders were selling the stock

(A) I and III

(B) I and IV

(C) II and III

(D) II and IV

987. Which of the following are TRUE statements regarding civil penalties that may be imposed for insider trading violations?

I. Civil penalties may be imposed only on registered persons.

II. The civil penalty may be up to three times the profit gained or the loss avoided on an illegal transaction.

III. A broker-dealer may be held liable if one of its registered representatives was not properly supervised while committing an insider trading violation.

IV. The violation is defined as buying or selling securities while in possession of material nonpublic information.

(A) I, III, and IV

(B) I, II, and III

(C) I and IV

(D) II, III, and IV

988. Which of the following is liable if a trade is made on material nonpublic information?

(A) The tippee

(B) The tipper

(C) Both (A) and (B)

(D) Neither (A) nor (B)

989. The CEO of OEC Corporation tells a lifelong friend that OEC will be announcing an acquisition of COE, Inc., the following week. The friend acts on this knowledge and purchases shares of COE and shorts OEC. Who violated insider trading rules?

(A) The CEO

(B) The lifelong friend

(C) Both the CEO and the lifelong friend

(D) Neither the CEO nor the lifelong friend

990. Which TWO of the following are the maximum penalties for insider trading violations?

I. 20 years in prison per violation

II. 25 years in prison per violation

III. $5 million per individual per violation

IV. $30 million per individual per violation

(A) I and III

(B) I and IV

(C) II and III

(D) II and IV

991. As part of FINRA's business continuity plan, member firms must provide the emergency contact information for ________ principal(s) of the firm to contact in the event of an emergency.

(A) one

(B) two

(C) three

(D) all

992. Business continuity plans (BCPs) must be reviewed

(A) annually by a principal of the firm

(B) semiannually by a principal of the firm

(C) annually by FINRA

(D) as needed by FINRA

993. A client is on an overseas trip and wishes for the brokerage firm to hold their confirmations and account statements until they return. Which of the following is TRUE regarding holding a client's mail?

(A) This is not allowed under any circumstances.

(B) This is allowed only with permission from FINRA.

(C) The firm may hold the client's mail up to three months.

(D) The firm may hold the client's mail indefinitely.

994–1,001 FDIC and SIPC

994. Which of the following is TRUE about SIPC?

(A) It is an agency of the U.S. government.

(B) Investment advisers are required to be members of SIPC.

(C) Banks selling municipal securities must be SIPC members.

(D) SIPC funding is made by member assessments.

995. The FDIC covers each

(A) depositor for up to $250,000

(B) investor for up to $250,000

(C) depositor for up to $500,000

(D) investor for up to $500,000

996. SIPC protects each separate customer up to

(A) $500,000 in cash and securities with no more than $250,000 cash

(B) $500,000 in cash and securities with no more than $100,000 cash

(C) $400,000 in securities and $100,000 cash

(D) $500,000 in securities and an additional $250,000 cash

997. SIPC provides coverage for which of the following securities held in a customer's account?

(A) Common stock

(B) Municipal bonds

(C) REITs

(D) All of the above

998. You have a new client who is going to open an individual cash account and an individual margin account in their name. At the same time, the client also wants to open a joint account with a spouse, a joint account with a son, and a corporate account. How many separate accounts is the investor covered for under SIPC?

(A) One

(B) Two

(C) Four

(D) Five

999. Mike Nugent and his wife, Mary, have individual accounts with ABCDE broker-dealer. Along with their individual accounts, they also have a joint account with rights of survivorship. Mike's individual account has $200,000 of stock, $50,000 of bonds, and $200,000 of cash. Mary's individual account has $100,000 of stock and $400,000 of cash. In the joint account, Mike and Mary have $100,000 of stock, $350,000 of bonds, and $200,000 of cash. If ABCDE declares bankruptcy, what would be the maximum SIPC coverage for all the accounts?

(A) $950,000

(B) $1,300,000

(C) $1,350,000

(D) $1,850,000

1000. If an investor is not fully covered under SIPC, they become a(n) ______________ of the bankrupt broker-dealer.

(A) secured creditor

(B) general creditor

(C) owner

(D) stockholder

1001. Which entity is the guarantor and insurer of bank savings accounts?

(A) The Fed

(B) SIPC

(C) The Treasury Department

(D) FDIC

2 Checking Your Answers

IN THIS PART . . .

Check your answers.

Read explanations that should aid in your study for the SIE Exam.

Chapter **13**

The Answers

Chapter 1 Answers

1. **A. the Securities Act of 1933**

The Securities Act of 1933 covers the sale of new issues (primary market). The Securities Act of 1933 was designed to provide more transparency in financial statements and to curb fraudulent activities of issuers. The Securities Act of 1933 also goes by a myriad of other names, such as the Paper Act, New Issues Act, Full Disclosure Act, and Truth in Securities Act.

2. **A. require full and fair disclosure regarding sales of new securities to the public**

The main purpose of the Securities Act of 1933 is to require the full and fair disclosure regarding sales of new securities to the public.

3. **B. the Securities Exchange Act of 1934**

The Securities Exchange Act of 1934 was designed to provide rules for the trading of outstanding securities in the over-the-counter (OTC) market and exchanges.

4. **C. the registration of securities**

The Securities Act of 1933 deals with new securities and issuers. The Securities Exchange Act of 1934 deals with outstanding securities.

5. **C. I, II, and IV**

The Trust Indenture Act of 1939 regulates all corporate bond issues exceeding $5 million. The only corporate bonds listed are equipment trust bonds. U.S. government T-bonds, municipal general obligation (GO) bonds, and municipal revenue bonds are exempt from the Trust Indenture Act of 1939.

6. **D. Treasury bonds**

The Trust Indenture Act of 1939 regulates all corporate bond issues exceeding $5 million. Since Treasury bonds are issued by the U.S. government, they are exempt from the Trust Indenture Act of 1939.

7. **D. I, II, III, and IV**

When a company files a registration statement with the Securities and Exchange Commission (SEC), it must include the issuer's name and description of its business, the names and addresses of all the company's control persons, what the proceeds will be used for, the company's capitalization, complete financial statements, any legal proceedings against the company, and so on.

8. **A. shelf registration**

A *shelf registration* allows the issuer to sell securities registered with the Securities and Exchange Commission (SEC) for up to three years from the effective (release) date. A shelf registration allows an issuer to time the sale of its securities with market conditions.

9. **B. shelf offerings**

The Securities and Exchange Commission (SEC) Rule 415 outlines the rules for shelf offerings (shelf registration). Typically, a company isn't going to sell all of its shares in one shot; it may want to wait another six months, a year, or two years before selling all of its authorized shares. Under SEC Rule 415, an issuer has up to two years to sell its registered securities without having to file a new registration statement.

10. **D. 3 years**

Shelf registration is a Securities and Exchange Commission (SEC) provision that allows an issuer to register a new issue without having to sell all the securities at one time. Shelf registration allows the issuer to hold back securities for up to three years without having to reregister them.

11. **A. 20**

The cooling-off period is when the Securities and Exchange Commission (SEC) is reviewing a company's registration statement before bringing new issues to market. The cooling-off period typically lasts about 20 days.

12. **B. II and III**

Be careful, any time you see something about the Securities and Exchange Commission (SEC), or any self-regulatory organization for that matter, approving or guaranteeing an issue, it's a false answer. The SEC just clears the issue. During the cooling-off period, the SEC reviews registration statements and may issue stop orders.

13. B. III and IV

Indications of interest for a new offering aren't binding on the customer or on the broker-dealer. For example, a customer may tell you that they want to buy 10,000 shares of Zamzow when it's available and then change their mind later. By the same token, the broker-dealer isn't obligated to have 10,000 shares available to sell to the customer when Zamzow becomes available.

14. D. Nothing.

Until a corporation has filed a registration statement with the Securities and Exchange Commission (SEC) for a new issue, an account executive can't do anything. After the registration statement has been filed, account executives can start obtaining indications of interest.

15. A. selling group members

A tombstone ad is print notice typically placed in newspapers or magazines. Companies use tombstone ads to make an announcement of a new issue of securities. Believe it or not, it got the name *tombstone ad* because the shape of the ad is typically in the shape of a headstone. The ad displays the names of the issuer, syndicate manager, and syndicate members but not selling group members.

16. A. I, III, and IV

Issuers can register securities on the state level by filing (notification), through coordination, or through qualification. The Series 63 and Series 66 exams explore this topic in much more detail. Communication was just thrown in there as a bogus answer choice because it looks something like the other words.

17. C. Qualification

The three types of state securities registration are notification (registration by filing), coordination, and qualification. If the securities are exempt from federal (SEC) registration but still must be filed with the state, the issuer would use registration by qualification.

18. A. Notification

The three types of state securities registration are notification (registration by filing), coordination, and qualification. If securities are to be sold by an established issuer who has previously sold securities within the state, they would register by notification (filing).

19. B. Coordination

When an issuer wishes to register securities to be sold with the SEC and states at the same time, they would do it by coordination. This type of registration is most often used for IPOs (initial public offerings).

20. D. all of the above

An investment banking firm is a financial institution that provides a variety of services for issuers and sometimes high-net-worth investors. As related to new issues, investment bankers advise issuers how to raise money, help the issuers comply with securities laws, and often help the issuers raise money by selling securities.

21. C. a syndicate

A syndicate is a group of at least two broker-dealers put together to help a corporation raise money by underwriting their securities and helping to sell them in the market.

22. B. the underwriter's agreement

The underwriter's agreement (agreement among underwriters) is not a part of the final or preliminary prospectus.

23. B. firm commitment

A *firm commitment underwriting* is one in which any unsold securities are retained by the underwriters. *All-or-none (AON)* and *mini-max* are types of best-efforts underwritings in which a certain quantity of securities must be sold, or the offering is canceled.

24. C. the agreement among underwriters

The agreement among underwriters (syndicate agreement) outlines the liabilities and responsibilities of each firm involved in the distribution of new securities.

25. C. standby

In this case, you're looking for the false answer. *All-or-none (AON), best efforts,* and *mini-max* are all types of bond underwritings. However, a *standby underwriting* is only for common stockholders. A standby underwriter purchases shares that aren't purchased by existing shareholders during a rights offering.

26. B. all-or-none

An all-or-none offering is one in which the underwriter(s) is responsible for selling all the securities, or the offering is canceled. The securities and the money are held in an escrow account until the entire offering is sold. In the event that the offering is canceled, the money is returned to the purchasers, and securities are returned to the issuer. All-or-none and mini-max are types of best-efforts underwritings.

27. B. Mini-max

A mini-max is a type of best efforts underwriting in which the syndicate has to sell a certain minimum amount of securities or the offering is cancelled.

28. C. obtain indications of interest from investors

The correct answer is Choice (C). However, look closely at Choice (B). The Securities and Exchange Commission (SEC) (or any self-regulatory organization [SRO] for that matter) never approves or guarantees an issue of securities; the SEC just clears the issue for investment. The preliminary prospectus is released when the issue is in registration during the 20-day cooling-off period. The preliminary prospectus has no price and no effective date and may be used only to obtain indications of interest from investors.

29. A. The managing underwriter

It is up to the managing underwriter to make sure the information placed in the prospectus is accurate. Remember, the SEC just reviews the prospectus and registration statement to make sure all required information has been covered. The SEC does not approve or guarantee any issue.

30. D. I and III

Remember, you're looking for the exception in this question. The preliminary prospectus (red herring) would include such items as the financial history of the company (including financial statements) and what the company is going to do with the funds being raised. However, the preliminary prospectus doesn't include the effective (release) date or the public offering price. The effective date and the public offering price would be included in the final prospectus.

31. C. preliminary prospectus

A preliminary prospectus is also known as a red herring because of the red lettering required on the first page. A preliminary prospectus includes much of the information required in a final prospectus except the final offering price.

32. A. may be used to help obtain indications of interest

The preliminary prospectus (red herring) is distributed to potential investors during the cooling off period. The main purpose is to help obtain indications of interest. Indications of interest are not binding on the client or broker-dealer.

33. B. I, II, and III

A preliminary prospectus includes the purpose for the funds and financial statements. Because a preliminary prospectus (red herring) is printed before the final offering price is established, it may include a projected price range that is subject to change.

34. B. I and IV

The nice thing about this question is that the titles *registrar* and *transfer agent* pretty much sum up what they do. The registrar works along with the transfer agent to maintain a record of stock and bondholders and to make sure that more shares aren't outstanding than there should be. The main function of a transfer agent is to transfer things like stock certificates, bond certificates, and proxies. The transfer agent also keeps a record of stock and bondholders.

35. D. Sending out proxies

Hopefully the word "transfer" in "transfer agent" led you to the correct answer. Yes, the transfer agent is responsible for transferring or sending things. Typically, the transfer agent is responsible for sending out proxies (voting by absentee ballot), cancelling old shares, sending out new shares, distributing dividends, and so on.

36. A. IPO

An IPO is an initial public offering and is the first time a corporation ever sells securities to the public.

37. D. 90 days after the effective date

If an initial public offering (IPO) will be traded initially on the Over-the-Counter Bulletin Board (OTCBB) or OTC Pink Market, brokerage firms that execute orders for customers to buy the stock must send a copy of the final prospectus with the confirmation (receipt of trade) within the first *90 days after the effective date.* For any other unlisted offering, the prospectus needs to be available for 40 days. For an IPO trading immediately on the NASDAQ or exchange, the final prospectus is necessary for the first 25 days of trading. The final prospectus includes items such as the Securities and Exchange Commission's (SEC) "we don't guarantee or approve" disclaimer, the offering price, use of proceeds, description of the underwriting, stabilization bid procedure, business history, investor risk, information about the management, financial information about the issuer, and so on.

38. D. 90 days

Initial public offerings (IPOs) that aren't sold on an exchange have a 90-day prospectus requirement. All other new offerings have a 40-day prospectus requirement.

39. D. Combined

This is a combined (split) offering. The 600,000 shares that are authorized but previously unissued shares are a primary offering, and the 400,000 shares are a large block of outstanding shares, so that's a secondary offering. When you put a primary and secondary offering together, it's called a combined offering.

40. **C. Secondary**

A *secondary offering* is a large block of outstanding or previously outstanding (treasury) stock. Remember, treasury stock was stock that was outstanding (trading in the market) and then at some point repurchased by the issuer.

41. **D. initial public offering**

An *initial public offering (IPO)* is the first time a corporation sells stock to the public (becomes publicly traded). When a corporation has an IPO, it can't have another one because it can go public only once. All new stock sold after the IPO is over is part of a primary offering. IPOs are usually quite risky investments and, therefore, aren't suitable for all investors.

42. **A. split**

A combined offering is also known as a split offering. A split offering is a combination of a primary (new securities) and a secondary (outstanding securities) offering.

43. **D. I and III**

A primary offering is the offering of new securities from the issuer. Primary offerings raise money for the issuer and would increase the number of shares outstanding. *Treasury stock* is stock that was outstanding and was repurchased by the issuer. Because treasury stock was previously issued, it's not new stock coming to the market and wouldn't be part of a primary offering.

44. **C. REITs**

Securities that are exempt from the registration requirements of the Securities Act of 1933 include U.S. government securities (Treasury bonds, Treasury bills, Treasury notes, and so on), municipal bonds, securities issued by banks, public utility stocks and bonds, and so on. However, real estate investment trusts (REITs) must register with the Securities and Exchange Commission (SEC).

45. **C. General obligation bonds**

General obligation bonds are local government securities that are exempt from SEC registration. All of the other choices must be registered with the SEC.

46. **B. I and IV**

Nonexempt securities are ones that must be registered with the SEC. Fixed annuities and non-negotiable CDs do not fit the definition of security and are therefore exempt from SEC registration. However, variable annuities and oil and gas limited partnerships must register and are therefore non-exempt.

47. A. I, II, and IV

Revenue bonds, which are a type of local government bond; Treasury bonds, which are federal government bonds; and securities issued by not-for-profit organizations are all exempt from SEC registration. However, variable annuities, not fixed annuities, must register.

48. D. TIPS

TIPS are Treasury Inflation Protected Securities issued by the U.S. government and therefore are exempt from the registration and prospectus requirements of the Securities Act of 1933.

49. D. Commercial paper

Commercial paper is corporate debt securities that mature in 270 days or less. Debt securities with a maturity of 270 days or less are exempt from Securities and Exchange Commission (SEC) registration.

50. C. I and IV

There is a difference between securities that are exempt because of whom the issuer is and transactions that are exempt. Exempt securities include U.S. government securities, municipal bonds, securities issued by banks, public utility stocks, securities issued by nonprofit organizations, and so on. Intrastate offerings, Regulation A offerings, Regulation D offerings (private placements), and so on are exempt transactions.

51. A. an offering of securities only within the issuer's home state

A Rule 147 offering is an intrastate (not interstate) offering that's exempt from the Securities and Exchange Commission (SEC) registration provided the issuer conducts business only in one state and sells securities only to residents of the same state. This also includes the 80% rule that states that at least 80% of the issuer's assets are located within the state and at least 80% of the offering proceeds are used within the same state.

52. C. an offering of securities to no more than 35 unaccredited investors within a one-year period

A Regulation D offering is a private placement that only allows up to 35 unaccredited investors per year to invest.

53. C. Regulation T

Regulation D, Regulation A+, and Rule 147 offerings are exempt transactions that are exempt from the full registration requirements of the Securities Act of 1933. Regulation T has to do with the extension of credit for margin and cash accounts.

54. **B. joint investors with a combined income of at least $200,000 for the current year and previous two years**

The list of accredited investors has expanded greatly, and this answer was close. However, because it says "joint" investors, you'd have to change the number to $300,000. The $200,000 would have worked for an individual investor.

55. **B. They are issued without using a prospectus.**

Regulation A+ Tier 2 offerings are offerings of securities valued at $75 million or less within a one-year period (Tier 1 — $20 million or less). Regulation A+ offerings are exempt from the full registration requirements of the Securities Act of 1933. Companies issuing securities through Regulation A+ offerings make an offering circular instead of a prospectus, which is available to all potential purchasers. An *offering circular* is somewhat of an abbreviated form of a prospectus.

56. **D. Private securities offerings are typically exempt from SEC registration.**

Private securities offerings (private placements) are typically exempt from SEC registration under Regulation D.

57. **D. All of the above**

All of the choices listed are considered accredited (sophisticated) investors.

58. **C. Either (A) or (B)**

Rule 144 covers the sale of restricted, unregistered, and control securities. If an investor wishes to sell these securities, the maximum they can sell every 90 days is 1% of the outstanding shares or the average weekly trading volume for the previous 4 weeks, whichever is greater.

59. **A. the sale of control stock**

Rule 144 regulates the sale of control and restricted securities in the secondary market. Included are how long the securities must be held, the type of sale, the limitation on the quantity of securities that can be sold, and so on.

60. **D. 42,500**

When the restricted stock is to be sold, a Form 144 must be filed with the Securities and Exchange Commission (SEC), which is good for 90 days. According to Rule 144, the most the investor can sell after holding the restricted stock for at least six months is the greater of 1% of the outstanding shares or the average weekly trading volume for the previous four weeks. You have to be careful to take just the previous four weeks, which in this case is the top four. Start by multiplying the 1% by the 4 million shares outstanding:

$$(1\%)(4\text{ million}) = 40{,}000$$

Next, determine the average weekly trading volume for the previous four weeks by adding together the quantity of shares sold and dividing by 4:

$$35{,}000 + 50{,}000 + 40{,}000 + 45{,}000 = 170{,}000$$

$$\frac{170{,}000}{4} = 42{,}500$$

This investor can sell a maximum of 42,500 shares.

61. D. All of the above

Even though a security is exempt from registration and prospectus requirements, such as U.S. government securities and private placements, it isn't exempt from the anti-fraud provisions in the Securities Act of 1933 or the Securities Exchange Act of 1934. Anti-fraud rules always apply — all issuers must provide accurate information to the public.

Chapter 2 Answers

62. A. I and III

Both preferred stockholders and common stockholders have ownership of a corporation. Bondholders are creditors, not owners.

63. C. preferred shares

Common and preferred stock are both equity securities which represent ownership of the issuing corporation. TIPS, debentures, and GO bonds are debt securities.

64. C. Stocks represent ownership in an issuing corporation.

Stocks are equity securities that represent ownership in the issuing corporation. Bonds are debt securities that represent a loan to the issuer. Warrants are long-term marketable securities that give the holder the right to purchase stock of the issuer at a fixed price.

65. B. common stock

All public corporations issue common stock. They may also issue bonds, preferred stock, and warrants, but they don't have to.

66. **C. Unpaid workers, IRS, secured creditors, general creditors, subordinated debenture holders, preferred stockholders, common stockholders**

In the event that a corporation declares bankruptcy, the corporate assets are distributed in the following way: unpaid workers, IRS, secured creditors, general creditors, subordinated debenture holders, preferred stockholders, and finally (if there's anything left) common stockholders.

67. **D. common shareholders**

In the event of a corporate bankruptcy, common stockholders have a residual claim on assets meaning that they are the last to get paid if there are any assets left.

68. **B. III and IV**

Common stockholders have a residual claim to the assets of the corporation at dissolution. Common stockholders are entitled to receive a report containing audited financial statements on a yearly — *not* monthly — basis. Stockholders do get to vote for stock splits but not dividends (whether cash or stock); the board of directors decides on dividends.

69. **C. I and II**

Stockholders can't vote for dividends. Stock and cash dividends are declared by the board of directors.

70. **B. Common stockholders**

All common stockholders (except if they purchased non-voting stock) receive voting rights. That same right is not afforded to preferred stockholders or bondholders.

71. **C. I and IV**

Common stockholders can vote for members of the board of directors (BOD) and for stock splits. However, stockholders do not have the right to vote for dividends whether they're stock or cash.

72. **A. I and III**

Common stockholders have limited liability because their loss is limited to the amount they invested. If the issuer goes bankrupt, the common stockholders don't owe money to anyone as a result of that bankruptcy. In addition, common stockholders have voting rights.

73. **D. 4,000**

Cain has a total of 4,000 votes (1,000 shares × 4 vacancies). Because HIT allows cumulative voting, Cain can vote the shares in any way he sees fit, even if he votes them all for one candidate. Statutory or regular voting would allow Cain to vote only up to 1,000 shares for each candidate.

74. C. 3,000 votes each for three candidates

This investor has a total of 8,000 votes (2,000 shares × 4 vacancies), which can be voted any which way because it's cumulative voting. The reason that Choice (C) doesn't work is because it would require 9,000 votes (3,000 votes × 3 candidates), and this investor has only 8,000.

75. B. Cumulative

Cumulative voting gives smaller shareholders a better chance to gain representation on the board of directors. Statutory (regular) voting gives you one vote per share owned times the number of vacancies on the BOD, which have to be split evenly. Cumulative voting gives you the same number of votes, but they don't have to be split evenly.

76. A. Ayla can vote by proxy.

If a stockholder is unable to attend the actual vote, they can vote by proxy (absentee ballot).

77. B. by telephone

Common shareholders who wish to vote can do so either in person or by proxy, which is basically an absentee ballot. However, common shareholders cannot vote by telephone.

78. B. It is stock that was previously authorized but still unissued.

Choices (B) and (C) oppose each other, so one of them has to be the answer to the question. Treasury stock is stock that was issued and subsequently repurchased by the company. Treasury stockholders have no voting rights and don't receive dividends.

79. D. repurchased stock

Choices (A) and (B) are wrong because stock represents ownership, and you can't own a percentage of the government. Treasury stock is stock that was outstanding in the market and subsequently repurchased by the issuer. Corporations repurchase their own stock sometimes to increase the demand for their outstanding shares or to avoid a takeover.

80. C. 950,000

Macrohard could have issued up to 2 million shares, but it issued only 1.1 million at this time. Macrohard repurchased 150,000 shares of its stock, which is called treasury stock. To determine the amount of shares outstanding, use the following formula:

$$\begin{aligned}\text{Outstanding} &= \text{Issued} - \text{Treasury}\\ &= 1{,}100{,}000 - 150{,}000\\ &= 950{,}000\end{aligned}$$

81. C. A stock split

Remember the par value on common stock has no bearing on the market value and is only used for bookkeeping purposes. So, the par value doesn't change for dividends, but it does change for splits. So, if a corporation decided to split its stock 2 for 1, the par value would be cut in half.

82. A. I and III

Unlike the par value of preferred stock and debt securities, the par value doesn't really matter too much to common stockholders. The par value of common stock is generally used for bookkeeping purposes of the issuer, and common stock is even sometimes issued with no par value. In the event of a stock split, the par value would be adjusted to reflect the split. And because stock is an equity security that represents ownership of the issuing corporation, there's no maturity date as there is with debt securities.

83. D. additional paid in capital

Remember the par value for common stock is only used for bookkeeping purposes. So, when a corporation issues stock, it is typically well above the par value. Any money received above par value is called additional paid in capital, paid in surplus, or capital surplus.

84. A. increase

Tender offers are when a corporation, person, or group attempts to take control of a particular corporation. They are attempting to buy enough shares in the market to gain control. To purchase enough shares, they offer a premium over the current market price for sellers willing to sell a large quantity of securities. Since the offer is at a premium, tender offers drive the price of the outstanding securities up.

85. C. A stock split

Par value for a common stock is used for bookkeeping purposes for the issuer and isn't of much use to investors. However, when a company does split its stock (such as 2 for 1), the par value would be reduced.

86. B. 200

This question is asking you how many additional shares the investor would have after the split. Because it's a 4-for-3 split, the investor would have four shares for every three that she had before. Start by multiplying the number of shares owned by four and dividing by three:

$$\frac{(600\text{ shares})(4)}{3} = \frac{2{,}400\text{ shares}}{3} = 800\text{ shares}$$

This investor originally had 600 shares and now has 800, so they received an additional 200 shares. You should be prepared to determine how many additional shares or the number of shares after the split because a Series 7 exam question could ask you to find either answer.

87. B. 1,250 ABC at $32

This is an uneven split. Because of the answers given, you probably don't need to set up an equation for this one. Dana is going to have five shares for every four they had before, so you know that the amount of shares must increase, and the price must decrease because Dana's overall value of securities didn't change. If you wanted to do the math to double-check your answer, first you'd multiply the 1,000 shares by 5 and then divide it by 4:

$$\frac{(1{,}000\text{ shares})(5)}{4} = \frac{5{,}000\text{ shares}}{4} = 1{,}250\text{ shares}$$

Then you multiply the price ($40) by 4 and then divide it by 5:

$$\frac{(\$40)(4)}{5} = \frac{\$160}{5} = \$32\text{ new market price}$$

88. B. 50 shares at $80 per share

This is a reverse split. Because of the answers given, you may not need to set up an equation for this one. Because it's a 1-for-2 reverse split, the investor is going to have one share for every 2 they had before. So, the shares have to go down. If the shares go down, the price has to go up. There is only one answer that works. However, here is how you do the equation:

$$\frac{(100\text{ shares})(1)}{2} = \frac{100\text{ shares}}{2} = 50\text{ shares}$$

Then you multiply the price ($40) by 2 and then divide it by 1:

$$\frac{(\$40)(2)}{1} = \frac{\$80}{1} = \$80\text{ new market price}$$

89. A. I only

Another primary issue of shares would dilute Declan's ownership because new shares would be coming to the market. Don't forget that when a corporation issues stock dividends, splits its stock, or makes a secondary offering, the percentage of equity does not change.

90. D. II and IV

The decision to either pay or not pay a dividend is decided by the board of directors. Since they are decided by the board of directors, there is no dividend guarantee.

91. **A. are not guaranteed**

Even though the board of directors declared a dividend this time, it has no bearing on future dividends. Future dividends can be higher, lower, or nonexistent.

92. **B. $24.65**

You solve this question by simply subtracting the amount of the dividend from the previous day's closing price:

$$\$24.95 - \$0.30 = \$24.65$$

93. **B. The ex-date**

The ex-date or ex-dividend date is the first day the stock trades without the previously declared dividend. Therefore, ABCDEF would have its stock price reduced on the ex-date to reflect the dividend.

94. **A. I and III**

The *ex-dividend date* is the first day a stock trades without a previously declared dividend. The ex-dividend date is one business day before the record date (except for mutual funds), and it's the date that the stock reduces by the amount of the dividend.

95. **D. To increase the demand for its stock**

The main reason a corporation splits its stock is to increase the demand. The most common unit of trading stock is 100 shares, which is called a *round lot.* If a stock is trading at a relatively low price, such as $20, most investors can afford to purchase 100 shares, and it helps keep trading active. However, say that the price of the stock increased to $100 per share; it would cost $10,000 to purchase a round lot. When this happens, trading slows down because not as many investors are able to pay that much for 100 shares. If that same corporation splits its stock 4 for 1, there'd be four times as many shares outstanding at a price of $25 per share, which most investors could afford.

96. **C. II and III**

When an investor receives a stock dividend, the amount of shares the investor owns increases, and the price decreases. The only answer that works is Choice (C). Remember: When an investor receives a stock dividend or stock split, the investor's overall value of investment doesn't change. You can also figure this out mathematically by multiplying the number of shares by the market price, like so:

$$(1{,}000 \text{ shares})(\$24 \text{ market price}) = \$24{,}000$$

This investor owns $24,000 worth of DIM stock, so they'll own $24,000 worth of DIM stock after the stock dividend. Your next step would be to figure out the new number of shares owned by the investor. The investor initially owned 1,000 shares and then received a stock dividend of 200 shares (20% × 1,000 shares):

$$1{,}000 \text{ shares} + 200 \text{ shares} = 1{,}200 \text{ shares}$$

$$\frac{\$24{,}000}{1200 \text{ shares}} = \$20 \text{ market price}$$

97. D. 525 shares valued at $52.38 per share

Your key here is that the overall investment value doesn't change. When investors receive a stock dividend, the number of shares has to increase, and the market price has to reduce. So out of the answer choices given, only one meets the criteria: Choice (D). First, you have to figure out the overall value of investment by multiplying the number of shares by the market price:

$$(500 \text{ shares})(\$55 \text{ per share}) = \$27{,}500$$

This investor had $27,500 worth of stock and will still have $27,500 worth of stock after the dividend. When this investor gets the 5% stock dividend, they'll get 5% more shares, which means that this investor now has 525 shares: 500 shares + 25 shares (5% stock dividend) = 525 shares. Divide the $27,500 by the new number of shares to find the new stock price.

$$\frac{\$27{,}500}{525 \text{ shares}} = \$52.38 \text{ per share}$$

98. C. I and III

Straight preferred stock does receive a fixed dividend and has higher preference than common stock in the event of issuer bankruptcy. However, holders of preferred stock don't have voting rights unless they don't receive expected dividends. Also, unlike bonds, preferred stock has no maturity date.

99. A. I and III

Preferred stock is an equity security like common stock because they both represent ownership of the corporation. Preferred stock is also similar to debt securities because they both have fixed income . . . one in the way of dividend and the other in the way of interest.

100. A. I only

Unlike common stock, which can pay dividends in the form of cash, stock, or product, preferred dividends can be paid only in the form of cash.

101. **A. fall**

Similar to debt securities, because of the fixed income, as interest rates rise, prices will fall. Conversely, if interest rates fall, prices will rise.

102. **C. II and III**

Unlike holders of common stock, preferred stockholders typically don't have voting rights unless not receiving expected dividends. In the event of corporate bankruptcy, preferred stockholders are senior to common stockholders and would receive liquidation assets (if any) before common stockholders.

103. **B. It is fixed and based on the par value.**

Unless variable (adjustable) rate preferred, which you can't assume, preferred dividends are fixed and based on a percentage of par value (typically $100).

104. **D. neither (A) nor (B)**

Unlike common stockholders, preferred stockholders do not have voting rights or preemptive rights. Preemptive right is the right to maintain proportionate ownership of the issuing corporation if they issue new shares. New shares would first be offered to existing stockholders.

105. **B. its par value**

Preferred stock dividends are based on a percentage of its par value. You can assume that the par value of preferred stock is $100 unless stated differently in the question. So, a 6% preferred stock would pay $6 a year in dividends. Dividends are typically paid quarterly.

106. **C. II and III**

Straight preferred stock is non-cumulative, which means that any missed dividends are not required to be paid by the issuer.

107. **C. They continue to accumulate on the company's books until they can be paid.**

When a corporation issues cumulative preferred stock, any past due dividends must be kept on the corporations books until the dividends can be paid. In addition, the corporate issuer cannot pay any common dividends until the past due and current dividends are paid to their cumulative preferred shareholders.

108. B. must pay any past and current preferred dividends before paying any dividends on its common stock

Since this is cumulative preferred stock, the issuer must pay all past due and current dividends on the cumulative preferred stock before paying any dividends on their common stock. Remember preferred stock is senior to common stock so it has a higher priority for dividends.

109. C. $7

If a company issues cumulative preferred stock, it's allowed to owe investors dividend payments. However, before the company pays a dividend to common stockholders, it must first make up any delinquent and current payments to the cumulative preferred shareholders. This company should be paying the preferred shareholders $4 per year (4% of $100 par). In the first three years, the company should have paid out $12 in dividends ($4 × 3 years). However, the company paid only $9, so it owes $3 from the first three years ($12 – $9) and $4 for the following year for a total of $7.

110. C. $11

Remember that because it's cumulative preferred stock, the corporation must make up any missed dividends to its cumulative preferred stockholders before paying a dividend to its common stockholders. In the first year, they shorted their preferred stockholders $2 per share because they were supposed to pay $6 ($100 par × 6%) and only paid $4. In the second year, they only paid $3 to their shareholders so they were shorted $3. So far, so good. However, the key to this question is that they want to pay a common dividend the following year, so you have to add the $6 in dividends for that year also. Here's how it looks:

$$(\$6-\$4)+(\$6-\$3)+\$6=\$11$$

111. B. $18

Since this is cumulative preferred stock, AylDec must make up any past due dividends plus the current one prior to making a dividend payment to the common shareholders. So, the current dividend is $6 (6% × 100 assumed par value) and $6 each for the previous two years for a total of $18.

112. D. convertible preferred stock

Typically, preferred stock trades somewhat close to its par value. Because it trades close to its par value, investors are subject to inflation risk. Inflation risk is the risk that the value of the security doesn't keep pace with the cost of living. Your client can minimize this risk by purchasing convertible preferred stock. Convertible preferred stock allows investors to convert their preferred stock into common stock of the same company at any time. Common stock is more likely to keep pace with inflation.

113. **B. convert their bonds for a fixed number of shares of ABCD common stock**

Holders of convertible bonds are allowed to convert their bonds into a fixed number of shares of common stock of the same company based on the conversion price.

114. **A. Convertible preferred**

Since convertible preferred stock can be converted into a set number of shares of the issuer's common stock, it typically trades pretty close to parity with the issuer's common stock.

115. **D. Convertible**

Since convertible preferred stock is tied to the value of the common stock, it would likely be more volatile in periods of stable interest rates than other types of preferred stock.

116. **C. It allows the issuer to issue preferred stock with a lower fixed dividend after the call date.**

First, you should have crossed off Choice (D) right away because equity securities, such as preferred stock, don't have a maturity date. Callable preferred stock is issued with a higher fixed dividend rate than non-callable because it's riskier for investors (more risk = more reward) because they may not be able to hold the stock as long as they want. Issuers will typically call their callable preferred stock and/or callable bonds when interest rates decrease. If interest rates decrease, issuers would be able to issue preferred stock with a lower fixed dividend and/or bonds with a lower coupon rate.

117. **D. dividend payments will stop once the shares have been called**

Once a corporation calls its shares, they stop trading in the market, and the dividend payments will stop. If you look at choices (C) and (D) you'll notice that they're saying two opposing things. This means that one of them had to be true.

118. **D. Callable preferred**

Because of the additional risk taken with callable preferred, which allows the issuer to call the preferred stock when they want, it would typically pay the highest dividend.

119. **B. HIJ would likely call their outstanding 6% callable preferred stock.**

When interest rates have dropped to where it doesn't make sense for an issuer to have their callable preferred shares in the market, they will call them. Now, they may issue new callable preferred stock with a lower dividend, but they will definitely call their outstanding convertible preferred stock.

120. C. callable

This is another one of those investing situations where more risk = more reward. From an investor's standpoint, purchasing callable securities is riskier than non-callable securities because the issuer decides when the security is called. For example, the issuer may call the security after one year when you were hoping to hold it at least ten years. Because an investor is taking that additional risk, callable securities pay a higher dividend or higher interest (bonds) than non-callable.

121. B. Participating

Participating preferred stock has a stated dividend, which is typically lower than dividends of other preferred stock. However, they do participate in dividends paid to common shareholders up to a point. So, their dividends could possibly end up higher than other preferred depending on the issuer's financial position.

122. A. an additional dividend of 3%

TUVs normal preferred dividend on the participating stock is 5%. However, this year they are going to get 8% because they are participating in the common stock dividend up to 8%. As such, they are receiving an extra dividend of 3%.

123. C. The interest rate is often tied to a benchmark rate like the Treasury bill rate.

The dividend on variable (adjustable or floating-rate) preferred is typically tied to a benchmark such as the Treasury bill (T-bill) rate. As that rate increases, so does the dividend on the variable rate preferred. If the T-bill rate decreases, so would the dividend.

124. A. Variable rate preferred

Since the dividends on variable (adjusting or floating-rate) preferred stock varies based on current interest rates, the price tends to remain more stable than other types of preferred stock.

125. A. Adjustable rate

Adjustable or variable rate preferred stock has a dividend that varies based on current interest rates. These rates are typically tied to a certain benchmark such as T-bills. So as interest rates increase, so does the dividend.

126. A. a receipt for a foreign security trading in the United States

An ADR is an American depositary receipt. ADRs are receipts for foreign securities traded in the United States. Besides the normal risks of investing in securities, holders of ADRs also face currency risk.

127. **C. it has low currency risk**

American depositary receipts (ADRs) facilitate the trading of foreign securities in U.S. markets. ADRs carry currency risk because distributions on them must be converted from foreign currency to U.S. dollars on the date of distribution. The trading price of the ADR is actually quite affected by currency fluctuation, which can devalue any dividends and/or the value of the underlying security.

128. **A. they help U.S. companies gain access to foreign dollars**

American Depositary Receipts (ADRs) are receipts for foreign securities trading in the United States. Therefore, they help foreign companies gain access to U.S. dollars, not the other way around. Investors don't receive the actual stock certificates; they receive a receipt representing a certain number of shares of the issuer. Investors of ADRs don't have voting rights. Dividends (if any) are paid in U.S. dollars.

129. **B. Common stock**

American Depositary Receipts are receipts for foreign securities traded in the United States. Each American Depositary Receipt typically represents one to ten shares of stock of a foreign corporation.

130. **D. As a way to diversify a portfolio**

American Depositary Receipts are receipts for foreign securities trading in the U.S. Many investors purchase ADRs as a way of diversifying their portfolio.

131. **D. I and III**

Many ADRs are listed on exchanges and Nasdaq. They trade in U.S. dollars and the price will fluctuate throughout the day like common stock.

132. **B. I and III**

ADRs (American Depositary Receipts) are issued to help raise money for foreign corporations. They are issued to help foreign corporations gain access to U.S. investors.

133. **D. rights are automatically received by preferred stockholders**

Rights are automatically received by common stockholders, not preferred stockholders. Each share of outstanding common stock receives one right. Rights are short-term (usually 30 to 45 days), and rights offerings typically have a standby underwriter to purchase the shares not purchased by stockholders.

134. B. A rights distribution to existing shareholders

Remember, the corporation is trying to raise money. Choices (A) and (C) would cost the corporation money, and Choice (D) would be a wash. However, having a rights distribution allows existing shareholders to purchase new stock at a discount and, thus, brings more money into the corporation.

135. A. I and IV

Rights are short term because they typically expire in 30 to 60 days. Warrants last several years and are even sometime perpetual (no expiration date), so they're long term.

136. C. They allow investors to buy unissued stock at a discount from market price

Rights allow investors the right to buy stock at a discount as soon as they are issued. However, warrants allow investors the right to buy stock at a premium to the market price when they are first issued. If the market price of the stock increases dramatically, investors will be able to buy the stock at a discount with the warrants. However, there are no guarantees that a stock price will increase.

137. A. It gives existing shareholders the right to purchase more shares at a discount if the issuer is offering more shares.

Rights or preemptive rights give existing shareholders the opportunity to purchase new shares of the issuer at a discount to help maintain proportionate ownership of the corporation. Rights are short term (typically 30–45 days) and may be exercised, sold, or allowed to expire. Shareholders receive 1 right for each common share owned.

138. A. warrants

Warrants are basically long-term options to buy stock from the issuer at a fixed price. Because they are just the right to buy stock and not the actual stock, they don't receive dividends.

139. C. They have voting rights.

Warrants give investors a long-term and sometimes perpetual right to buy stock from the issuer at a fixed price. They are marketable, meaning that they may trade separately. Because warrants aren't the underlying security until the holder actually uses the warrants to purchase stock, they don't receive dividends. The answer that is *not true* is Choice (C). Warrant holders don't have voting rights.

140. B. they are non-marketable securities

Warrants *are* marketable securities, which means that they can be traded separately in the market. Warrants have longer maturities than rights because they typically have a maturity of up to ten years and sometimes longer. Rights typically have a maturity of only 30 to 45 days. When initially issued, warrants are usually combined in a unit with the issuer's bonds. The exercise price of the warrants would be at a price higher than the market price of the issuer's common stock.

141. **B. I and III**

Warrants are most often issued with a corporation's other securities, such as debt securities, to make an offering more attractive. Because of this, warrants are often called "sweeteners" because they're sweetening the deal. Statement II uses the word *perpetual*, which means never ending. Warrants typically provide a long-term and sometimes perpetual interest in the issuer's common stock. Holders of warrants have no voting rights until exercising their right to buy the common stock.

Chapter 3 Answers

142. **A. borrower**

Issuers of bonds are borrowing money from investors.

143. **C. II and III**

Bondholders are lending money to the issuer and are taking the position of a creditor.

144. **B. $1,000**

When holding a bond until maturity, an investor will receive par value. Assume par value is $1,000 unless stated differently in the question.

145. **C. $10,137.50**

The first thing you have to do is convert the fraction to a decimal. So, a bond trading at 101⅜ would convert to a bond trading at 101.375 (3/8 = 0.375). Next, you have to remember that these $1,000 par value bonds aren't actually trading at 101.375. The 101.375 is a percentage of par, so the bonds are actually trading at (101.375%)($1,000 par) = $1,013.75.

Next, because the investor is purchasing ten of these bonds, you have to multiply your answer by 10: ($1,013.75)(10 bonds) = $10,137.50.

146. **A. Nominal yield**

The only yield found on the indenture of a bond is the nominal yield or coupon rate. The reason the other yields can't be on the indenture of a bond is because they change as the market price changes.

147. C. $10,000 plus $300 interest

This one was a little tricky. Probably your first inclination was to go for the $10,000 answer because an investor gets paid par value at maturity, and since this investor had 10 bonds, they would receive $10,000 (10 × $1,000 par). However, you have to remember that bonds with a stated coupon rate pay interest up until the time they mature. So, this investor would receive the $10,000 plus the last semiannual interest payment for the 10 bonds for $300.

148. B. the credit rating

The reason you wouldn't find the credit rating on a bond is because the credit rating would change if the issuer's financial condition changes. They may have a AAA rating now but in three years, who knows?

149. B. I and IV

The coupon rate or nominal yield of the bond is 5.5%, which means that the bond is paying $55 per year ($1,000 assumed par value × 5.5%). Since most bonds pay interest semiannually (twice a year), the semiannual interest payments are $27.50 ($55/2).

150. B. $2,250

The coupon rate is based on the par value of the bonds, not the purchase price or market value. Ayla purchased $100,000 par value of bonds with a coupon rate of 4½%. This means that Ayla will receive $4,500 (4½% × $100,000) in interest per year. However, you can assume (unless told differently in the question) that bonds pay interest semiannually (every six months). So, you need to divide the annual interest by 2 to get $2,250 ($4,500/2).

151. C. receive $60 annual interest until the bond matures

Since the coupon rate is 6%, Mr. Bear will receive $60 per year interest (6% of $1,000 par) broken down into two semiannual payments of $30 each until the bond matures.

152. B. $20.00

To determine the annual interest, you have to multiply the coupon rate (4%) by par value ($1,000): (4%)($1,000) = $40 annual interest.

Because bonds pay interest semiannually (twice a year), the investor will get paid $20 ($40/2) every six months.

153. **B. I and III**

The indenture of a bond is a legal contract between the issuer and the bondholder. The indenture includes items such as the nominal yield (coupon rate), the maturity date, collateral backing the bond (if any), coupon payment dates, and callable and convertible features. The rating and the yield to maturity can't be included in the indenture because neither of them is static. The rating changes if the issuer's financial condition changes, and the yield to maturity changes when the market value changes.

154. **A. A balloon maturity uses components of not only term maturities but also serial maturities.**

With a balloon maturity a portion of the bond is paid off in successive years like a serial bond, but it has one big final payment (balloon payment) due at the final maturity date like a term bond.

155. **A. a percentage of dollar price**

Term bonds are also called *dollar bonds* because they're quoted according to a percentage of dollar price. For example, a term bond that's trading for $990 would be quoted as 99 (99% of $1,000 par).

156. **B. Term**

Term bonds are all issued at one time, and they all mature at one time.

157. **B. term bond**

Term bonds are all issued at one time and all mature at one time so the issuer will have a big payment due at the maturity date. In order to have the funds available for that big payment, the issuer will put money aside in a sinking fund. Typically, the money in the sinking fund is invested in safe securities such as U.S. Treasury securities.

158. **C. Serial**

Term bonds are all issued at one time and all mature at one time, so they typically have a sinking fund available to pay off the debt. Serial bonds have one issue date, but an equal amount of bonds mature each year sometime in the future (such as 20% on year 26, 20% on year 27, 20% on year 28, 20% on year 29, and 20% on year 30). Balloon issues are issued at the same time and mature in subsequent years like serial bonds but have a balloon payment at the end (such as 10% on year 26, 10% on year 27, 10% on year 28, 10% on year 29, and 60% on year 30). Series bonds are kind of the opposite of serial bonds because they're issued on different dates but all mature on the same date.

ANSWERS 101–200

159. C. Balloon

A balloon issue has a portion of the bonds maturing prior to the final maturity date. At the final maturity date, the largest payment (a balloon payment) is due.

160. A. series

Bonds can be issued with term, serial, or balloon maturity but not series maturity. Bonds may be issued in series, but they are each their own separate bond issue.

161. D. a lien on property owned by HIJ Corp.

This is one of those questions that takes you on a ride full of superfluous information you don't need. All you need to know is what the bonds are secured by. In this case, you're dealing with mortgage bonds, which are secured by a lien on property owned by HIJ. In the event that HIJ failed to pay principal and/or interest to its bondholders, property owned by HIJ would be sold to generate the money to make the payments.

162. B. I and II

Corporations may issue unsecured bonds, such as debentures, subordinated debentures, and income bonds, or secured bonds, such as mortgage bonds, equipment trust bonds, income bonds, and guaranteed bonds. However, *double-barreled bonds* and *revenue bonds* are types of bonds issued by municipalities.

163. C. an equipment trust bond

Equipment trust bonds (or equipment trust certificates, ETCs) are typically issued by transportation companies, such as trucking companies, airlines, and railroads. These secured bonds are backed by rolling stock (assets on wheels). In the event of default, the rolling assets backing the bonds would be sold to pay off bondholders.

164. D. Both (A) and (C).

Equipment trust bonds (or equipment trust certificates, ETCs) are typically issued by transportation companies, such as trucking companies, airlines, and railroads. These secured bonds are backed by rolling stock (assets on wheels). The trustee holds the titles to the assets backing the bonds and in the event of default, the assets backing the bonds would be sold to pay off bondholders.

165. B. backed by stocks and bonds owned by the issuer

Collateral trust bonds are typically issued by holding companies that hold securities of other companies. In the event of default, the debt holders receive the securities held in trust. A trustee hired by the issuer is responsible for the safeguarding of the securities and transferring the assets in the event of default.

166. B. One that is backed by the assets of another company

A *guaranteed bond* is one that's backed by the assets of another company (typically a parent company).

167. D. debenture

Unlike equipment trust bonds, mortgage bonds, and collateral trust bonds, debentures are not backed by any of the issuer's assets. With all else being equal, debentures are riskier than secured bonds and would, therefore, pay a higher coupon rate.

168. A. It has a claim that is lower than other debt securities but higher than the issuer's preferred stock.

In the event of corporate bankruptcy, subordinated debentures have a lower claim than all of the other debt issues but higher than the common and preferred stock.

169. C. investment grade debentures

Whether investment grade or not, debentures are junior debt, which are not secured by any collateral.

170. B. income bonds

The one you need to stay away from is income (adjustment) bonds. Income bonds are typically issued by failing businesses (bankruptcy or reorganization). As such, the bondholders receive only the interest and principal if the issuer has enough money to pay it. Income bonds are extremely risky, but if the company turns around, the reward can be high. Income bonds are typically issued at a deep discount. All of the other answer choices would be proper recommendations for an investor who is risk-averse.

171. C. Income bonds

Income (adjustment) bonds trade without interest (trade flat) unless the board of directors declares payments. These bonds are typically issued at a deep discount by companies that are in financial trouble.

172. D. Adjustment bonds

Adjustment (income) bonds would be ideal for Bad Luck Corp. The interest and/or principal on adjustment bonds doesn't have to be paid unless the company becomes profitable.

173. **C. Income bonds**

Income or adjustment bonds are bonds issued by corporations in financial trouble and are typically trying to reorganize after coming out of bankruptcy. The interest on income bonds is not paid until the issuer is in a financial position to do so. These are very speculative securities.

174. **C. remains fixed**

The coupon rate (nominal yield) of a bond remains fixed for the life of the bond unless the coupon rate is variable, which you can't assume and it would have to be stated in the question.

175. **B. increased**

Interest rates and the market prices of outstanding bonds go in opposite directions. So, as interest rates decrease, the prices of outstanding bonds will increase and vice versa.

176. **D. nominal yield**

The only yield that could be included on the indenture of a corporate bond is the nominal yield (coupon rate). None of the other choices could be placed on the indenture of a corporate bond because they don't remain fixed. The yield to maturity, yield to call, and current yield change over time and when the market price changes.

177. **A. The current yield is equal to the yield to maturity.**

For bonds trading at par, the nominal yield, current yield, yield to maturity, and yield to call would all be equal.

178. **C. annual interest by the market price**

To determine the current yield on a bond, you divide the annual interest by the market price of the bond.

179. **A. 4.19%**

The coupon rate represents the annual rate of interest. In this case, the coupon rate is 4.25%, which means that the investor will receive $42.50 (4.25% of $1,000 par) per year broken down into two semiannual payments.

U.S. government bonds, such as Treasury bonds (T-bonds), are quoted in 32nds, not decimals, so pay close attention to the security in the question.

The market price of the bond is

$$101.16 = 101\frac{16}{32} = 101.50\% \text{ of } \$1{,}000 \text{ par} = \$1{,}015.00$$

Finally, to determine the current yield, use the following formula:

$$\text{Current yield on a bond} = \frac{\text{Annual interest}}{\text{Market price}} = \frac{\$42.50}{\$1,015.00} = 0.0419, \text{ or } 4.19\%$$

180. **C. 4.35%**

To determine the current yield of a bond, you have to divide the annual interest by the market price. The annual interest is $40, and the market price is $920:

$$\text{Current yield} = \frac{\text{Annual interest}}{\text{Market price}} = \frac{\$40}{\$920} = 0.0435, \text{ or } 4.35\%$$

181. **C. 6.36%**

To determine the current yield of a bond, you have to divide the annual interest by the market price. Since the semiannual interest is $35, the annual interest is $70 ($35 × 2). You can use the following formula:

$$\text{Current yield} = \frac{\text{Annual interest}}{\text{Market price}} = \frac{\$70}{\$1100} = 0.0636, \text{ or } 6.36\%$$

182. **C. premium**

Basis is the same as yield to maturity. If the yield to maturity is lower than the 7% coupon rate (nominal yield), the bond is trading at a premium.

183. **C. below 6%**

Since this investor purchased the bond at a premium (above 100 or $1,000 par), the highest yield would be the coupon rate or nominal yield. Progressively, the yields would go down from there from the current yield, yield to maturity, and yield to call if the bond is callable.

184. A. A 5% bond yielding 7%

When the question says "yielding," it's talking about the yield to maturity (YTM). Since the coupon rate on answers (C) and (D) is above the YTM, they are both premium bonds that would cost more than $1,000 to purchase. Since the coupon rate and YTM are the same on answer (B), the cost of that bond would be $1,000. So, the only answer that works is answer (A) because the YTM is greater than the coupon rate, so the bond must be selling at a discount below $1,000.

185. D. I, II, and IV

The best way to visualize a bond selling at a discount and how it affects the yields is by setting up a seesaw, like the following. Because the bond is selling at a discount, the price is below par value, so the left side of the seesaw has to be lowered.

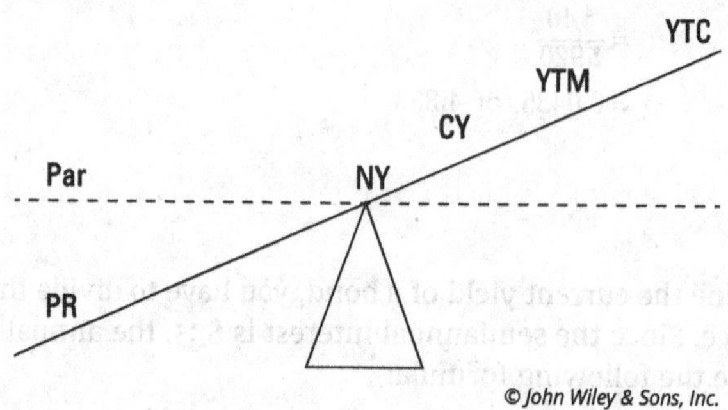

With the left side lowered, you can see that the market price (PR) is below par value, the current yield (CY) is greater than the coupon rate (NY = nominal yield), and the yield to maturity (YTM) is greater than the current yield. However, because rates and prices have an inverse relationship, if interest rates declined, outstanding bond prices would rise above par, not below par.

186. D. 5.75%

Since this bond was purchased at a premium (above par), the yield to maturity (YTM) has to be below the coupon rate of 6%. The only possible answer that could work is answer (D).

187. B. It is greater than 5%

For bonds trading at a premium, the yields go as follows from highest to lowest: nominal yield, current yield, yield to maturity (basis), and yield to call. Since the yield to maturity is 5%, the nominal yield (coupon rate) has to be higher than that.

188. **A. I and III**

One point on a bond equals 1% ($10 on a $1,000 par bond). A basis point is 1/100 of a point, or 10 cents. In this case, because the bond increased by 50 basis points (1/2 a point), it increased by 0.50% or $5.

189. **A. $10**

One point on a bond is 1% of $1,000 par or $10.

190. **A. Default risk**

Moody's, Standard & Poor's, and Fitch rate the likelihood of default of bond issuers. The likelihood of default relates to the chances that investors won't receive their expected interest payments or par value at maturity.

191. **C. I, II, and III**

The top four Moody's ratings — Aaa, Aa, A, Baa — are considered investment grade, and everything Ba and below are considered speculative or "junk" bonds. Remember, S&P, Moody's, and Fitch rate the creditworthiness of debt securities.

192. **D. I, II, III, and IV**

The liquidity (marketability) of a bond depends on many factors, including the rating (the higher, the more liquid), the coupon rate (the higher, the more liquid), the maturity (the shorter, the higher the liquidity), call features (non-callable bonds are more liquid), the current market value (the lower, the more liquid), and the issuer (the more well known, the more liquid).

193. **A. IV, III, II, I**

The top four S&P (Standard & Poor's) investment ratings — AAA, AA, A, and BBB — are considered investment grade and have a relatively high degree of safety. Each rating can be broken down even further by adding plusses and minuses. For example, in the AA rating, you'd have from highest to lowest: AA+, AA, AA–. So, the first thing you need to look at is the letter rating and then whether it has any plusses or minuses. Out of the choices listed, AAA is the highest, AA is the next highest, AA– is the one after that, and A+ is the lowest. You can assume for test purposes that the lower the rating, the higher the yield (more risk = more reward).

ANSWERS 101–200

194. A. IV, III, II, I

The top four Moody's investment ratings — Aaa, Aa, A, and Baa — are considered investment grade and have a relatively high degree of safety. Each rating can be broken down even further by adding numbers 1, 2, and 3. For example, in the Aa rating, you'd have from highest to lowest: Aa1, Aa2, Aa3. So, the first thing you need to look at is the letter rating and then whether it has any numbers next to it. Out of the choices listed, Aaa is the highest, Aa2 is the next highest, Aa3 is the one after that, and A1 is the lowest. You can assume for test purposes that the lower the rating, the higher the yield (more risk = more reward).

195. B. maturity

Additional features added to bonds would be whether they're callable, puttable, convertible, and so on. However, the maturity date is not considered an additional feature.

196. D. allows the issuer to call in their bonds prior to the maturity date if in their best interest

A call feature on a bond gives the issuer the right to call in the bonds prior to maturity. Issuers would likely call their bonds if interest rates drop and they can issue bonds with a lower coupon rate.

197. D. Little call protection

This is one of those questions where you have to look at things from a corporation's point of view rather than an investor's point of view. From a corporation's point of view, having to pay a high coupon rate, having a put feature, and having to pay a high call premium aren't desirable. However, having little call protection on callable bonds that it issued would be the best. Call protection has to do with the number of years an issuer has to wait before calling its bonds.

198. C. The investor decides when to exercise the call privilege.

You're looking for the false answer in this question. The investor doesn't decide when the bonds are called, the issuer does.

199. B. the amount an issuer must pay above par value when calling its bonds early

A call premium is the amount over par value paid by an issuer if calling its bonds in the early years.

200. D. The amount that the issuer must pay to investors for calling its bonds early

A call premium is the amount that the issuer must pay to investors for calling its bonds early. When a corporation issues callable bonds, it typically has to pay a call premium (an amount over par value) as a disincentive for calling its bonds early. The issuer, not the investor, is the one that decides when the bonds are called.

201. D. II and III

The issuer would likely call their bonds if interest rates fall so that they could issue debt securities with a lower coupon rate. Investors would likely put their bonds if interest rates rise so they could purchase bonds with a higher coupon rate.

202. C. allows ABDC bondholders the right to convert their bonds into ABDC common stock

A convertible feature on a corporate bond allows the bondholder to convert their bond into common stock (not non-voting common stock) of the same issuer.

203. A. $20

You can assume that the par value for a bond is $1,000, so, if the bond is convertible into 50 shares of stock, the conversion price is $20 ($1,000/50 shares).

204. A. Allow the bond to be called.

The best way to determine what's best for the investor is to determine the amount of money he'll receive for the call, for selling the bond in the market, and for converting the bond. Whichever is highest is the best for the investor.

Allowing the bond to be called: $1,020 (102% of $1,000 par)

Selling the bond in the market: $980 (98% of $1,000 par)

Converting the bond and selling the stock: $1,000 (25 shares × $40)

For an investor holding the convertible bond, the best alternative is to allow the bond to be called because the investor will receive $1,020, which is higher than the other two alternatives.

205. D. 25

As with some of the questions you'll see on the real Series 7 exam, this question includes information that isn't necessary to answer the question. Don't let the test writers take you on a ride that you don't need to be on. Just focus on the information you need to answer the question.

The conversion ratio is the amount of shares a convertible bond (or stock) is convertible into. You can use the following formula:

$$\text{Conversion ration} = \frac{\text{Par}}{\text{Conversion price}} = \frac{\$1{,}000}{\$40} = 25 \text{ shares}$$

In this case, assuming that the par value for the bonds is $1,000, an investor would receive 25 shares of TUV's common stock if converting one of his bonds.

206. D. $1,120

The first step you have to take with convertible bond questions is to get the shares. To determine how many shares the bond is convertible into, use the following formula:

$$\text{Conversion ration} = \frac{\text{Par}}{\text{Conversion price}} = \frac{\$1{,}000}{\$25} = 40 \text{ shares}$$

To determine the parity price of the stock, multiply the number of shares by the market price of the stock: (40 shares) ($ 28) = $1,120.

207. A. I and III

First, get the shares that the bond is convertible into, using the following formula:

$$\text{Conversion ration} = \frac{\text{Par}}{\text{Conversion price}} = \frac{\$1{,}000}{\$50} = 20 \text{ shares}$$

To determine the parity price of the stock, multiply the number of shares by the market price of the stock: (20 shares)($42) = $840.

The bond is trading for $830 (83% of $1,000 par), and it's convertible into $840 worth of stock. This means that the bonds are trading below parity, and converting the bonds would be profitable.

208. B. $1,200

Parity price is when the convertible security is convertible into the same dollar amount of the security it's being converted into. So, when you're dealing with questions that are asking for parity price, you must first determine the conversion ratio, which will sometimes be given. The conversion ratio is the amount of shares the bond is convertible into. You can use the following formula:

$$\text{Conversion ration} = \frac{\text{Par}}{\text{Conversion price}} = \frac{\$1{,}000}{\$20} = 50 \text{ shares}$$

Assume that pare value is $1,000 unless told differently. In this case, after using the equation, you can see that the conversion ratio is 50 shares. To determine the parity price, use the following information:

parity price of the bond = market price of the stock × conversion ratio parity price of the bond = $24 × 50 shares = $1,200

So, in this case, if the bond is trading below $1,200, it may make sense for the investor to convert the bond.

209. **A. are all issued in book-entry form**

U.S. Treasury securities such as T-bills, T-notes, T-bonds, TIPS, and so on are all issued in book-entry (electronic) form so investors cannot receive the actual certificates. Some pay semiannual interest while others are issued at a discount and mature at par and make no interest payments. In addition, most of the U.S. Treasury securities are issued in a minimum denomination of $100, not $1,000.

210. **D. I, II, III, and IV**

Initial maturities for U.S. Treasury bills are 4, 8, 13, 17, 26, and 52 weeks.

211. **B. I, II, and IV**

This question is a little tricky. The keyword to this question is *earn.* Although holders of Treasury bills and Treasury STRIPS don't receive interest payments, they do receive interest. Treasury bills and Treasury STRIPS are issued at a discount and mature at par value, and that difference is considered interest. Treasury bondholders receive interest payments once every six months. However, Treasury stock is stock that was issued and subsequently repurchased by the issuing corporation. Stockholders never receive interest but sometimes receive dividends.

212. **A. issued at a maturity of 20 years or more**

At the present time, U.S. Treasury bonds are issued with maturities of either 20 or 30 years.

213. **C. III, I, II**

Treasury bills are issued with maturities of one month, three months, six months, and one year. Treasury notes are issued with maturities of more than one year to ten years. Treasury bonds are issued with maturities of 10 years to 30 years.

214. **B. 32 weeks**

Treasury bills are short-term U.S. government securities. Initial maturities include 4 weeks, 8 weeks, 13 weeks, 17 weeks, 26 weeks, and 52 weeks.

215. **B. Treasury stock**

Treasury bills, Treasury STRIPS, and Treasury bonds are all U.S. government securities and are directly backed. However, Treasury stock is stock that has been repurchased by a corporate issuer.

216. C. Treasury STRIPS

Treasury STRIPS (T-STRIPS or Treasury receipts) can be purchased in many different maturities. Obviously in this case, Mary should purchase ones with 15-year maturities. They are purchased at a discount, mature at par value, and don't make interest payments along the way, so Mary doesn't have to worry about reinvestment risk. The longer-term STRIPS can be purchased at a deep discount to par value, and all STRIPS mature at par value.

217. D. a percentage of par value

As with corporate bonds U.S. Treasury notes (T-notes) interest is stated as a percentage of par value. So, a 4% Treasury note with a par value of $1,000 would pay $40 per year interest (4% × $1,000).

218. A. pay interest semiannually and mature at par value

T-bonds (Treasury bonds) are long-term bonds issued by the U.S. government. They mature at par value and holders receive semiannual interest payments.

219. B. Treasury STRIPS

Treasury STRIPS are interest payments stripped and bundled from U.S. government bonds and notes. They are issued at a discount, mature at the face value, and do not pay interest along the way.

220. D. TIPS

As with T-bonds and T-notes, TIPS (Treasury Inflation Protected Securities) pay interest every 6 months. However, the interest payments on TIPS adjust according to inflation or deflation.

221. A. Treasury STRIPs

Treasury STRIPS are made up of bundled interest and principal payments stripped from Treasury bonds and notes. Treasury STRIPs are issued at a discount and mature at the face value without making interest payments along the way.

222. A. Treasury bills

Treasury bills (T-bills) are short-term U.S. government debt securities that mature in one year or less. They are issued at a discount and mature at par value. The difference is earned interest. Unlike some other U.S. government securities, holders of Treasury bills do not receive interest payments.

223. D. I, II, III, and IV

All of the choices listed are direct obligations of the U.S. government, which provides a high degree of safety.

224. A. Ginnie Mae (GNMA)

GNMA is directly backed by the full faith and credit of the U.S. government. FNMA and FHLMC have the implied backing of the U.S. government but are not quite as safe as GNMA.

225. B. I and IV

Money market securities are short-term debt securities that mature in one year or less. As such, they are considered safer and would provide a lower return than longer-term debt securities.

226. A. short-term debt

Money market instruments are short-term debt securities that typically have maturities of one year or less.

227. C. I, III, and IV

Money market instruments are short-term debt securities that mature in one year or less. Banker's acceptances, commercial paper, and Treasury bills are all considered money market instruments. However, T-notes (Treasury notes) are not short term because their initial maturity is 2, 3, 5, 7, or 10 years.

228. B. II and III

Money market securities are typically quite liquid (easily tradable). However, because they are short-term and investors are not taking as much risk as holding a longer-term security, the returns are typically lower. In addition, because they mature much more quickly, investors may have to invest the money they receive at maturity at a much lower rate depending on prevailing interest rates. Answer IV is correct but it is not a risk.

229. A. Common stocks

Money market instruments are short-term debt securities. Capital market instruments include long-term bonds, common stock, and preferred stock.

230. C. debt securities with a fixed income and short-term maturity

Money market instrument are short-term (typically one year or less) bonds with a fixed income.

ANSWERS 201–300

231. D. federal funds

All member banks have to keep a percentage of their deposits available on a daily basis (reserve requirements). If one bank has excess reserves, it can loan money to another bank to help them meet their reserve requirements. These are usually overnight loans, and they're made with federal funds; the interest rate charged is the federal funds rate.

232. A. I, III, and IV

Corporate commercial paper matures in 270 days or less and is exempt from the Securities and Exchange Commission (SEC) registration. It's issued at a discount and matures at par value and, therefore, trades without accrued interest. Unlike some other corporate debt securities, commercial paper isn't backed by the issuer's assets.

233. D. 270 days

Corporate commercial paper is a money market instrument. To be exempt from the Securities and Exchange Commission (SEC) registration, commercial paper has a maximum expiration of 270 days.

234. A. Commercial paper

So the question is telling you that TUBBB only needs the money for a short period of time to raise money for seasonal inventory. The only one of the choices that works is answer (A) because commercial paper is short-term debt that matures in 270 days or less.

235. C. I and III

The difference between regular bank CDs and negotiable CDs is that negotiable CDs are considered money market instruments that can be sold in the market to other investors. Additionally, negotiable CDs typically require an initial investment of $100,000 or more.

236. A. Negotiable CDs can be traded in the secondary market whereas regular CDs cannot.

Both negotiable CDs (certificates of deposit) and regular CDs have a fixed rate of return, but negotiable CDs can be traded in the secondary market and regular CDs cannot.

237. B. Banker's acceptances

Banker's acceptances (BAs) are a time draft used by companies to help finance international trade. Banker's acceptances are short-term and typically have a maturity of 270 days or less.

238. **B. Treasury bills**

Treasury bills (T-bills) are U.S. government securities that mature in one year or less. Since they are issued by the U.S. government, they have little to no risk and would therefore be suitable for this investor looking to buy a house.

Chapter 4 Answers

239. **A. issuers**

The Municipal Securities Rulemaking Board (MSRB) establishes rules that broker-dealers, bank-dealers, and municipal advisors must follow when engaging in transactions of municipal securities. Issuers aren't subject to MSRB rules.

240. **C. The Supreme Court**

The Supreme Court established regulations that made interest payments on municipal bonds federally tax-free and interest payments on U.S. government bonds state tax-free.

241. **B. II, III, and IV**

General obligation (GO) bonds are issued to fund non-revenue-producing facilities and are backed by the taxing power of the municipality. Because the people living in the municipality will be paying additional taxes to back the bonds, they do need voter approval. Also, GO bonds are subject to a debt ceiling, which is the maximum amount of money that a municipality may borrow to meet its needs.

242. **B. I and III**

Municipal general obligation (GO) bonds and double-barreled bonds are backed by the full faith and credit and taxing power of the municipal issuer. Double-barreled bonds are backed by a revenue-producing facility, and, if the revenues are insufficient to be able to pay the principal and interest on the bonds, they're backed by the municipality.

243. **B. I and II**

Municipal bonds are government bonds issued by states and local governments.

244. **C. Property taxes**

Property taxes (ad valorem taxes) are the largest source of funding for municipal general obligation (GO) bonds, not revenue bonds.

245. D. all of the above

Although the largest backing for municipal general obligation bonds is property taxes, they are also backed by traffic fines, licensing fees, sales taxes, and so on.

246. C. II and IV

Municipal revenue bonds are supposed to be self-supporting. The revenues received from the revenue-producing facility backing the bond are supposed to be enough to cover the debt. So, they don't require voter approval and aren't subject to a debt ceiling because they aren't backed by taxes.

247. A. property taxes

Property taxes are the largest source of backing for general obligation (GO) bonds, not revenue bonds. Revenue bonds are self-supporting and backed by user fees of the revenue-producing project or facility.

248. B. Property taxes

Property taxes are the largest source of backing for general obligation (GO) bonds, not revenue bonds. What's important to revenue bond investors is the *feasibility study* (how much sense the income producing project makes), *the flow of funds* (priority of payments from revenues), and *rate covenants* (a promise to adequately charge users of the facility).

249. B. I and II

General obligation (GO) bonds require voter approval prior to being issued because they're mostly backed by taxes on people living in the municipality. GO bonds are issued to fund non-revenue-producing facilities, such as schools and jails. A municipality would issue revenue bonds to fund revenue-producing projects, such as toll roads and airports. Revenue bonds are backed by users, not taxes.

250. B. the dated date

The dated date is the first day that a bond starts accruing interest and isn't a factor in the marketability of a bond. However, the credit rating, the maturity date, and the issuer's name are all important and would affect the marketability of a bond.

251. C. the call feature makes the bonds more marketable

Looking at Choices (A) and (C), you'll notice that they directly oppose each other, so the chances are extremely high that one of those is the correct answer. You're looking for the answer that's the exception in this case, so it has to be Choice (C). The call feature of a bond doesn't make the bond more marketable; it makes it less marketable. Therefore, the issuers would have to pay higher coupon rates to attract investors.

252. D. I, II, III, and IV

All of the choices listed are important. General obligation (GO) bonds are backed by the full faith, credit, and taxing power of the municipality. Although the largest backing for GO bonds is property (ad valorem) taxes, they're also backed by items such as license fee and fines. The issuer's home state is important because if purchasing a tax-free municipal bond within your own home state, the interest will be triple tax-free. You'd also want to see a growing population trend because that means that more people will be backing the bonds. Obviously, bonds being backed by a wealthy community are better than ones backed by a poor community. You'd also want to see a diversity of industry within the tax base because that would help a community grow.

253. C. Municipal bonds

The interest received on municipal bonds is federally tax-free. Because Gary is in the highest income-tax bracket, they can save more money by investing in municipal bonds. This strategy will put Gary on equal footing with other investors because neither high-income no low-income investors have to pay federal taxes on the interest received from municipal bonds. Therefore, municipal bonds are more advantageous to investors in high income-tax brackets.

254. D. I, II, III, and IV

Actually, all of the choices given are important. The higher your client's tax bracket, the bigger the advantage for buying municipal bonds. If a client purchases municipal bonds issued from within his home state, he'll have the advantage of them being triple tax-free. The bond's rating and maturity are important depending on the risk tolerance of your client.

255. C. default risk

Municipal bond insurance is a credit enhancer that insures municipal bonds against default risk. Default risk is the risk that interest and principal payments won't be received. In the event that the issuer fails to make expected payments, the insurance company will make them. Insured municipal bonds are typically rated AAA.

256. D. a state

Overlapping (coterminous) debt is important to not only taxpayers but also purchasers of municipal general obligation (GO) bonds. Overlapping debt has to do with debt being shared by more than one municipality. An example would be a town that's responsible for a portion of the county's debt. People who live in a county are also responsible for a portion of the state's debt. However, states can't be overlapped because one state isn't responsible for a portion of another state's debt.

257. **A. property tax**

The largest backing for municipal general obligation (GO) bonds is property taxes. The credit rating of GO bonds is highly dependent on the municipality's tax collection record, the number of people living in the municipality, property values, whether it's a limited tax GO bond or unlimited tax GO bond, and so on. Unlike revenue bonds, GO bonds typically require voter approval prior to being issued.

258. **C. They are issued to fund revenue-producing facilities.**

GO (general obligation) bonds are issued to fund non-revenue-producing facilities. Municipal revenue bonds are issued to fund revenue-producing facilities.

259. **D. I, II, and IV**

Revenue bonds are backed by the revenue-producing facility and are supposed to be self-sustaining. Raising money by issuing revenue bonds to build toll roads, airports, and sports stadiums all make sense because the revenues from these projects would be used to pay off bondholders. However, if a municipality wanted to build a new library, it would issue GO bonds because libraries don't make enough money to be self-sustaining.

260. **B. II and III**

Revenue bonds are typically lower rated than general obligation (GO) bonds because GO bonds are backed by taxes. As such, revenue bonds do not require voter approval to be issued.

261. **A. The municipal issuer will most likely default on the next interest payment.**

If the revenues are not sufficient to pay the next interest payment, the issuer will default on that bond issue.

262. **A. the maturity date of the issue will typically exceed the useful life of the facility backing the bonds**

In this case, you need to find the exception. The maturity of revenue bonds may be 25 to 30 years, but the facility being built by the income received from the revenue bond issue is usually expected to last a long time, if not a lifetime. Revenue bonds may be issued by interstate authorities, such as tolls, and the interest and principal on the bonds is paid from revenue received from the facility backing the bonds. In addition, revenue bonds aren't subject to a debt ceiling (maximum tax that can be imposed on people living in the municipality); general obligation bonds are.

263. **C. They are backed by a corporation.**

An industrial development revenue (IDR) bond is a municipal bond that's backed by a private company. The municipality uses the lease payments that the private company makes to pay principal and interest on the bonds. Therefore, IDRs are the riskiest municipal bonds.

264. **D. IDRs**

IDRs (industrial development revenue bonds; also IDBs or IRBs) are municipal bonds backed by a corporate lessee. Because they may be non-public purpose bonds, the interest received from these bonds may be subject to alternative minimum tax (AMT).

265. **D. Industrial development revenue bonds**

Industrial development revenue bonds (IDRs, IRBs, or IDBs) are typically issued to fund buildings or acquire factories for private-sector companies. As such, the interest income from the IDRs is subject to alternative minimum tax (AMT) calculation.

266. **A. Rate covenants**

A rate covenant would be on the indenture of a revenue bond, not a general obligation (GO) bond. However, per capita debt (debt per person), assessed property values, and the tax collection history of the municipality would all certainly affect the credit rating of a GO bond.

267. **D. covenants**

Covenants are promises stated on the indenture and are important for investors of revenue bonds, not general obligation bonds. An example is an insurance covenant in which the issuer promises to adequately insure the income-producing facility backing the bonds.

268. **C. insurance covenants**

You're looking for the exception in this question. Covenants are promises placed on the indenture of revenue bonds, not general obligation bonds. However, general obligation (GO) bonds are subject to a debt ceiling and are backed by items such as property taxes and traffic fines.

ANSWERS 201–300

269. A. I and II

When analyzing municipal general obligation (GO) bonds, investors should be concerned with the tax base, efficiency of the government, existing debt, debt per capita, and so on. If investing in municipal revenue bonds, an investor should be concerned about covenants and flow of funds.

270. B. *The Bond Buyer*

The Bond Buyer provides the best source of information about municipal bonds in the primary market. *The Bond Buyer* includes the 40-Bond Index, 20-Bond index, 11-Bond Index, Revenue Bond Index (RevDex), the visible supply, and the placement ratio.

271. C. Notice of sale

When a municipality wants to inform potential underwriters that it's taking bids for a new issue, it would post an official notice of sale in *The Bond Buyer*.

272. C. A syndicate that could sell the issue with the lowest cost to the municipality

The issuer will determine the winning bid on the lowest cost. The issuer will take into consideration the coupon rate (the lower, the better) and the selling price (the higher, the better).

273. A. the bond rating

The official notice of sale is an official invitation from a municipality, asking for broker-dealers to bid on a new issue of municipal bonds. The official notice of sale includes the date, time and place of sale, the bond maturity date, interest payment dates, any call provisions, the amount of good faith deposit, a description of the issue, and so on. The rating of the bond issue comes from ratings companies, such as Moody's and Standard & Poor's, and isn't determined until the bond is issued.

274. D. I, II, III, and IV

The official notice of sale is published in *The Bond Buyer* and is designed to solicit bids from underwriters for a new issue of municipal bonds. Included in the official notice of sale is all the information needed by underwriters to come up with a bid for the new issue, such as the name of the issuer, a description of the issuer, type of bond (GO, revenue, double-barreled), any bidding restrictions, required interest payment dates, the dated date, any call provisions, maturity structure (long term, short term), denomination of certificates, the name of the bond counsel, the name of the trustee, and so on.

275. A. IV, III, II, I

Typically, a syndicate sets up the way their orders are to be filled as follows: presale, syndicate (group-net), designated, member.

276. C. is backed by excise taxes

Special tax bonds are municipal bonds backed by excise taxes such as additional taxes on fuel, tobacco, alcohol, business licenses, and so on.

277. B. A special assessment bond

This project would most likely be funded by a special assessment bond. With a special assessment bond, only the people who will benefit from the new sewer project will be taxed at a higher rate to pay for the principal and interest on the bond.

278. A. They are backed by charges on the benefitted property.

Special assessment bonds are types of municipal bonds that are backed by taxes on the properties that benefit. For example, say that people who live a few blocks from you got all new streetlights and sidewalks. Why should you pay additional taxes to pay for their streetlights and sidewalks? The answer is, you shouldn't, and that's where special assessment bonds come into play. In this case, just the properties that benefit will be taxed at a higher level, while yours stays the same.

279. D. double-barreled bonds

Double-barreled bonds are kind of a combination of revenue and general obligation bonds. Revenue bonds are typically 100% supported by revenues generated by the revenue-producing facility. If it's a double-barreled bond and if the revenues aren't high enough to pay interest and/or principal on the bonds, the revenues are supplemented with municipal taxes.

280. D. I and IV

A double-barreled bond is a combination of revenue and general obligation (GO) bonds. If the revenues from the revenue-producing facility fall short, the bonds will be backed by the full faith and credit (taxing power) of the municipality.

281. A. they are backed by U.S. government subsidies

New housing authority (NHA) bonds are also known as public housing authority (PHA) bonds or simply housing authority bonds. NHA bonds are issued to build or repair low-income housing. Besides the rental income, these bonds are considered quite safe because they're backed by a subsidy from the U.S. government and are typically rated AAA.

282. B. Public housing authority bonds

Public housing authority (PHA) bonds are municipal bonds issued to finance the repair or construction of low-income housing. These bonds are extra safe because even though they're technically municipal bonds, they're guaranteed by the federal government. As with most other municipal bonds, their interest is exempt from federal taxation.

283. A. A moral obligation bond

A moral obligation bond is a revenue bond in which the state legislature has the authority, but no legal obligation, to provide financial backing for the issuer in the event of default.

284. A. BABs

BABs (Build America Bonds) are taxable municipal bonds issued to raise money for infrastructure projects, such as bridges, tunnels, and roads. There are two types of BABs: *tax credit BABs,* in which holders receive tax credits from the U.S. Treasury equal to 35% of the coupon rate, and *direct payment BABs,* in which the issuer receives tax credits from the U.S. Treasury equal to 35% of the coupon rate. Direct payment BABs are more commonly issued than tax credit BABs. Therefore, investors would likely receive a higher coupon rate than tax credit BABs.

285. B. Direct payment BABs

Direct payment BABs (Build America Bonds) are bonds issued to fund infrastructure projects, such as bridges, roads, and tunnels, where municipalities receive tax credits from the U.S. government of 35% of interest paid to investors. Because municipality is receiving a tax credit, it can issue the bonds with higher coupon rates than comparable bonds.

286. D. Build America Bonds (BABs)

Build America Bonds (BABs) were created for the purpose of allowing municipalities to borrow money for infrastructure projects (roads, bridges, and such). Although BABs are federally taxable, the issuer or investor receives a tax credit of 35% of the coupon rate. If the issuer receives the tax credit (direct payment), the issuer would be able to issue the bonds at a high coupon rates to make them more attractive to investors. If investors receive the tax credit, the amount of taxes paid could be less than the tax credit or refund the investors would receive.

287. A. provide short-term financing

Municipalities issue short-term notes, such as RANs (revenue anticipation notes), BANs (bond anticipation notes), TANs (tax anticipation notes), and CLNs (construction loan notes), to provide interim financing until a permanent long-term bond issue is floated, until tax receipts increase, or until revenue flows in.

288. **B. AONs**

Municipal notes are short-term debt securities issued by municipalities to provide interim financing while waiting for other revenues to come in. Municipal notes include TANs, RANs, TRANs, BANs, CLNs, PNs, and GANs. AON (all-or-none) is an order qualifier, not a type of municipal note.

289. **B. Tax anticipation notes**

The key phrase in this question is *temporary cash flow shortage*, which tells you that the municipality needs to issue short-term debt securities. So, you can cross off Choices (C) and (D) because revenue bonds and general obligation (GO) bonds are long term. That leaves you with the construction loan notes or *tax anticipation notes*. Because construction wasn't mentioned anywhere in the question, the best answer is *tax anticipation notes* because a municipality is always collecting taxes.

290. **A. federal government funds**

GANs provide interim financing for the municipality while waiting for grant money from the federal government.

291. **D. I, II, III, and IV**

All of the choices listed are municipal notes. Municipal notes are issued to provide short-term financing. The maturity of municipal notes is one year or less.

292. **B. municipal notes**

Moody's investment grade (MIG) ratings are applied to municipal notes, such as BANs, RANs, TANs, CLNs, and so on.

293. **C. MIG1**

A bond anticipation note (BAN) issued by municipalities is backed by bonds that will be issued. Municipal notes are short term and are rated by Moody's, using the Moody's investment grade (MIG) scale. MIG1 is the best rating available for a municipal note.

294. **D. MIG3**

Moody's uses three ratings for municipal notes: MIG1, which is the best quality; MIG2, which is high quality; and MIG3, which is adequate quality. Municipal notes not rated in the top three ratings are given the rating of SG, which means speculative grade.

295. D. GOs

Moody's investment grade (MIG) determines the creditworthiness of municipal notes (short-term municipal bonds). PNs (project notes), TRANs (tax and revenue anticipation notes), and CLNs (construction loan notes) are all types of municipal notes. However, GOs are general obligation bonds issued to provide long-term financing for a municipality and can't have an MIG rating.

296. A. likelihood of default

As with corporate bond ratings, municipal bond rating companies such as S&P and Moody's are mainly concerned with the likelihood that interest and principal payments will not be paid.

297. C. an official statement

Qualified Tuition Plans are also known at Section 529 plans. They are municipal fund securities, which are state sponsored so they must be sold by an official statement like other municipal securities.

298. D. LTGOs

Section 529 plans (qualified tuition plans), ABLE (Achieving a Better Life Experience) accounts, and LGIPs (Local Government Investment Pools) are all types of municipal fund securities. LTGOs (Limited-Tax General Obligation) bonds are general bonds issued in which the backing municipality is limited on the property taxes they can collect from the people in their municipality backing the bond.

299. A. qualified tuition plans

Municipal fund securities include Section 529 savings plans (qualified tuition plans), ABLE (Achieving a Better Life Experience) accounts, and LGIPs (local government investment pools).

300. D. 529

A Section 529 savings plan provides for specialized savings accounts to be set up for investors. These plans are also known as qualified tuition plans (QTPs) because they're designed to allow money to be saved for qualified expenses for higher education (colleges, postsecondary trade and vocational schools, postgraduate programs, and so on). As of 2018, tuition expenses at elementary public schools, secondary public schools, religious schools, and private schools have been added to the list.

301. **B. ABLE**

ABLE (Achieving a Better Life Experience) programs are designed for people with provable disabilities and their families. ABLE accounts allow these individuals and families to put aside after-tax dollars in a special account. Any earnings or distributions are tax-free as long as they are used to pay for qualified disability expenses.

302. **C. LGIP**

LGIPs (local government investment pools) are established by states to provide other local government entities a short-term investment vehicle for investing their excess funds.

303. **C. The interest is not taxable, but any capital gains are taxable.**

The interest received on municipal bonds is federally tax free, but capital gains on any security are taxable.

304. **A. I only**

Interest on municipal bonds is federally tax-free, but capital gains on all securities are fully taxed. Interest on U.S. government bonds is state tax-free but is taxed at the federal level. Cash dividends on stock are always taxable.

305. **B. GO bonds**

For Series 7 purposes, you can assume that municipal bonds have the lowest yields of all bonds. You may have chosen T-bonds (Treasury bonds) because they would be the safest, but then you didn't take into consideration the tax advantage of investing in municipal bonds. Municipal GO (general obligation) and municipal revenue bonds have lower yields because the interest investors receive is federally tax-free. Therefore, municipalities are able to offer lower pre-tax yields to investors than with other debt security investments.

306. **B. Tito's tax bracket**

To determine the best investment for Tito, you must do a taxable equivalent yield (TEY) calculation. To accomplish this, you need to know Tito's tax bracket. Remember, the interest received from municipal bond investments is federally tax-free, and investors in higher tax brackets will save more money by investing in municipal bonds when compared to other debt securities. The formula for TEY is as follows:

$$\text{TEY} = \frac{\text{Municipal yield}}{100\% - \text{Investor's tax bracket}}$$

ANSWERS 301–400

307. C. 4% GO bond

To determine the best after-tax investment for an individual investor, look for municipal bonds. A general obligation (GO) bond is a municipal bond in which the interest received is exempt from federal taxation. To compare all the listed bonds equally, you need to determine the GO bond's taxable equivalent yield (TEY), using this formula:

$$\begin{aligned} TEY &= \frac{\text{Municipal yield}}{100\% - \text{Investor's tax bracket}} \\ &= \frac{4\%}{100\% - 28\%} \\ &= \frac{4\%}{72\%} \\ &= 5.56\% \end{aligned}$$

For this investor, the taxable equivalent yield is 5.56%, which is higher than all the other bonds listed. The 5.56% represents the coupon rate needed on a taxable bond to be equal to the 4% that they'd be receiving on the federally tax-free bond.

ANSWERS 301–400

308. A. The general obligation bond has a higher after-tax yield.

Because the interest on municipal general obligation bonds is federally tax-free, you have to work out the taxable equivalent yield (TEY) by using the following formula:

$$\begin{aligned} TEY &= \frac{\text{Municipal yield}}{100\% - \text{Investor's tax bracket}} \\ &= \frac{5\%}{100\% - 28\%} \\ &= \frac{5\%}{72\%} \\ &= 6.94\% \end{aligned}$$

For this investor in the 28% tax bracket, purchasing a 5% municipal bond is equivalent to purchasing a 6.94% corporate bond. This means that the 5% municipal bond has a higher after-tax yield than the 6% corporate bond.

309. B. 4.14%

As compared to starting with a municipal yield and trying to find the taxable equivalent yield (TEY), in this case, you're starting with a corporate bond and trying to find the municipal equivalent yield (MEY). You can use the following formula to determine the MEY:

$$\begin{aligned} MEY &= (\text{Taxable bond yield})(100\% - \text{Investor's tax bracket}) \\ &= (6\%)(100\% - 31\%) \\ &= (6\%)(69\%) \\ &= 4.14\% \end{aligned}$$

The MEY is 4.14%, which means that for an investor in the 31% tax bracket, purchasing a 4.14% municipal bond is equivalent to purchasing a 6% taxable bond.

310. C. I, II, and III

Interest received from municipal bonds issued by the U.S. territories Guam, Puerto Rico, and U.S. Virgin Islands is triple tax-free (exempt from federal, state, and local taxes). You'd probably also want to let your client know that purchasing municipal bonds issued by their own state would also be triple tax-free.

311. D. I, II, and III

Actually, all of the choices listed are important. The *state of residence* is important because if a client purchases a municipal bond issued by their own state, they'll receive triple tax-free interest. *The tax bracket* is important because the interest on municipal bonds is federally tax-free, so they're more advantageous to investors in higher tax brackets. And, finally, if municipal bonds don't fit into a client's *investment objectives*, they shouldn't be recommended.

ANSWERS 301–400

312. A. 5% municipal general obligation (GO) bond

To determine the answer for this question, you need to figure out the taxable equivalent yield (TEY) for this investor on the municipal bond because the interest is federally tax free. You can use the following formula:

$$\begin{aligned} \text{TEY} &= \frac{\text{Municipal yield}}{100\% - \text{Investor's tax bracket}} \\ &= \frac{5\%}{100\% - 24\%} \\ &= \frac{5\%}{76\%} \\ &= 6.58\% \end{aligned}$$

After doing the calculations, you can see that for this investor, buying a 5% municipal bond would be equivalent to buying a corporate bond yielding 6.58% after taxes. Since none of the other answer choices are that high, a 5% municipal bond would be best for this investor.

313. D. It is exempt from federal, state, and local taxes.

When purchasing a municipal bond issued within your home state, the interest received is triple tax-free and is exempt from federal, state, and local taxes. Additionally, if you purchase a bond issued by a U.S. territory (such as Puerto Rico, U.S. Virgin Islands, Guam, Samoa, and Washington, D.C.), the interest is also triple tax-free. If you purchase a bond issued by another state, the interest is exempt from federal taxes only.

314. D. I, II, III, and IV

Under MSRB Rule G-15, the confirmation (receipt of trade) must include the customer's name, the capacity of the broker-dealer (agency or principal trade), the par value of the securities, trade date, execution price, whether it was a purchase or sale, the settlement date, yield or dollar price, CUSIP number (if there is one), and so on.

315. B. 2 business days after the trade date

Municipal bonds settle the regular way in two business days after the trade date (T+2).

316. C. the customer's signature

A confirmation includes all the particulars about the trade but does not require the signature of the customer.

317. B. for a minimum of 3 years and easily accessible for 2 years

All municipal advertising must be approved by a principal of the firm and must be held for at least 3 years and easily accessible for 2 years.

318. D. a municipal securities principal

All advertisements relating to municipal securities must be approved by a municipal securities principal (manager) or general securities principal prior to being sent to customers or potential customers. All advertising sent out by a firm (municipal or otherwise) must be approved by a principal.

319. C. Buying a client season passes to the Yankees

According to MSRB rules, no municipal securities brokers or dealers shall give (directly or indirectly) a gift in excess of $100 per year to any person other than a partner or employee of the dealer. However, normal business expenses, such as business meals, airline tickets, and hotel expenses, are exempt. So, sending a client a picture of yourself in an $80 frame may be inappropriate (or not), but it's not a violation. However, buying season tickets for the Yankees would go way and beyond the $100 limit and wouldn't be deemed a business expense.

320. D. Whatever is fair and reasonable

There is no set rule as far as the percentage that a municipal broker-dealer may charge when buying or selling municipal securities. Since this trade was executed out of the broker-dealer's inventory, you would expect that the amount that the broker-dealer would charge would be relatively low. The rule is "whatever is fair and reasonable," meaning that if the broker-dealer expended a lot of effort getting the securities, they would not be in violation if charging extra.

321. B. I, III, and IV

The indenture of a revenue bond would include items such as the maturity date, interest payment dates, the coupon rate, the legal opinion, covenants, the flow of funds, and so on. However, anything that's subject to change, such as the rating, wouldn't be placed on the indenture of a bond.

322. D. bond counsel

The legal opinion is a statement by a bond counsel (attorney) affirming that the interest received from a bond issue meets the requirements to be exempt from federal taxation. All municipal bonds must be accompanied by a legal opinion unless the issue is marked as ex-legal (a municipal bond that trades without a legal opinion).

323. D. guaranteeing timely payment of interest

A municipal bond counsel prepares the legal opinion for new municipal bonds. The main function of a municipal bond counsel is to make sure that it's valid and binding on the issuer and meets the laws that will make it federally tax-free. However, municipal bond counsels don't guarantee timely payment of principal and interest.

324. A. issue is without condition or restriction

An unqualified legal opinion means that the municipal issuer meets all conditions without restrictions such as liens or judgments.

325. D. The official statement

The official statement is similar to a prospectus but for a municipality, not a corporation. In the official statement, investors would be able to find out what the bond funds will be used for, the tax base, tax collection history, interest payment dates, the maturity date, insurance backing the bonds, and so on.

326. D. the preliminary official statement

Because a municipal issuer prepares the preliminary and official statements, they don't need to be approved by a municipal securities principal. However, most of the things that happen within your firm, such as opening accounts, transactions in accounts, and advertisements sent out by your firm, do need to be approved by a principal (manager) of the firm.

327. A. official statement

Municipal bonds don't have a prospectus, but they do have an official statement. The official statement gives investors the most information about the issuer and the bond issue.

328. **D. Once a year**

Broker-dealers and municipal securities dealers must send yearly statements to their clients, which may be in electronic form (emails and such). These statements must let the clients know that their firm is registered with the SEC and MSRB. The statement must let clients know their protections, how they can make a complaint to the proper authority, and so on.

329. **B. I and II**

Advertisements include promotional literature (written and electronic), circulars, market letters, seminar text, press releases, and so on. Preliminary official statements, official statements, offering circulars, and so on are not considered advertisements.

330. **B. $250 per election**

According to MSRB Rule G-37, the maximum contribution allowed for a municipal finance professional (MFP) to a candidate running for a local government office is $250 per election. If a particular candidate is running in a primary and a general election, the MFP may contribute a total of $500 ($250 for the primary election and $250 for the general election).

331. **D. I, II, III, and IV**

MSRB Rules G-8 and G-9 cover what records brokers, dealers, and municipal securities dealers must keep. Certainly, all of the choices listed must be kept. If you're wondering what blotters are, they're original entry records of all customer purchases and sales.

332. **C. 6 years**

Although FINRA requires that customer complaints need to be kept on file for 4 years, the Municipal Securities Rulemaking Board requires customer complaints to be kept on file for at least 6 years.

333. **A. the highest available bid price or the lowest available ask price**

It is required that broker-dealers make every attempt to try to get their customers the best price. The best price is the inside market (highest bid and lowest ask prices).

334. **D. II and IV**

Broker-dealers, principals, or agents cannot guarantee that a customer will not lose money. In addition, they may not share in gains and losses in a customer's account unless they set up a joint account and have a proportional sharing agreement arranged.

335. A. $100 contribution to a candidate for whom a municipal finance professional (MFP) may vote

Municipal finance professionals are allowed to make political contributions for up to $250 per election per candidate for whom they're allowed to vote. They're not allowed to make political contributions for individuals they're not allowed to vote for.

Chapter 5 Answers

336. C. 10%

According to the Investment Company Act of 1940, out of the 75% that must be diversified, a diversified investment company may not own more than 10% of outstanding shares of another company. In addition, the investment company cannot invest more than 5% of its diversified assets into one issuer's securities.

337. D. Circling or highlighting a particular section of the prospectus

Whether the prospectus is for a mutual fund or any other security, you may not alter it in any way, even if the customer asks you to.

338. C. 7 days

Mutual fund redemption must be completed within 7 calendar days.

339. B. is responsible for the safekeeping of the fund's cash and securities

The custodian bank of a mutual fund is responsible for the safekeeping of the fund's cash and securities.

340. B. Affiliated persons of an investment company are not allowed to trade the fund's portfolio of securities but are allowed to buy or redeem shares of the fund

Affiliated persons of investment companies (persons affiliated with the manager of the fund, the custodian bank, and owners of 5% or more of the outstanding shares of the fund) are not allowed to trade securities within the fund's portfolio of securities. However, affiliated persons are certainly allowed to buy and redeem shares of the fund like regular public customers.

341. A. There is no limit.

Mutual funds are open-end funds that can continually issue new shares . . . there is not limit.

342. **C. They charge commissions to customers who purchase shares.**

Open-end investment companies (mutual funds) do not charge a commission; they charge a sales charge added to the NAV.

343. **D. They may be purchased on margin**

Since all mutual fund shares are new securities, they may not be purchased on margin and must be paid for in full. However, once an investor has held mutual fund shares for at least 30 days; they can be moved to a margin account.

344. **B. Closed-end**

In both open- and closed-end funds, the NAV indicates the performance of the fund's portfolio. If the NAV (net asset value) and POP (public offering price) move in opposite directions, the fund must be a closed-end fund. The price of a closed-end fund not only depends on the performance of the securities held but also on supply and demand. In an open-end fund, the NAV and POP must move in the same direction since the price depends solely on the performance of the securities held by the fund.

345. **C. $27.52 plus a commission**

Closed-end funds charge a commission added to the POP (public offering price). Open-end funds charge a sales charge, which is built into the POP (public offering price), except for no-load funds which do not charge a sales charge.

346. **D. II, III, and IV**

Closed-end investment companies make a one-time offering of new shares and then trade in the market like other equity securities. Closed-end investment companies may also issue preferred stock and bonds in addition to common stock.

347. **A. II and III**

Closed-end funds are typically listed on an exchange and have a fixed number of shares outstanding. Closed-end funds must be sold to another investor and are not redeemable. In addition, closed-end funds may issue common stock, preferred stock, and bonds.

348. **B. closed-end funds**

Closed-end funds have a fixed number of securities outstanding. After the initial public offering, investors much purchase or sell the securities in the market because the securities cannot be redeemed with the issuer.

349. C. Growth fund

All of the other funds listed will provide investors with current income because they invest in bonds paying interest and possibly stocks paying dividends. However, growth funds invest in companies that are trying to expand their business. This means that they don't pay much in the way of dividends; they reinvest their profits back into the company.

350. A. I and II

Fixed unit investment trusts invest in a portfolio of debt securities, and the trust terminates when all of the debt securities held mature. A participating unit investment trust chooses a portfolio of mutual funds to hold, which remain fixed, and the trust terminates at a predetermined date. The return on the participating unit investment trusts depends on the performance of the funds held.

351. D. investment objectives

Although all of the choices listed are important, investor's should start at a fund's investment objectives. For example, is the customer looking for growth, income, growth and income, a tax-advantaged investment (municipal bond fund), and so on? When the client determines the type of fund, they can then start comparing the performance and expenses of those types of funds from several issuers prior to making a decision.

352. B. investors are prohibited from redeeming the money market fund for a year

Money market funds are types of mutual funds that hold short-term debt securities. The NAV of the fund is set at $1. They do offer a check-writing feature; they are no load (no sales charge); and the compute dividends daily and credit them monthly. However, investors are not prohibited from redeeming their funds for a year; they can redeem at any time.

353. D. income fund

Although hedge funds, growth funds, and aggressive growth funds have capital appreciation potential, they don't provide current income. Income funds invest in stocks paying dividends and bonds paying interest. Therefore, the best choice for this investor would be an income fund or some sort of bond fund.

354. B. Aggressive growth fund

Aggressive growth funds invest in the common stock of relatively new companies or companies with a high chance of growth looking for capital gains for their investors.

355. **A. Hedge funds can purchase commodities and foreign currencies while mutual funds cannot.**

Answers (B), (C), and (D) are applicable to both hedge funds and mutual funds. However, hedge funds are allowed to make more speculative investments and purchase things that aren't securities such as commodities and currencies.

356. **C. They purchased a lot of securities on margin.**

When a hedge fund or individual is purchasing securities on margin, they have a leveraged position. Although purchasing or selling short securities on margin increases gains when the securities go in your direction, it accelerates losses if the securities go in the wrong direction.

357. **C. attempt to achieve high returns for their investors by taking riskier strategies and investing in higher-risk investments**

Hedge funds take riskier strategies like purchasing on margin or selling short. In addition, they purchase things like options, currencies, and commodities, which aren't available to mutual fund companies.

358. **B. A sector fund investing in high-tech stocks**

Investors interested in current income would purchase some sort of bond or income fund. Investors interested in current income would not purchase a fund that invests in high-tech stocks because they are growth companies. Growth companies usually do not pay dividends but invest their earnings back into the company to expand or purchase new equipment.

359. **A. sector**

Sector funds invest in specific industries, such as automotive, pharmaceutical, energy, technology, and so on.

360. **D. hedge fund**

Hedge funds are the most speculative (riskiest) type of fund. Hedge funds are available to accredited investors and are allowed to execute trades that other funds cannot.

361. **A. I and III**

Private-equity funds are only available to sophisticated (accredited) investors and are exempt from SEC registration. As part of their investment strategy, they may purchase private companies and/or purchase enough shares of public companies to gain control.

362. C. II and III

The interest on municipal bonds is federally tax free. When purchasing a municipal bond fund, the tax-free interest is passed through to investors by way of a dividend. However, capital gains, even on municipal bonds, is always taxable.

363. B. a municipal bond fund

The interest received on municipal bonds is federally tax-free. Therefore, they are of a bigger advantage to investors in higher income tax brackets. When purchasing municipal bond funds, the dividends received by investors that represent the flow-through of interest received from the municipal bonds held by the fund are not taxable.

364. B. life-cycle fund

Life-cycle funds are pretty interesting and would meet this client's needs perfectly. As investors grow older, they typically do not have the ability to assume as much risk as younger investors. In most cases, investors adjust their portfolio every so often to move a larger percentage into fixed-income securities as they get older to minimize risk. Life-cycle (target-date) funds adjust the portfolio of securities held on their own. The investment adviser for the fund will rebalance the securities held by the fund every so often by selling off equity securities held by the fund and purchasing more fixed-income securities. Clients interested in investing in life-cycle funds should choose one with a target retirement date in line with their own needs.

365. D. 13 months

A letter of intent deals with mutual fund breakpoints. It allows investors up to 13 months to purchase enough of a fund in order to receive a breakpoint right away. The mutual fund holds shares in escrow until the investor purchases enough of the fund for the breakpoint. If the investor doesn't purchase enough in those 13 months, the mutual fund issuer will sell some shares held in escrow to make up for the lost sales charge fees.

366. A. Yes, with no restrictions

Even if under the letter of intent, investors can always redeem their shares. If they received a reduced sales charge, the issuer will sell some shares held in escrow to make up the difference between what the investor should have paid in sales charges and what they actually did.

367. B. life-cycle funds

Life-cycle or targeted-date funds change the securities that the fund holds as it gets closer to that targeted date. As the fund gets closer to the targeted date it will start purchasing more fixed-income securities (bonds) and sell some of its equity securities (stocks).

368. D. I, II, and III

Letters of Intent allow mutual fund investors to receive a breakpoint (discounted sales charge for large dollar purchases) right away as long as they purchase enough of the fund within 13 months to receive the breakpoint. It may be backdated for up to 90 days so that the 13-month period can apply to a previous purchase. The issuer may hold shares in escrow to make sure the investor lives up to the terms of the Letter of Intent.

369. C. 90 days

By signing a letter of intent, an investor is able to take advantage of a breakpoint (reduced sales charge) right away even though not purchasing enough to receive a breakpoint. A letter of intent allows an investor up to 13 months to purchase enough to receive the breakpoint. Letters of intent can be backdated for up to 90 days (3 months), so they can apply to previous purchases.

ANSWERS 301–400

370. D. 8½% of the amount

The maximum sales charge for a mutual (open-end) fund is 8½% of the amount invested.

371. C. 8½%, which is built into the public offering price

The maximum sales charge for a mutual fund is 8½% of the amount invested. This means that investors purchase at the public offering price, which already has the sales charge built in.

372. B. 5.30%

With mutual funds, the sales charge is built into the public offering price (POP) so you have to subtract the net asset value (NAV) from the POP and then divide that by the POP. Check out the following equation:

$$\text{Sales charge \%} = \frac{\text{POP} - \text{NAV}}{\text{POP}} = \frac{\$22.60 - \$21.40}{\$22.60} = \frac{\$1.20}{\$22.60} = 5.3\%$$

373. A. 3%

With mutual funds, the sales charge is built into the public offering price (POP) so you have to subtract the net asset value (NAV) from the POP and then divide that by the POP. Remember that since this investor received a breakpoint, you have to use the public offering price for this investor. Check out the following equation:

$$\text{Sales charge \%} = \frac{\text{POP} - \text{NAV}}{\text{POP}} = \frac{\$41.55 - \$40.30}{\$41.55} = \frac{\$1.25}{\$41.55} = 3\%$$

374. B. they are available to investment clubs

Breakpoints are reduced sales charges for investors purchasing a large dollar amount of a fund. They are not available to investment clubs or partnerships.

375. B. 5.08%

With mutual funds, the sales charge is built into the POP so you have to subtract the NAV from the POP and then divide that by the POP. You can use the following equation:

$$\text{Sales charge \%} = \frac{\text{POP} - \text{NAV}}{\text{POP}} = \frac{\$37.62 - \$35.71}{\$37.62} = \frac{\$1.91}{\$37.62} = 5.08\%$$

376. C. $28.23

To determine the public offering price (POP) for a mutual fund, you have to divide the net asset value (NAV) by 100% minus the sales charge percent. Use the following equation:

$$\text{POP} = \frac{\text{NAV}}{100\% - \text{sales charge \%}} = \frac{\$27.24}{100\% - 3.5\%} = \frac{\$27.24}{96.5\%} = \$28.23 \text{ per share}$$

377. C. $55.90

To determine the public offering price (POP) for a mutual fund, you have to divide the net asset value (NAV) by 100% minus the sales charge percent. Use the following equation:

$$\text{POP} = \frac{\text{NAV}}{100\% - \text{sales charge \%}} = \frac{\$53.66}{100\% - 4\%} = \frac{\$53.66}{96\%} = \$55.90 \text{ per share}$$

378. A. It will be used to purchase fractional shares.

The additional money will be used to purchase fractional fund shares. So, it would not be unusual for a mutual fund investor to have an account statement that says that they own 442.718 shares of a fund.

379. D. 1,690.331 shares

Because this investor is depositing enough to receive a breakpoint, the investor will not be paying the regular POP (public offering price). So, to determine what this investor will be paying per share, you have to calculate his POP. Look at the following equation:

$$\text{POP} = \frac{\text{NAV}}{100\% - \text{sales charge \%}} = \frac{\$14.20}{100\% - 4\%} = \frac{\$14.20}{96\%} = \$14.79 \text{ per share}$$

Okay, you got the difficult part of the question completed. Now all you have to do is divide the dollar purchase by Mr. Smith's cost per share. Don't let the fact that you may end up with fractional shares confuse you because you're allowed to purchase fractional shares of mutual funds.

$$\frac{\$25{,}000 \text{ invested}}{\$14.79 \text{ per share}} = 1{,}690.331 \text{ shares}$$

380. B. Mutual funds

Mutual funds are open-end funds that are purchased from and redeemed with (sold to) the issuer. When redeeming mutual fund shares, the investor will receive the NAV (net asset value).

381. A. Class A

With Class A shares, the investor pays the load (sales charge) when purchasing shares of the fund. These funds are typically better for long-term investors because they usually have lower expense ratios, and they have breakpoints for large dollar purchases.

382. D. Class D

Class D shares are considered no load because the fund doesn't charge a fee for the purchase or a fee for the redemption.

383. A. Front-end load

Front-end load (Class A) is the most common way investors purchase mutual fund shares. Class A shares are better for long-term investors, and investors are paying the sales charge at the time of purchase.

384. B. expecting to redeem their shares in a short-period of time

Class C shares are level load and are better for investors looking to hold their mutual fund shares for a short period of time. Investors holding Class C shares pay a periodic fee (quarterly or yearly), which will turn out to be more expensive than the up-front costs of purchasing Class A shares over the long haul.

385. D. Face amount certificate company

Face amount certificate companies are similar to zero-coupon bonds because they are purchased at a discount and mature at face value. Very few face amount certificate companies are around at this point.

386. A. I and III

UITs offer securities that may be redeemed with the issuer. However, UITs issue securities only once. UITs may also be purchased from and sold by underwriters.

387. **C. Variable annuity**

The three types of investment companies are management companies, which include closed-end funds and open-end funds, face amount certificate companies, and unit investment trusts. Variable annuities are insurance company products and are considered securities because of the investment part, which is the separate account.

388. **B. UIT**

A UIT (unit investment trust) invests in a fixed portfolio of securities so there is nothing to manage . . . therefore, no management fee.

389. **A. UIT**

UITs (unit investment trusts) invest in a fixed portfolio of securities. Since the trust is a fixed portfolio, the trust would not need a manager to supervise the money invested. Therefore, UITs do not charge a management fee.

390. **D. lower operating costs**

UITs (unit investment trusts), have a fixed (unmanaged) portfolio of securities so they will have lower operating costs when compared to mutual funds, which are managed.

391. **A. municipal bonds**

Tax-free funds invest in municipal bonds because the interest received on those bonds is federally tax free. The fund is allowed to pass on that tax-free interest to investors by way of a dividend.

392. **A. mutual funds cannot be purchased on margin**

New securities cannot be purchased on margin for at least 30 days. Since mutual funds are new securities, they are not marginable. However, investors who have held onto mutual fund shares for over 31 days can place them in margin accounts and borrow money against them.

393. **C. II and III**

The interest on municipal bonds is federally tax-free. When purchasing a municipal bond fund, the tax-free interest is passed through to investors by way of a dividend. However, capital gains, even on municipal bonds, is always taxable.

394. **D. I, II, and IV**

In this question you are looking for the differences between exchange-traded funds (ETFs) and mutual funds. Unlike mutual funds, ETFs can be sold short; they can be purchased on margin; and they provide real-time pricing not forward pricing like mutual funds. What is similar is that both ETFs and mutual funds represent a basket or portfolio of securities.

395. B. I and IV

Exchange traded funds (ETFs) are purchased and sold at the current bid and ask prices based on supply and demand. Mutual funds have forward pricing, which means that the purchase price will be at the next computed public offering price, and the redemption price will be at the next computed NAV (net asset value).

396. B. I and IV

ETFs (exchange traded funds), because they aren't new securities like mutual funds, can be purchased on margin. Also, the purchase and sale price of ETFs changes throughout the day as trades take place. Mutual funds are forward priced meaning that if you purchase or redeem during the day, you get the next computed public offering price or redemption price, which is typically computed at the end of the trading day.

397. B. ETF

ETFs (exchange traded funds) are designed to track an index, so the securities held by the fund typically don't change. In addition, after the IPO (initial public offering) the securities are traded in the market and not redeemed with the issuer so the expense ratio would be low when compared to the other investments listed.

398. A. I and III

Unlike mutual funds which have forward pricing and can only be purchased and redeemed with the issuer, exchange traded funds (ETFs) trade between investors throughout the day (no forward pricing). In addition, ETFs typically have low operating costs and expense ratios when compared to mutual funds because the portfolio is designed to track an index such as the S&P 500, and the securities held by the fund are not actively managed.

399. C. The next computed bid price

When investors redeem shares of a mutual fund, they are essentially selling shares back to the issuer. When investors sell, they sell at the bid price. The bid price for a mutual fund is the NAV (net asset value). Because mutual funds hold so many different securities, there is no current bid or ask price. Mutual funds use forward pricing so investors selling shares are selling them at the next computed bid price, which is typically at the end of the trading day.

400. D. next computed ask price

Mutual fund trades are not executed until the next close. Shares are purchased at the next computed ask price and sold at the next computed bid price.

401. A. Growth fund

Growth funds invest in a diversified portfolio of more speculative stocks of relatively new and existing companies looking for big increases in their stock prices.

402. A. Balanced fund

Balanced funds are a combination of growth funds and income funds. They invest in common stock, preferred stock, long-term bonds, and short-term bonds attempting to get growth by the way of common stocks and income by the way of fixed-income securities.

403. C. Money market fund

Money market funds invest in short-term debt securities (money market instruments). They are always no load (no sales charge), and investors are given a checkbook as a way of redeeming shares. Typically, there are restrictions on writing checks such as $250 minimum, you can only write 4 checks per month, and so on.

404. A. international

International funds invest in securities issued by foreign companies. Besides the risk of funds of U.S. securities, investors of international funds face the political risk and currency risk associated with foreign investments.

405. C. the ask price plus a commission

When exchange traded funds (ETFs) are trading in the market, they sell at the market price, not the NAV. So, purchasers would buy at the ask price and pay a commission. Sellers would sell at the bid price and get charged a commission.

406. B. An inverse exchange-traded fund

Exchange-traded funds (ETFs) are funds that track a basket of securities or an index such as the S&P 500, Nasdaq 100, Russell 2000, or even specific sectors. Inverse ETFs (short funds) are constructed to take advantage of a declining market. Inverse ETFs are often purchased by investors to hedge their portfolios against falling prices. Answer Choices (A) and (D) are out because mutual funds cannot be sold short.

407. A. the performance of the securities held in the separate account

The investment return on a variable annuity is based on the performance of the securities held in the separate account. Variable annuities are issued with an assumed interest rate (AIR), which means that the insurance company is expecting to get investors a return of that percentage. However, if the securities held in the separate account underperform, the payouts will decrease; if the securities held in the separate account perform better than expected, the payouts will increase.

408. **D. Fixed annuities and variable annuities**

Fixed and variable annuities are designed to provide retirement income for their investors. The stream of payments is guaranteed for life of the policyholder. Depending on whether the investor chose a fixed annuity or variable annuity, the amount of the payments may or may not be guaranteed.

409. **A. Payments will continue for the life of the annuitant.**

A mortality guarantee provides for payments to the annuitant for their life even if they live beyond their life expectance. Because it is a variable annuity, the payments will change based on the performance of the securities held in the separate account.

410. **C. the payout is guaranteed by the insurance company**

Unlike a variable annuity, with a fixed annuity the investor is taking no investment risk because the insurance company is guaranteeing the payout from their general account. Instead of the investor taking the investment risk, the investment risk is taken on by the insurance company.

411. **D. the performance of the securities held in the separate account**

The performance of the securities held in the separate account is of primary importance to holders of variable annuities because it will affect their payouts.

412. **C. I and III**

Variable annuities are insurance company products so they have to be registered with the state insurance commission. In addition, because they have an investment element in the way of the separate account, they must also be registered with the SEC.

413. **D. All of the above.**

Since annuities are set up as retirement plans, there is an early withdrawal penalty of 10% added to the investor's tax bracket on the amount of money withdrawn prior to age 59½. However, that 10% penalty is typically waived for first-time homebuyers, those over age 55 and separated from work, death, or disability.

414. **C. Fixed annuities**

Fixed annuities are not considered investment companies since the payout is guaranteed by the issuing insurance company.

415. **B. fixed annuities**

Since the payout on a fixed annuity is guaranteed, they are not regulated by the Investment Company Act of 1940. Fixed annuities are exempt from SEC registration, and the payouts are made out of the insurance company's general account, not a separate account. Since fixed annuities have a fixed payout, they are subject to purchasing power risk. You need an insurance license but not a securities license like a Series 7 to sell fixed annuities.

416. C. investors are protected against capital loss

Variable annuities have a separate account that is professionally managed and often contains mutual funds. Variable annuities are much more likely to keep pace with inflation than fixed annuities. However, variable annuity investors are not protected against capital loss the way that holders of fixed annuities are.

417. B. It will be higher.

If the return in the separate account is higher than the AIR (assumed interest rate) for a particular month, the payout for the following month would be higher. Conversely, if the return is lower than the AIR, the payout would be lower than the AIR for the following month.

418. A. the holder of the policy

Annuities are retirement plans issued by insurance companies. The big difference with fixed and variable annuities is that in variable annuities the investment risk is on the policyholder. In a fixed annuity, the insurance company holds the investment risk. Variable annuities are riskier but more likely to keep pace with inflation.

419. D. the designated beneficiary

If the owner of a variable annuity dies during the accumulation (pay-in) phase, the death benefit will be paid to the designated beneficiary. The death benefit is typically the total of all investments plus any earnings. It is typically paid in a lump sum, and the beneficiary would be responsible for paying taxes on the earnings (amount received over the deceased's cost basis) at the beneficiary's tax rate.

420. A. II only

Accumulation units are similar to shares of a mutual fund. A variable annuity holder purchases accumulation units during the pay-in phase. During the pay-out phase, the accumulation units are converted into annuity units. So, in order for a variable annuity to have accumulation units, there had to be a pay-in phase. Out of the choices listed, the only one that had a pay-in phase was the periodic payment deferred annuity.

421. D. Single payment deferred annuity

This investor has a large amount of money right now, so they will likely make a single (lump-sum) payment. Since they are only 25 years old, they will defer payments until retirement. Single payment deferred annuity would work best for this investor. As a side note, answer Choice (A) is bogus because the insurance company will not pay out without an investor depositing money first.

422. B. payment deferred immediate annuity

Choices (A), (C), and (D) are all possible ways of purchasing a variable annuity. However, an insurance company is not going to let you collect on an annuity when not a single payment has been made, as stated in Choice (B).

423. C. $2,520

Since it is a non-qualified annuity, the investor was already taxed on the $38,000 invested. This means that they were not taxed on the $9,000 that the account appreciated in value ($47,000 – $38,000). So, the first money withdrawn will be the taxable part.

$$\$9000 \times 28\% = \$2520$$

424. D. A fixed number of annuity units based on the value of the accumulation units

When a variable annuity is annuitized during the payout phase, investors receive a fixed number of annuity units based on the value of the accumulation units. The part that is variable with a variable annuity is that the payouts will vary based on the value of the securities held.

425. C. II and III

During the surrender period (typically around the first 5 years) of a variable annuity, the number of accumulation units increases since the investor continues to deposit money and/or reinvest money earned from investments to purchase more units. During the annuity period, the number of annuity units liquidated each month remains the same, but the value of the units varies.

426. A. Straight-life annuity

Annuities are retirement plans issued by insurance companies. Straight-life annuities are annuities with no beneficiaries and, therefore, provide the largest monthly payout. When the investor dies, the insurance company is not required to pay a beneficiary. Life annuity with period certain, joint and survivor annuities, and unit-refund annuities have named beneficiaries to be paid if the policyholder dies early.

427. A. Life income annuity

Since the life income annuity (life annuity) payments cease at the death of the annuitant, they have the highest monthly payments. Joint and last survivor annuities have the lowest monthly payments.

428. B. mortality guarantee

Actually, the only answer that wasn't made up was answer Choice (B). Holders of variable annuities receive payments for life even if they live beyond their life expectancy. The insurance company assumes the mortality guarantee.

429. B. joint life with last survivor

Joint life with last survivor would suit this investor's needs perfectly. Although these types of plans are typically set up for spouses, there's no reason this mother cannot set one up with a child. In this case, payments would be made until the last remaining survivor passes. Obviously, the payments would be lower than straight life because the insurance company will go by the life expectancy of the daughter, not the mother.

430. A. Life with period certain

This investor can choose an annuity policy set up as life with period certain. In this case, they can choose a policy that will pay a minimum of 10 years, whether they're living or not. If they die prior to the 10-year period, the remaining payments will go to a named beneficiary.

431. D. The investor is buying a varying number of accumulation units each month.

When purchasing an annuity, an investor is buying accumulation units. Depending on the value of the securities held in the separate account, the amount of accumulation units an investor is able to purchase each month with the same amount of money varies.

432. C. I and IV

In variable life insurance policies, the minimum death benefit is guaranteed, but the cash value is not guaranteed. Based on the performance of the securities held in the separate account, the death benefit may increase, but may never decrease below the minimum. The cash value (surrender value) varies depending on the performance of the separate account and is not guaranteed.

433. A. Variable life

Variable life insurance has a fixed premium, and the death benefit is fixed as to a minimum but not a maximum. If the securities held in the separate account outperform the expected return, the death benefit increases. Unlike variable life, variable universal life has a flexible premium. In this case, if the securities held in the separate account underperform, the death benefit and cash value are not guaranteed.

434. D. performance of the securities in the separate account

As with variable annuities, variable life insurance policies also have a separate account with investments chosen by the policyholder. The performance of the securities held in that separate account affect the value of a variable life insurance policy.

435. D. II and IV

Unlike variable life policies, variable universal (flexible premium) life policies, the premium is not fixed, and if the securities held in the separate account perform poorly, the death benefit and cash value will suffer because they're not guaranteed.

436. C. both a securities license and an insurance license

Reps selling variable life or variable universal life policies must have an insurance license because they're insurance products and a securities license because of the investment portion of the policies.

Chapter 6 Answers

437. B. I and IV

In order for a partnership to not be taxed as a corporation, they must avoid at least two corporate characteristics. The easiest corporate characteristics for a partnership to avoid are having a perpetual life (partnerships are set up for a finite period of time) and having free transferability to partnership interest. Because of the approval process, limited partnerships are some of the most difficult investments to get in and out of.

438. B. an oil and gas limited partnership

If Marge is looking to add some liquidity (ease of trading) to her portfolio, an oil and gas limited partnership would not make sense. Limited partnerships (DPPs) are some of the most difficult investments to get in and out of. Limited partnerships require not only approval of the registered rep but also require approval of the general partner of the limited partnership. Limited partnership investors not only need a certain minimum deposit, but would also need to have liquidity in other investments in case the limited partnership needs additional funds to meet its goal.

439. B. they may participate in management decisions since they have a tremendous amount of risk

The general partner(s) make the management decisions, not the limited partners.

440. A. General Partners

The limited partners are the main investors of a limited partnership. The general partner(s) has/have the fiduciary responsibility to run the partnership to the best of their ability.

441. D. They must end on a predetermined date or end by vote

Unlike corporations that are formed with the idea of having a perpetual life, limited partnerships are set up for a predetermined date or goal. The only way they can dissolve the partnership prior to that is by a vote of the limited partners.

442. **C. II, IV, I, III**

When a limited partnership dissolves, secured creditors are paid first, then general creditors, after that, limited partners, and finally general partners.

443. **B. I and III**

General partners are not allowed to borrow money from the partnership. In addition, they cannot manage two partnerships that are in direct competition with each other. For arguments sake, a general partner cannot be running two partnerships that are building commercial buildings near to each other.

444. **A. a majority vote by the limited partners only**

Since there are not shareholders in a limited partnership, Choice (D) is out. To dissolve a limited partnership prior to the preset dissolution date requires a majority vote of the limited partners only.

445. **A. an active role and unlimited liability**

A general partner has an active role in managing the partnership and has unlimited liability. A limited partner has an inactive role and limited liability.

446. **D. both (A) and (B)**

All limited partnerships must have at least one general and one limited partner.

447. **D. All of the above**

All of the choices listed are benefits of investing in a limited partnership. Investors are certainly getting (or hoping for) professional management by way of general partner(s). Also, because a partnership isn't taxed as a corporation, the gains and losses are passed through to investors. In addition, limited partners' losses are limited to the amount invested plus any additional loans, if needed.

448. **C. The ability to participate in management decisions**

DPPs (direct participation programs) are professionally managed by the general partner(s). If a limited partner decides to get involved with management decisions, they will lose their liability protection and open themselves up to being sued.

449. **A. I, II, and IV**

Limited partnerships pass through gains and income to the limited partners, who are responsible for reporting those gains and losses to the IRS. Certain real estate limited partnerships may receive federal tax credits from the U.S. government. DPPs do not have free transferability of shares because all limited partners must go through an approval process.

450. **B. General partners assume more risk.**

The risk assumed by a limited partner is limited to the amount invested plus any additional loans. However, because general partners can be sued as a result of the partnership, they assume unlimited risk.

451. **D. Real estate**

Non-recourse debt is available to limited partners in real estate direct participation programs (DPPs) only. Non-recourse debt involves pledging partnerships' assets as collateral for a loan, and the limited partners aren't held personally responsible.

452. **B. General partners**

Since general partners are the ones who manage the partnership, they are the last ones to be paid when the partnership is dissolved. Secured creditors are the first to be paid; then general creditors; after that, limited partners; and finally, general partners.

453. **C. I, III, and IV**

Tangible assets are for items such as equipment. They may be depreciated on either a straight-line basis (writing off the same amount each year) or an accelerated basis (writing off more in the early years and less in the later years). Typically, these assets will have salvage value at the end of the partnership and can be sold.

454. **B. II and III**

When a real estate DPP owns apartments, houses, or buildings, they can rent them out and receive current income. Additionally, they hope to have capital growth by way of the value of the properties they own going up in value.

455. **C. providing a bulk of the capital for the partnership**

The general partner is responsible for running and making decisions for the partnership. However, the limited partners provide the bulk of the capital.

456. **B. Lack of liquidity**

Because of the approval process required for becoming a limited partner, DPPs are pretty illiquid.

457. **A. I, II, and III**

Limited partners can't make management decisions for the partnership; that is the job of the general partner(s). However, limited partners may inspect the books, compete with the partnership (invest in another competing partnership), and vote to terminate the partnership.

458. **C. I, II, and IV**

Limited partnerships require a subscription agreement to accept new limited partners, a certificate of limited partnership to be filed with the Securities and Exchange Commission (SEC) and states, and a partnership agreement (agreement of limited partnership) that outlines the rights and responsibilities of the general and limited partners.

459. **C. Partnership agreement**

The partnership agreement lays out the rights and responsibilities of the limited and general partner(s).

460. **A. Certificate of limited partnership**

A limited partnership (DPP) must file a certificate of limited partnership with the SEC (Securities and Exchange Commission) prior to a public offering. The subscription agreement is the paperwork a general partner must sign prior to accepting a new limited partner. The agreement of limited partnership states the rights and responsibilities of the limited and general partners.

461. **D. A subscription agreement**

A general partner would sign a subscription agreement to accept a new limited partner.

462. **D. An oil and gas limited partnership**

Limited partnerships require written proof of the customer's financial background. Both the broker-dealer and the general partners must verify that the customer has a high enough net worth, enough money to invest now, and more money to invest in the future if necessary.

463. **D. Real estate investment trusts**

You'll notice that all the partnerships require proof of the investor's financial status. The reason is because investors are not only responsible for an initial investment but may also be required to invest more money if needed. Such is not the case for real estate investment trusts (REITs).

464. **B. Bylaws**

Bylaws (corporate charters) are required for corporations, not limited partnerships. However, all partnerships require a certificate of limited partnership, an agreement of limited partnership, and a subscription agreement for new investors.

465. **C. The partnership is fully taxed by the IRS.**

Remember, you're looking for a false answer for this question. If you look at Choices (C) and (D), you can see that they're opposing answers, so it has to be one of them. One of the advantages of being a partner in a limited partnership is that all gains, losses, expenses, and income flows through to the limited and general partners. Remember that partnership passive gains and passive income can be written off only against passive losses.

466. **B. cash distributions**

When a limited partner receives a cash distribution, it reduces the cost basis because the limited partner is receiving some money back. The cost basis is derived from cash contributions, recourse and non-recourse debt of the partnership, and any property contributed to the partnership.

467. **A. I only**

Direct participation program (DPP) losses are deemed to be passive losses under IRS rules. Passive losses can be used to offset only passive gains from another direct participation program (partnership).

468. **C. depletion deductions**

Depletion deductions can be claimed only on natural resources that can be used up. Because real estate can't be used up, real estate partnerships can't claim depletion deductions.

469. **D. Both (A) and (B).**

All tax liabilities flow through to the investors, whether they be limited or general partners.

470. **B. Depletion deductions**

Depletion deductions can only be used for limited partnerships that deal with natural resources that are being depleted, such as taking oil from the ground.

471. **A. REIT**

A REIT is a real estate investment trust and is not a type of direct participation program (DPP).

472. **D. You should not recommend a limited partnership.**

The key to this question is that Mary has all of the rest of her money tied up in non-liquid investments. Partnerships require not only an initial investment but also the limited partners to come up with additional funds if needed. It's your job as a registered rep to pre-screen investors prior to having an investor submit a subscription agreement to a general partner. Part of that pre-screening process is to make sure that a potential limited partner has liquidity in other investments. In this case, Mary isn't a good fit for a limited partnership. However, you may want to recommend that Mary invest in real estate investment trusts.

473. C. appreciation

The main concern of investors of undeveloped (raw) land limited partnerships is appreciation potential. Their hope is that land purchased by the partnership can be purchased cheaply and sold sometime in the future at a much higher price.

474. A. income

Income programs are a type of oil and gas direct participation program (DPP), not a real estate DPP.

475. D. All of the above

Intangible drilling costs (IDCs) are write-offs for drilling expenses. These items have no salvage value and include things like wages, fuel, insurance, repairs, hauling of equipment, and so on.

476. B. Depletion

Depletion deductions can only be claimed on partnerships that deal with natural resources such as oil and gas. All of the other choices are standard deductions that can be made by partners.

477. A. Exploratory

Oil and gas exploratory (wildcatting) partnerships drill in areas not knowing if resources are available.

478. A. Limited partnerships

Limited partnerships are among the most difficult securities to purchase or sell because investors have to have enough money to invest and have liquidity in other securities in case the partnership needs more money. Additionally, each limited partner must be approved by the general partner(s).

479. B. can be depreciated yearly but have salvage value at the end of the program

Tangible drilling costs are for things such as equipment, which can be written off yearly but will have salvage value at the end of the program because the equipment is still worth something.

480. C. Capital appreciation potential

You're looking for the false answer in this question. Equipment leasing limited partnerships make money by leasing out equipment. The equipment leased out gets worn out or outdated, so capital appreciation potential makes no sense. However, a steady stream of income, depreciation deductions, and operating expenses to offset revenues are all advantages of investing in an equipment leasing program.

481. B. I and III

Public assisted housing and historic rehabilitation programs receive federal tax credits from the U.S. government.

482. A. Exploratory

IDCs are intangible drilling costs and are associated only with oil and gas partnerships. IDCs are highest in the first year of operation; therefore, exploratory (wildcatting) is the best answer. IDCs are usually completely deductible in the first year, and they include expenses, such as fuel costs, insurance, wages, and supplies.

ANSWERS 401–500

483. D. sold

Depletion has to do with reducing the amount of a mineral resource, such as oil and gas. Depletion deductions are based on the amount of oil and gas sold, not extracted from the ground and put in storage.

484. B. II only

Out of the choices given, the only partnership that could claim depletion deductions is oil and gas. Depletion deductions can be claimed only on a natural resource that has been used up (depleted). However, all three of the types of partnerships listed can claim depreciation deductions.

485. C. II and III

Unlike limited partners, general partners take an active role in the partnership and face unlimited liability, because if the partnership fails, they can be sued.

486. A. I, II, III

Income programs have the least risk because they purchase income-producing wells and sell what comes out of the ground. And exploratory (wildcatting) programs are the riskiest because they purchase land in unproven areas, hoping they find oil.

487. A. Oil and gas exploratory program

You should direct John to invest in a partnership that produces immediate write-off to offset the gains from the real estate DPP. Oil and gas exploratory (wildcatting) programs have immediate write-offs as they're searching and/or drilling for oil. Oil and gas exploratory programs drill in unproven areas. Write-offs include things such as payroll, equipment, fuel, and leasing or purchasing land. Exploratory programs are the riskiest oil and gas DPPs but have the highest return if oil or gas is reached.

488. D. income oil and gas programs

To claim depletion deductions, the partnership has to be depleting a natural resource. Of the choices given, only oil and gas programs deal with a natural resource. Exploratory programs (ones that are looking for oil) don't have depletion deductions until they actually hit oil and start pumping it from the ground, like income programs.

489. B. developmental program

Oil and gas exploratory programs drill in unproven areas. Oil and gas developmental programs drill in proven areas. Oil and gas income programs take over existing, productive areas. Oil and gas combination programs are a combination of all three.

490. C. An income program

Because your client is set on investing in an oil and gas program and is risk-averse, you should put them in the safest program, which is an income program. Income programs invest in already producing wells, so the risk is minimal as compared to the other programs. However, the potential reward isn't going to be as high as the other programs.

491. C. A combination program

Oil and gas combination programs offer diversification between exploratory, developmental, and income producing areas.

492. A. I and III

Both equity REITs and hybrid REITs, which are a combination of equity and mortgage REITs, derive part of their income from rent collected from property that is owned.

493. C. double-barreled

Double-barreled bonds are ones issued by municipalities and aren't types of REITs (real estate investment trusts). The three basic types of REITs are

- Equity REIT: Purchases properties
- Mortgage REIT: Invests in construction and/or mortgage loans
- Hybrid REIT: A combination of equity and mortgage REITs

494. C. 90%

A REIT (real estate investment trust) must distribute at least 90% of its income to shareholders to avoid taxation as a corporation.

495. D. trusts

As their name would suggest REITs (real estate investment trusts) are organized as a trust. The assets of the REIT are held in trust and shares of that trust are sold to investors. So, they are equity securities.

496. B. real estate investment trusts

You can assume that for all direct participation programs (DPPs) that investors will have to meet minimum financial requirement and be able to prove it to the general partner(s). Real estate investment trusts (REITs) can be purchased like a regular stock without the invest having to prove their financial situation.

497. A. They are registered as investment companies under the Investment Company Act of 1940.

Although there are some similarities between REITs and investment companies, they aren't classified as investment companies.

498. D. Publicly traded REITs

All publicly traded REITs (real estate investment trusts) must be registered with the SEC.

499. D. All of the above.

A hybrid REIT (real estate investment trust) is a combination of an equity REIT and a mortgage REIT. Hybrid REITs may receive interest from mortgages and generate income from capital gains and/or rent.

500. C. Private REITs

Private (private placement) REITs (real estate investment trusts) are REITs that may be sold privately without SEC registration.

501. **A. registered non-listed REIT**

PNLRs are public non-listed REITs (registered non-listed REITs). These REITs are registered with the SEC but don't trade on a major exchange. These REITs are not quite as liquid as REITs that trade on exchanges.

502. **B. rental income and capital gains from properties sold**

Equity REITs take equity positions in real-estate properties. Their income is derived from rent collected or profits made when properties are sold.

Chapter 7 Answers

503. **C. 100 shares of the underlying security**

Most option contracts represent 100 shares of the underlying security.

504. **C. $65**

This is a fairly easy question if you remember that options are for 100 shares unless otherwise stated in the question. It's as simple as taking the premium increase and multiplying it by 100.

$0.65 \times 100 = \$65$

505. **B. 9 months**

Standard option contracts are issued with 9-month expirations. Long-term equity anticipation securities (LEAPS) have expirations of up to 39 months.

506. **B. I and IV**

Buying calls is a bullish strategy because the investor wants the price of the underlying security to increase. For example, if an investor purchased an ABC 30 call option, the investor would want the price of the stock to go above 30. If the price of ABC increases above 30, the investor could exercise the option to buy the stock at 30 and sell it in the market for a higher price. In addition, selling in-the-money put options is also a bullish strategy because the seller wants the price of the underlying security to increase. When selling a naked option, the most an investor can hope to make is the premium received. Therefore, the seller would not want the put option to go into the money more; they would want the underlying stock to increase in value.

507. C. Long a put or short a call

Investors who are long a put or short a call would deliver a stock when the option is exercised. Here is the breakdown: Long a call — the right to buy the stock

Long a put — the right to sell the stock

Short a call — the obligation to sell the stock

Short a put — the obligation to buy the stock

508. B. Long a DIM put

The best hedge (protection) for an investor who owns a stock is to purchase a put option on the same security at the current market price or higher. In the event the stock price starts declining, the investor would be able to exercise the put option and sell the stock at the strike price of the option.

509. D. buyers of puts and writers of calls

If someone is bearish on a particular security, they want the price to decrease. With no other positions in the underlying stock, both buyers of puts and writers of calls want the price of the underlying stock to decrease.

510. A. right to buy stock at a fixed price

The buyers of options, whether calls or puts, have the right to buy (call options) or sell (put options) the underlying security at a fixed price.

511. D. neither the buyer nor seller would have a profit if the option is exercised

The breakeven point is the same for both the buyer and seller. It is the point at which if the option is exercised, they'll both break even, so neither will have a profit or loss.

512. A. I and III

Buying puts and selling calls are bearish positions, meaning the investor wants the price of the underlying security to decrease. The buyer of a call option has the right to buy the stock, so the seller of a call has the obligation to sell the stock if the option is exercised.

513. B. Buying a DWN put option

You should have knocked out Choice (A) right away because buying a call option is a bullish strategy used when you believe the price of the security is going to increase. Now, Choices (C) and (D) would work, but they aren't the cheapest options. Buying a straddle is ideal when you aren't sure which direction the stock is going because you are buying a put and buying a call. When shorting a stock, an investor has to come up with 50% of the market value. Buying a put is the best answer because it is a bearish strategy, and investors can have an interest in a large quantity of securities for a small outlay of money.

514. **C. obligation to buy stock at a fixed price if exercised**

The purchasers of options always have the *right* and the writers (sellers) have the *obligation* to live up to the terms of the contract if exercised. Here it is in a nutshell:

Buy a call — right to buy stock

Buy a put — right to sell stock

Sell a call — obligation to sell stock

Sell a put — obligation to buy stock

515. **A. I, III, and IV**

Call options go in-the-money when the market price is greater than the strike (exercise) price. Put options go in-the-money whenever the market price is lower than the strike price. Therefore, the only option that is not in the money when UPP is trading at 43.50 is short a 40 put.

516. **A. have the right to buy 100 shares of DEF stock at a fixed price**

Buyers of equity call options are buying the right to purchase 100 shares of the underlying stock at a fixed price.

517. **A. owning put options on the same stock with a higher strike price**

All of the other answers would cover a call option sold except owning a put. Owning a put with the same strike price or higher would cover the sale of a put option, not a call option.

518. **B. The writer must deliver cash equal to the in-the-money amount.**

When an index option is exercised, cash, not the securities in the index, must be delivered. The cash the writer must deliver in this case is equal to the in-the-money amount multiplied by 100.

519. **C. $350.00**

This customer purchased the option for $3.50 per share and since options are for 100 shares unless otherwise stated in the question, the customer paid $350.00.

520. D. II and IV

Since the investor sold a call option against the stock they own (covered call), they are limiting the upside potential because if the option goes in the money prior to expiration, it will be exercised. Also, because they bought the stock and sold the option, their loss is limited to the amount they paid for the stock minus the amount they received for selling the option.

521. D. have the obligation to buy 100 shares of LMN stock at a fixed price if exercised

Buyers of put options have the right to sell stock at a fixed price, so sellers of put options have the obligation to purchase that stock at a fix price if exercised.

522. C. Long an ABC call option

This investor shorted ABC common stock, so they want the price of ABC to decrease. What would cost the investor money is if the price of ABC increases. So, this investor can purchase a call option on ABC to protect themself in case the price of ABC increases.

523. C. The option is in-the-money.

Call options go in-the-money when the price of the underlying security trades above the strike (exercise) price. In this case, the underlying stock price is at 33, and the strike price of the option is 30, so it's 3 points in-the-money. In case you were wondering, there is no such thing as negative intrinsic value, which is Choice (D).

ANSWERS 501-600

524. C. ABC May 50 call

You need to remember the phrase "call up and put down." I believe that this will help you remember that call options go in-the-money when the price of the stock goes above the strike price and put options go in-the-money when the price of the stock goes below the strike price. Choice (A) is in-the-money because the price of the stock is below the put price of 45. Choice (B) is in-the-money because the price of the stock is above the 35 call strike price. Choice (D) is in-the-money because the price of the stock is below the 55 put strike price. However, Choice (C) is out-of-the-money because the price of the stock is below the 50 call strike price.

525. C. LMN Nov 80 call

Call options go in-the-money when the market price goes above the strike price and put options go in-the-money when the stock price drops below the strike price. In this case, the only one that is not out-of-the-money is Choice (C), because that one is in-the-money.

526. **B. The investor has received $300 for the call contract.**

Since this investor is short, they sold (wrote) the option. Therefore, they have the obligation to live up to the terms of the option and deliver 100 shares of XYZ at $50 per share if exercised. This investor received $300 for selling the call contract.

527. **C. II and III**

When a call or put option expires unexercised, the seller of the option gets to keep the premium received, and the buyer loses the premium paid.

528. **D. I, II, and III**

All of the choices listed are important factors in an option's premium. If the underlying security is subject to wide price swings, the option has more of a chance of going in-the-money and sellers would expect a higher premium for taking more risk. Also, when comparing two options with everything equal except the expiration month, the one with the longer time until maturity would have a higher price because it has more of a chance of going in-the-money. Remember, an option's premium is made up of intrinsic value (how much the option is in-the-money) and time value. If the intrinsic value goes up, the premium goes up.

529. **C. 12.25**

An options premium (P) is made up of intrinsic value (I) and time value (T). This option has an intrinsic value (an in-the-money amount) of 12 because it is a 40 call option, and the stock is at 52. Call options go in-the-money when the price of the stock goes above the strike price. So, the premium has to be at least 12. Since the option is only two days away from expiration, the time value has to be really small, so the only choice that works is (C).

530. **C. $0**

The intrinsic value is based on how much the option is in-the-money. Call options go in-the-money when the market value goes above the strike price. In this case, the market value is below the call option strike price, so the intrinsic value is $0. You cannot have a negative intrinsic value.

531. **A. When the underlying stock is below the exercise price**

Put options go in-the-money when the price of the underlying security drops below the exercise (strike) price. When an option is in-the-money, it has intrinsic value; the investor doesn't have to be in a profitable position.

532. B. 4

To determine the time value of an option, you can use the following equation:

$P = I + T$

P = the Premium of the option

I = the Intrinsic value of the option (how much it's in the money)

T = the Time value of the option

$9 = 5 + T$

$T = 4$

The premium in this case is 9. The intrinsic value is 5 because call options go in-the-money when the stock price goes above the strike price. To determine the intrinsic value, just subtract the 50 strike price from the market price of $55. With the premium at 9 and the intrinsic value at 5, the time value would have to be 4.

533. D. 3.5

The premium of an option is made of intrinsic value (how much the option is in-the-money) and time value (the longer the maturity, the higher the premium). In this case, the option is not in-the-money because put options go in-the-money when the price of the stock goes below the strike price. That means that the price of the stock would have to be below $45, which it isn't. That means that because there is no intrinsic value, the premium is made up entirely of time value. So, the time value is 3.5.

ANSWERS 501–600

534. B. Let the option expire

If an option has no intrinsic value at expiration, it is not in the money. Options not in the money at expiration would expire without being exercised.

535. C. may purchase stock at a predetermined price

The holder (owner) of a call option has the right to purchase the underlying security at a fixed price. Call options go in-the-money when the price of the stock goes above the strike price. In order for the holder to profit, it has to go enough above the strike price for the holder to recoup the premium paid plus some.

536. A. I and III

When writing (selling) an option with no other positions, the maximum potential gain is the premium received. To determine the break-even point for a call option, you have to add the premium to the strike price.

537. C. the exercise price plus the premium

To determine the breakeven point on a call option (whether buyer or seller), you have to add the exercise (strike) price plus the premium. This works because call options go in the money when the price of the underlying security increases. If it increases exactly enough for the buyer to recoup the premium, they have reached a breakeven point. The breakeven point is the same for the buyer and seller.

538. B. $1,625

This investor purchased 5 calls at a premium of $325 each (3.25 × 100 shares) per option that expired worthless. So, all you need to do is multiply $325 × 5 options.

$325 × 5 = $1,625

539. C. II and III

You have to remember that sellers (writers or shorters) of options always face more risk than the buyers; the buyers risk is limited to the amount invested. However, sellers of put options do not face a maximum loss potential that is unlimited because put options go in-the-money when the price of the stock drops below the strike price, and it can only go down to 0. Sellers of uncovered calls face a maximum loss potential that is unlimited because call options go in-the-money when the price of the stock increases above the strike price, and the seller would have to purchase the stock at a price that could keep going higher. Additionally, investors who short stock (answer II) face a maximum loss potential that is unlimited because they are bearish and lose money when the price of the security increases and there is nothing to stop the price from increasing. Investors who have sold covered calls do not face an unlimited maximum loss potential because they already have the stock to deliver if exercised.

540. A. above the exercise price plus the premium paid

In order for an investor to profit from a long call position, they would have to exercise the option when the market price is above the exercise (strike) price plus the premium paid.

541. D. $41.75

When you are determining the breakeven point for an individual option, the current market value does not fit into the equation. You just have to look at what the investor paid for the option and the strike price. Call options go in-the-money when the price of the stock goes above the strike price. In this case, since Mr. Couture paid 1.75 for the option, the breakeven point would be $41.75.

40 + 1.75 = $41.75 breakeven point

542. D. the exercise price minus the premium

To determine the breakeven point on a put option (whether buyer or seller), you have to subtract the premium from the exercise (strike) price. This works because put options go in-the-money when the price of the underlying security decreases below the strike price. If it decreases exactly enough for the buyer to recoup the premium, the buyer has reached a breakeven point. The breakeven point is the same for the buyer and seller.

543. A. $700

This is a relatively easy question. You can use an options chart, but it probably isn't really necessary for questions like this. Since the question does not mention anything about this investor having any other stock or option positions, you are just dealing with the individual option. Since this investor sold the option, the most they can hope to make is the premium received. The premium received is $700 (7 premium × 100 shares per option).

544. C. 43

When buying or selling a call option with no other positions, you need to add the premium to the strike (exercise) price to get the breakeven point. In this case, it doesn't matter whether this investor was purchasing or selling the option because both break even at the same price.

$40 + 3 = 43$

545. D. The option is exercised when the price of the underlying stock is below the strike price minus the premium.

When selling an uncovered put option, an investor has taken a bullish position. The maximum potential gain is the premium received. In other words, the investor does not want the option to be exercised because they will start losing money and possibly even end up taking a loss. Therefore, Choice (D) is the correct answer.

546. B. $415

When selling an individual option, the maximum potential gain is the premium. When looking at the exhibit, the first column is the market price of RST; the second column is the strike prices; and everything to the right of that column are the premiums. To find the premium for a Dec 50 put, find the Dec column (the last one) and the 50p row (the bottom one), and where they intersect, you will find the premium. In this case, it is 4.15, which represents a price of $415 because options are for 100 shares.

547. A. Strike price minus the premium

When writing (selling) a naked (uncovered) call option, the maximum loss is unlimited. However, when writing a naked put option, the maximum loss is the strike (exercise) price minus the premium. Put options go in the money when the price of the stock drops below the strike price. This means that a put option can go only so far in-the-money because the price of the underlying stock can only drop to zero. Therefore, the maximum loss per share would be the strike price less whatever Mr. Drudge received per share when he sold the option.

548. **C. (Strike price – the premium) × 100 shares × 10 options**

When selling an uncovered (naked) put option, the most the seller could lose is the strike price minus the premium multiplied by 100 shares and then by 10 options. Put options go in-the-money when the price of the stock goes down below the strike (exercise) price. Because the stock can only go down to zero, the seller can lose money from the strike price down to zero less the premium received. However, because options are for 100 shares, you have to multiply that answer by 100 shares and then by the 10 options the customer sold.

549. **D. Unlimited**

When purchasing a call option with no other positions on the underlying security, the maximum potential gain is unlimited because there is nothing keeping the stock from continuing to increase in price.

550. **A. $350**

When purchasing a call option with no other positions on the underlying security, the maximum potential loss is the premium paid. In this case, the investor purchased the option for $350 (3.5 × 100 shares per option).

551. **C. 36.5**

Call options go in the money when the market price of the stock goes above the strike price. So, to determine the breakeven point for a call option, you have to add the strike price and the premium (call up). So, in this case, you have to add the premium of 6.5 to the strike price of 30.

30 + 6.5 = 36.5 breakeven point

552. **A. $700**

When shorting (selling or writing) an option with no other positions on the underlying security, the maximum potential gain is the premium received. This investor received a premium of $700 (7 × 100 shares per option), so that's the maximum potential gain.

553. **D. Unlimited**

When writing (selling or shorting) a call option with no other positions on the underlying security, the maximum potential loss is unlimited. Remember, call options go in-the-money when the price of the underlying security goes above the strike (exercise) price. There is no limit to how high the underlying security can go, so the maximum potential loss for a seller of a call option is unlimited.

554. **C. 49.5**

Call options go in-the-money when the market price of the stock goes above the strike price. So, to determine the breakeven point for a call option, whether buying or selling, you have to add the strike price and the premium (call up). So, in this case, you have to add the premium of 4.5 to the strike price of 45.

45 + 4.5 = 49.5 breakeven point

555. **C. the strike price minus the premium**

The best way to determine a breakeven point for an investor who has an option position only is to remember "call up" and "put down." Since this is a put option, you need to put down by subtracting the premium from the strike price. This answer would have been the same whether the investor was long the put or short the put.

556. **B. $4,400**

When dealing with put options that go in-the-money when the market price declines, there will not be an unlimited maximum gain or loss. Declan purchased the option for 6, so their maximum potential loss is $600 ($6 × 100 shares per option). To determine the maximum potential loss, you just subtract the premium from the strike (exercise price).

50 − 6 = 44

This gives you both the breakeven point. If you multiply that by 100 shares per option, you'll get a maximum potential gain of $4,400 ($44 × 100 shares).

557. **A. 56**

To determine the breakeven point for a put option, remember put down (subtract the premium from the strike price) because put options go in the money when the price of the underlying security drops below the strike price.

60 − 4 = 56

558. **A. $6**

The maximum potential loss when purchasing an option with no other positions on the underlying security is the premium paid. In this case, the investor paid $6 per share.

559. **A. 34**

The easiest way to determine the breakeven point for an individual option is to remember:

Call up: Add the premium to the call strike price.

Put down: Subtract the premium to the put strike price.

40 − 6 = 34

560. A. 31.5

Put options go in-the-money when the price of the stock goes below the strike price. Therefore, this stock has to go 3.5 points below the strike price of 35 for this investor to break even.

35 − 3.5 = 31.5 breakeven point

561. C. 68.38

A lot of information is included in this question that is not needed to get the answer. Put options go in-the-money when the price of the stock goes below the strike (exercise) price. To get the answer, all you need to do is put down (subtract the premium from the strike price). In this case, you need to subtract 6.62 from 75.75 − 6.62 = 68.38 breakeven point.

562. A. $800

When selling an option with no other positions, the maximum potential gain is the premium received. Since options are for 100 shares, you have to multiply the premium of 8 by the 100 shares. $8 × 100 shares = $800.

563. B. $4,200

When selling a put option with no other positions, the maximum potential loss per share is determined by subtracting the premium from the strike price. This is true because put options go in the money when the price of the underlying security drops below the strike (exercise) price. So, you subtract 3 from 45 to get a breakeven point of 42 (45 − 3 = 42). Multiply that by 100 shares to get your answer.

42 × 100 shares = $4,200 maximum potential loss

564. B. 32

Since this is a put option, you can determine the breakeven point by using *put down* — subtracting the premium from the strike (exercise) price.

40 − 8 = 32 breakeven point

565. D. Closing purchase

When Melissa originally (wrote) sold the options, it was an initial or opening transaction. Since Melissa sold those options, it's an opening sale. To get out of that position, Melissa would need to close the options. So, since Melissa has to purchase the options, it is a closing purchase.

566. D. Closing sale

I think that you will find this question easier if you break it down into two parts. First you have to look at whether it is an initial purchase or sale, or at whether the customer is getting rid of an option position. In this case, the customer is getting rid (closing) of an option position. Next, is the customer buying (purchasing) or selling themself out of the position? This customer owns the option, so they have to sell themself out of the position. This means that you would mark the option order ticket as a closing sale.

567. B. $75 gain

The easiest way for you to see what is going on is to set up an options chart. This investor wrote (sold) the RST put for a premium of 3.25, so you have to put $325 (3.25 × 100 shares per option) in the "Money In" side of the chart because the investor received the money for selling the option. Next, the option was exercised, so you have to put $4,000 (the 40 strike price × 100 shares per option) in the "Money Out" side of the chart because "puts switch," meaning that the exercised option has to go on the opposite side of the chart from the premium. After that, the investor sold the 100 shares of stock in the market for $37.50 per share for a total of $3,750, which goes in the "Money In" side of the chart because the investor received money for selling the stock. Total up the two sides, and you will see that the investor had received $4,075 and spent $4,000 for a miniscule profit of $75.

Money Out	Money In
$4000	$325
	$3750
$4000	$4075

ANSWERS 501–600

568. B. $200 gain

I feel the best way to visualize equations like this and not make a careless mistake is to set up an options chart. An options chart is simply a money in / money out chart. So, the investor sold the 70 put for 5, and you have to put $500 ($5 × 100 shares per option) on the Money In side of the chart. Next, the investor sold the 80 call for 4, so you have to put $400 on the Money In side of the chart. Next, the investor closes the put for 4 and the call for 3, so you have to put $400 and $300 on the Money Out side of the chart because to close means do the opposite of what was done originally. Total up the two sides, and you'll see that this investor had $200 more in than out ($900 – $700). This means that this investor had a $200 gain.

Money Out	Money In
$400	**$500**
$300	**$400**
$700	**$900**

569. A. $1,100 gain

I feel the best way to visualize equations like this and not make a careless mistake is to set up an options chart. An options chart is simply a money in / money out chart. This investor purchased the 60 call option for 4, so you have to put $400 out ($4 × 100 shares per option) because that's what they spent. Next, it said that it went up to $75 just prior to expiration, which doesn't require you to do anything because it's not an action, it's just giving you information. Next, the investor exercised the option, so you have to put $6,000 ($60 strike price × 100 shares) under its premium because calls same (the premium and strike price go on the same side of the chart). After that, they sold the 100 shares received by exercising the option. The market price is $75, so you have to put $7,500 on the Money In side of the chart because that's what they received for selling the shares. Total up the two sides, and you'll see that this investor has a $1,100 gain ($7,500 – $6,400).

Money Out	Money In
$400	$7,500
$6,000	
$6,400	**$7,500**

570. A. $400 gain

I feel the best way to visualize equations like this and not make a careless mistake is to set up an options chart. An options chart is simply a money in / money out chart. Alyssa wrote (sold) the call for 9, so you have to put the $900 received ($9 × 100 shares per option) on the Money In side of the chart. The underlying stock price then increased to $45, which doesn't require you to do anything. Then, the call was exercised, so you have to put the $4,000 (40 strike price × 100 shares) under the $900 premium because calls same (the premium and strike price go on the same side of the chart). Next, Alyssa bought the stock in the market at $4,500 ($45 × 100 shares) to meet the obligation. Since that was money spent, put the $4,500 on the Money Out side of the chart. Total everything up, and you'll see Alyssa had a gain of $400 ($4,900 – $4,500).

Money Out	Money In
$4,500	$900
	$4,000
$4,500	**$4,900**

571. C. $300 gain

I feel the best way to visualize equations like this and not make a careless mistake is to set up an options chart. An options chart is simply a money in / money out chart. This investor bought the put option for 7, so you have to put $700 ($7 × 100 shares per option) on the Money Out side of the chart. TTT dropped to 50 just prior to expiration, so you don't have to do anything with that information yet. Now, the investor purchased the stock in the market at the market price of $50 per share, so you have to put $5,000 ($50 × 100 shares) on the Money Out side of the chart. And then, the investor exercised the put, so you have to put $6,000 ($60 strike price × 100 shares) on the Money In side of the chart because puts switch (the premium and strike price go on opposite sides of the chart). Total up the two sides, and you'll see that this investor had a gain of $300 ($6,000 – $5,700).

Money Out	Money In
$700	$6,000
$5,000	$
$5,700	$6,000

572. B. $300 loss

You probably don't need an options chart for this one, but I'll do it anyway. An options chart is simply a money in / money out chart. This investor purchased the call for 9, so you have to put $900 ($9 × 100 shares per option) on the Money Out side of the chart. Next, the investor closed the option for 6. Closing means do the opposite. So, this investor originally purchased the option, so to close they're going to sell the option. In this case, they're selling it for $600 (6 × 100 shares), so you have to put that on the Money In side of the chart. This investor had $300 more out than in ($900 – $600), so that's the loss.

Money Out	Money In
$900	$600

573. A. $400 gain

I feel the best way to visualize equations like this and not make a careless mistake is to set up an options chart. An options chart is simply a money in / money out chart. Melissa bought the 100 shares of HHH common stock at $50 per share, so you have to put $5,000 ($50 × 100 shares) on the Money Out side of the chart. Next, Melissa received $600 ($6 × 100 shares per option) for selling the call, so you have to put that on the Money In side of the chart. After that, Melissa sold the HHH stock at $52 per share, so you have to put $5,200 ($52 × 100 shares) on the Money In side of the chart. Then, Melissa closed the option for $400 (4 × 100 shares). Since Melissa originally sold the option, she purchased the option to close it, so the $400 has to go on the Money Out side of the chart. Total up the two sides, and you'll see that Melissa had $400 more in than out ($5,800 – $5,400), so that is the gain.

Money Out	Money In
$5,000	$600
$400	$5,200
$5,400	**$5,800**

574. **B. I, II, and III**

The OCC (Options Clearing Corporation) sets the contract sizes, the strike prices, and the expiration dates. However, the premium is based off of the intrinsic value (how much the option is in-the-money) and time value (the amount of time until the option expires).

575. **C. $4,500**

The aggregate exercise (strike) price of an option is the exercise price multiplied by the number of shares per option (100 unless otherwise stated in the question).

$45 – 100 shares = $4,500 aggregate exercise price

576. **D. clearing member**

A clearing member is a member of FINRA that has been admitted to membership in the OCC (Options Clearing Corporation).

577. **C. buying a WXY 45 put option**

To have a delta neutral position, an investor has to be fully hedged; for example, owning 100 shares of WXY stock and owning an at-the-money put on that same stock. So, it is offsetting long and short positions.

578. **D. Selling short 1,000 shares of HIJ**

A net delta position is when the investor has enough shares (either long or short) to offset the option position. Since this investor is short 10 put options, which go in-the-money when the price of the underlying security goes below the exercise (strike) price, they need to offset that by selling short 1,000 shares of HIJ. Remember, options are for 100 shares, so 10 options would be 1,000 shares. By selling short, this investor has the potential for making money when the price of the security drops along with the potential for losing money on the options sold when the price of the security drops.

579. **A. the number of option contracts that a person can hold on the same side of the market**

Position and exercise limits are the number of options an investor can hold or exercise on the same side of the market. By the same side of the market, I mean bullish or bearish positions. So, this means that an investor is limited to a certain number of bullish option positions (buying calls and/or selling puts) and a certain number of bearish potions (buying puts and selling calls).

580. C. The strike price is lowered to reflect the dividend.

For any open orders for options, the price of the strike (exercise) price of the option will be lowered to reflect the dividend to be paid on the ex-dividend date. For example, if one of your customers had a limit order to purchase 10 XYZ Oct 40 call options at 4 and XYZ announced a 40-cent dividend, your customer would now have a limit order to purchase 10 XYZ Oct 39.60 call options at 4. Your customer can keep it at a strike price of 40 by placing a DNR (do not reduce) order so the option order would remain the same on the ex-dividend date.

581. D. I, II, III, and IV

When a customer purchases or sells an option, they must receive a confirmation. The confirmation must include the type of option (call or put), the underlying security or index, the expiration month, the strike price, the number of contracts, the premium, the trade date, the settlement date, long or short, opening or closing transaction, whether it was done on a principal or agency basis, the amount of commission, and so on.

582. B. OCC

The OCC (Options Clearing Corporation) is the issuer and guarantor of all listed options. The OCC decides which securities will have options, their strike prices, and their expiration dates. In addition, the OCC guarantees that option holders will be able to exercise their options.

583. B. II, I, IV, III

When a customer is interested in purchasing or selling options, you must first send them an ODD (Options risk Disclosure Document). The ODD is not an advertisement but lets the customer know the risks of investing in options. Next, a ROP (Registered Options Principal) must approve the account. Then, the trade can be executed. Finally, within 15 days of the approval of the account, the customer must sign and return the OAA (Options Account Agreement). The OAA basically states that the customer understands the risks and rules regarding option transactions.

584. A. a registered options principal

A registered options principal (ROP) is responsible for approving all options accounts. In addition, they must approve all options transactions and approve all options advertising. To become a ROP, you must pass a Series 4 exam.

585. C. within 15 days after approval of the account

Investors must receive an ODD at or prior to the approval of the account. However, investors must sign and return an Options Account Agreement within 15 days after approval of the account.

586. **B. The premium decreases the cost basis.**

Selling covered calls reduces the cost basis. I think the best way to see this is if I give you sample numbers. Let's say that an investor purchased stock for $50 per share and then sold a covered call for 3. They originally spent $50 per share and then got $3 back, so their cost basis was reduced from $50 to $47 ($50 – $3).

587. **B. 5:30 p.m. EST on the third Friday of the expiration month**

The last trade of an option is 4:00 p.m. EST on the third Friday of the expiration month. The last exercise is 5:30 p.m. EST on the third Friday of the expiration month. And, options expire 11:59 p.m. EST on the third Friday of the expiration month.

588. **B. Random selection**

The OCC (Options Clearing Corporation) chooses which firm to receive the exercise notice randomly only. When the firm receives the exercise notice, they choose which customer's options to exercise randomly, first in, first out, or any other method fair and reasonable.

589. **D. I, II, III, and IV**

Options of the same series have the same stock, same expiration month, same strike price, and same type (calls or puts).

590. **B. within 15 days after approval of the account**

The options account agreement (OAA or options agreement) must be signed and returned within 15 days after approval of the account. The customer would first receive an options risk disclosure document (ODD or options disclosure document), and then the account would be approved by an options principal. Once approved, the customer has 15 days to sign and return the options account agreement.

591. **B. 4:00 p.m. EST on the business day of expiration**

The last time an investor can trade an option is 4:00 p.m. EST (3:00 p.m. CST) on the business day of expiration, which you can assume is the third Friday of the expiration month.

592. **C. Selling uncovered calls**

When purchasing an option, the most you can lose is the premium. Therefore, option sellers always face more risk than option buyers. When selling uncovered call options, the maximum loss potential is unlimited because call options go in-the-money when the price goes above the strike price. In theory, the price of the stock can keep going up. Put options go in-the-money when the price of the stock goes below the strike price. Because the price can only go to zero, the maximum loss potential when selling an uncovered put is not unlimited.

593. **A. at or prior to approval of the account**

The options disclosure document (ODD or options risk disclosure document) must be sent to customers at or prior to approval of the account. So, it's the ODD first, the account gets approved, the trade takes place, and finally the customer has to send in a signed options account agreement (OAA) within 15 days after approval.

594. **D. 11:59 p.m. EST on the business day of expiration**

Listed options expire on the third Friday of the expiration month at 11:59 p.m. Eastern standard time.

595. **D. the premium**

The OCC (Options Clearing Corporation) sets the exercise (strike) price, the amount of shares per option, and the expiration date of an option. The premium is based on supply and demand.

596. **C. II and III**

Two options of the same class have the same stock and the same type. Answer I includes a call and a put while answer IV has different underlying stocks.

597. **C. based on size**

When exercising an option, the firm can choose a customer by any method except based on size (the number of contracts that each investor sold).

598. **A. one**

Options settle in one business day after the trade date (T+1).

599. **B. the customer cannot establish any new options positions**

The options account agreement (OAA) must be signed and returned by the customer within 15 days after approval of the options account. If not signed and returned, the customer cannot establish any new options positions.

600. **B. the registered rep**

The first one responsible to determine whether a customer can handle the risk of investing in options is the registered representative. If the registered rep believes the customer is suitable, it is up to the registered options principal (ROP) to determine the size and types of option transactions are okay for this customer.

601. **D. the customer with the largest position**

Although the OCC can choose the firm randomly only, the firm chosen can choose the customer to assign the exercise notice to by FIFO (first in first out), random selection, or any other method fair and reasonable. However, they cannot choose the customer based on size (the amount of option contracts held).

602. **B. T+2**

This one may have been a little bit tricky. You probably remember that option transactions settle in one business day (T+1). However, this is a stock transaction because the investor exercised the option to purchase stock. Stock transactions settle regular way in two business days after the trade date (T+2).

Chapter 8 Answers

603. **C. I, II, and III**

Although it may be helpful, it is not required for you to know whether or not a new customer has an account at another brokerage firm. However, you do need to know the customer's citizenship, whether or not their name appears on the SDN (Specially Designated Nationals) list, and whether or not they work for another broker-dealer.

604. **C. the individual's educational background**

The individual's Social Security number, date of birth, and residential address are all required from a customer when opening an account. Although the individual's educational background would be helpful to have, it's not required.

605. **D. all of the above**

When opening an account for a client, you should help determine the risk tolerance and investment goals. Part of that includes looking at the client's financial and nonfinancial considerations. Some of the nonfinancial considerations are the customer's age, marital status, number of dependents, employment status, and employment of other family members.

606. **C. I, III, and IV**

Statements I and IV were probably a given. But you also need the type of account that the customer is opening (cash, margin, corporate, and so on), the customer's age and marital status, and the customer's occupation and employer. You don't need the customer's educational background.

607. **D. I, II, III, and IV**

All of the information listed needs to be on the new account form. In addition, you also need the Social Security number (or tax ID if a business), the occupation and type of business, bank references, net worth, annual income, if the customer is an insider of a company, and the signature of the registered rep and a principal.

608. **A. customer identification programs**

Under the USA Patriot Act, all financial institutions must maintain customer identification programs (CIPs). It's up to the financial institution to verify the identity of any new customers, maintain records of how they verified the identity, and determine whether the new customer appears on any suspected terrorist list or terrorist organization. As part of the identification program, they must obtain the customer's name, date of birth, address (no P.O. boxes), and Social Security number.

609. **A. CIPs**

The USA Patriot Act requires financial institutions, such as broker-dealers and banks, to maintain CIPs (customer identification programs) to help prevent money laundering and the financing of terrorist organizations. Financial institutions are required to look at the Specially Designated Nationals (SDNs) list published by the Office of Foreign Asset Control (OFAC) to see whether any of their new customers are on the list. If a new customer is on the list, their assets will be frozen, and your firm must cease doing business with them.

610. **A. The customer's**

If the customer is opening a cash (not margin) account at your firm, their signature is not required on the new account form. However, the signature of the registered representative and the principal's signature are both required.

611. **D. I, II, III, and IV**

Actually, all of the choices listed would likely change the investor's investment objectives. Typically, as an investor grows older, they will likely want to take less risk. By the same token, investing for one person or two people as in someone getting married or divorced would change the investment objectives. Also, as people gain investment experience, they will likely be more open to more speculative investments. Plus, you can assume that as an investor has more family responsibilities, they will want to take less risk.

612. **D. I, II, III, and IV**

Logically, all of the choices listed would change an investor's investment objectives. Certainly, aging and having a child would most likely mean that an investor wouldn't take as much risk. Depending on the terms of a divorce, an investor may want to invest in something that would provide regular income. However, winning a lot of money in a lottery would most likely mean that an investor would be able to take additional risk.

613. C. II and III

Yes, believe it or not, a customer's signature isn't required on a new account form. However, if you're opening a new account for a customer, you'd have to fill out and sign the new account form and have it signed by a principal (manager) of the firm.

614. D. The client's investment objectives

The most important consideration is the client's investment objectives. You'd hope that the client's age, marital status, and financial needs should help your client determine their investment objectives. Investment objectives include current income, capital growth, tax-advantaged investments, preservation of capital, diversification, liquidity, and speculation.

615. D. Corporate bonds

Your client is looking for total return, which is growth and income. At the current time, 100% of their portfolio is invested in stocks, which provide only growth potential. They also need to invest in fixed-income securities, like corporate bonds, which provide income to meet their investment objective.

616. A. The registered representative must determine the client's suitability.

The registered representative should get the customer's investment objectives and suitability prior to making a recommendation. A principal's approval isn't required for a registered representative to make an investment recommendation to a client.

617. C. The stock of new corporations

Investors looking for capital growth are more speculative investors. These investors are looking to invest money now, hoping that the investment will grow at a rapid rate. To meet that objective, the investor should invest in stock of new corporations.

618. A. I and II

Liquidity has to do with ease of trading. The more liquid a security is, the easier it is to trade. To get the answer for this question, you have to find the two answers that aren't liquid. Municipal bonds usually aren't very liquid because they're usually thinly traded. Direct participation programs are some of the most difficult investments to get in and out of, so they're not liquid.

619. B. Municipal bonds

Because your client is in the highest tax bracket, they should have some tax-advantaged investments, like municipal bonds or municipal bond funds, in their portfolio. Because the interest received from municipal bonds is federally tax-free, high income tax bracket investors save more tax money by investing in them.

620. C. I and IV

An investor who has an investment objective of speculation (aggressive growth) would purchase securities that have a potential for growth, such as sector funds or technology stocks. The risk of investing in sector funds and technology stocks is high, but if the investments become profitable, the reward can be quite high. Speculative investors are looking to purchase securities at a low price and sell them at a much higher price.

621. A. MMA would open a numbered account for Chael.

Numbered (street-named) accounts are very common at broker-dealers. If Chael wants to remain anonymous, they can have the broker-dealer set up their account as a numbered account. All order tickets would contain a number or code; however, the broker-dealer must have a signed document on file by Chael, stating that they are the owner of the account.

622. A. The client must sign a written statement attesting to ownership of the account.

Numbered accounts are also known as street-name accounts. To open an account for a client in street name, the customer must sign paperwork attesting to responsibility for the account. Because accounts of different investors can't be commingled (combined), the firm must keep this client's account segregated from other clients' accounts held in street name.

623. C. I, II, and III

A registered rep may open a minor's account by a custodian (UGMA account), a corporate account by a designated officer, and a partnership account by a designated officer. However, registered reps aren't permitted to open an individual account in the name of a third person.

624. A. A parent and a minor daughter

A joint account is one in the name of more than one adult. An account for an adult and a minor would be an UGMA (Uniform Gifts to Minors Act) or UTMA (Uniform Transfer to Minors Act) account. Both UGMA and UTMA accounts are custodial accounts in the name of the adult for the benefit of the minor.

625. A. The entire account would be transferred to Mrs. Faber.

This account was set up as joint tenants with rights of survivorship (JTWROS). When an investor with a JTWROS account dies, the investor's portion of the account is transferred to the remaining survivors of the account (in this case, Mrs. Faber). Most married couples set up their joint accounts this way to avoid probate issues.

626. **B. Tenancy in common**

In a joint tenancy in common (TIC) account, if one investor dies, that investor's portion of the account is transferred into the investor's estate while the remainder of the assets are transferred to the survivors. Persons may or may not have equal ownership of the account. The account may be divided based on percentage of money contributed.

627. **B. The deceased party's portion of the account is transferred to their estate.**

In a joint account with tenants in common (TIC), if one investor dies, the deceased party's portion of the account is transferred to their estate. In a joint account with rights of survivorship, the entire account is transferred to the survivors of the account.

628. **C. if one partner dies, that partner's portion in account is passed on to their estate**

Since answers (B) and (C) are in opposition to each other, one of them must be the answer. In a joint tenant with rights of survivorship account (JTWROS), if one partner dies, that partner's portion of the account goes to the remaining survivors of the account. Since we're looking for the false answer, you have to go with answer (C).

629. **C. Joint tenants with rights of survivorship**

Most married couples set up accounts as joint tenants with rights of survivorship (JTWROS). In the case that one of the spouses dies, the assets of the account are transferred to the remaining spouse.

630. **D. The account is transferred to the former minor.**

Under the terms of the Uniform Gifts to Minors Act (UGMA), the account must be handed over to the former minor when they reach the age of majority. You won't be expected to know the age of majority because it varies from state to state, but it's typically between the ages of 18 and 21.

631. **A. That partner's portion of the account is transferred to their estate**

Accounts set up as joint with tenants in common have the assets of a deceased partner transferring to yjrot estate.

632. **B. I and III**

Fiduciary accounts, such as UGMA and UTMA accounts, are required to follow the prudent man rule or legal list of the state in which the account is set up. The prudent man rule or legal list establishes a guideline of appropriate investments for fiduciary accounts. There isn't a FINRA list of approved investments for minors' accounts.

633. A. a parent and a minor daughter

A joint account is an account in the name of more than one adult. That means that Choice (A) doesn't work. UGMA accounts are designed for situations in which you have one minor and one adult.

634. B. An account for a minor daughter

An individual may open an account and trade the account for a minor without a written power of attorney. However, if a client wants to open and trade an account for a spouse or for a partner, they'd need them to sign a power of attorney, giving them the authorization to open the account and execute trades.

635. B. corporate resolution

In order for a corporation to open a cash account, it must send the brokerage firm a copy of its corporate resolution, which says who will have trading authority for the account. In order for the company to open a margin account, it must send the brokerage firm a copy of its resolution and charter (by-laws).

636. B. I and IV

UGMA (Uniform Gifts to Minors Act) accounts are custodial accounts set up with one minor and one custodian per account. Any taxes due are paid by the minor, not the custodian.

637. B. Certificates are endorsed by the minor.

UGMA (Uniform Gifts to Minors Act) accounts are custodial accounts set up with one minor and one custodian per account. The accounts are set up in the custodian's name for the benefit of the minor. Because the minor is legally too young to endorse any paperwork or certificates, the custodian endorses them.

638. C. custodial account

UGMA (Uniform Gift to Minors Act) accounts are custodial accounts. These accounts are managed by a custodian for the benefit of the minor. The custodian has full control over the account and has the right to buy or sell securities, exercise rights or warrants, hold securities, and so on. The custodian must do what is in the best interest of the minor. When the minor reaches the age of majority, which varies from state to state, the account is transferred to the former minor. An UGMA account can have only one custodian and one minor.

639. A. I only

A power of attorney or trading authorization is required for discretionary accounts. In this case, an individual is giving trading authorization to their registered rep or broker-dealer. All discretionary orders must be marked as such at the time they're entered for execution. These types of accounts must be monitored closely by a principal to make sure that there's no excessive trading for the purpose of generating commission (churning).

640. **B. corporate resolution**

For a corporation to open a cash account, you or your firm would need to receive a copy of the corporate resolution. The corporate resolution tells you who has trading authority for the account. If the corporation was opening a margin account, you'd need a copy of the corporate resolution and the corporate charter. The corporate charter (by-laws) lets you know that the corporation is allowed to purchase securities on margin according to their own by-laws.

641. **B. margin account**

A customer's signature is required to open a margin account, but not a cash account.

642. **C. The Federal Reserve Board**

The Federal Reserve Board (Fed or FRB) sets Regulation T and maintenance requirements for margin accounts.

643. **D. I, II, III, and IV**

For any new account, a new account form must be filled out by the broker-dealer. Since this is a margin account, a margin agreement must be signed, and the broker-dealer must obtain a copy of the corporate charter (bylaws), which would need to state that the corporation is allowed to purchase or sell short on margin. In addition, since it a corporate account, you would need to know who in that corporation has the authority to trade the account — that's where the corporate resolution comes in.

644. **C. I, III, and IV**

Because of the additional risk taken in margin accounts, customers must sign a margin agreement before executing any trades. The margin agreement is broken down into the credit agreement, a hypothecation agreement, and a loan consent form. A risk disclosure document needs to be sent out prior to opening an options account.

645. **A. The credit agreement**

The credit agreement discloses the terms for borrowing, which includes the interest rate to be charged on the debit balance, the broker-dealer's method of computation, and how and when the interest rate may change. There's no such thing as a *margin interest rate form*, so Choice (D) is obviously wrong.

646. D. I, II, and IV

Margin accounts are always held in street name (in the name of the broker-dealer for the benefit of the customer). Because the customer borrowed money from the broker-dealer to purchase the securities, the customer would be required to pay interest on the money borrowed (the debit balance; DR). In addition, a portion of the securities (140% of the DR) may be pledged as collateral for a bank loan by way of rehypothecation. However, a decrease or increase in the market value of the securities doesn't affect the debit balance.

647. B. allows the broker-dealer to loan a customer's margined securities to other investors

A loan consent form is required only for margin accounts, not cash accounts. Although technically it isn't required, almost all firms require that customers sign it prior to opening a margin account. The loan consent form allows the broker-dealer to loan a margin customer's securities to other investors or broker-dealers, typically for the short sale of securities.

648. D. Risk disclosure document

Because of the additional risk involved when purchasing securities on margin, all margin customers must receive a risk disclosure document prior to opening the account. The risk disclosure document covers some of the broker-dealer's rules and outlines the risks like "investors may lose more money than initially deposited." Because of the additional risk involved, not all investors are good candidates for margin accounts. As far as the other answers go, the credit agreement, the hypothecation agreement, and the loan consent form are all part of the margin agreement.

649. C. Regulation U

The Federal Reserve regulation that covers bank loans made to customers for the purpose of buying securities is Regulation U. Regulation T covers broker-dealer loans to customers.

650. A. The short sale of a corporate stock

All short sales of corporate stocks must be executed in margin accounts because of the unlimited loss potential.

651. C. only if permitted in their partnership documentation

As with corporations that wish to trade on margin, partnerships must also provide paperwork to the broker-dealer (a partnership resolution) that shows that they have agreed that they would be able to trade on margin.

652. B. in the name of the broker-dealer

Because the customer is borrowing money to purchase or sell the securities short, the securities are held in the name of the broker-dealer. This makes it easier for the broker-dealer to be able to sell off securities or close the margin account if the customer doesn't come up with payments if needed.

653. D. 25% on a long margin account and 30% on a short margin account

The Fed set the minimum maintenance requirements for long margin accounts at 25% and short margin accounts at 30%. These may be increased by the broker-dealer if they're not willing to take that much risk.

654. A. I and II

Securities that are marginable include stock and bonds listed on an exchange, NASDAQ stocks, non-NASDAQ stocks approved by the Fed, and warrants. However, mutual funds and IPOs (initial public offerings) can't be purchased on margin because they're new issues. New issues can't be purchased on margin for at least 30 days. However, after you've held mutual fund shares for more than 30 days, they can be transferred to a margin account.

655. C. $25,000

A day trader is an individual who purchases and sells the same security within the same day in an attempt to take advantage of price fluctuations. Pattern day traders are individuals who execute four or more day trades within five business days. The minimum equity for a pattern day trader is $25,000.

656. B. $1,200

The key to this question is that it is an initial transaction in a margin account. So, in this case, the customer purchased $1,200 (100 shares × $12) of securities. Reg T (50%) of that amount would be $600 ($1,200 × 50%). That would be the correct answer if it were an existing margin account. However, since they are just opening the margin account, they would either have to deposit the Reg T amount if more than $2,000, $2,000, or pay in full if the purchase is less than $2,000, which in this case it is. Therefore, Alyssa would have to deposit $1,200.

657. B. $1,800

Because this is the initial transaction in a margin account, different rules apply. After the margin account is open, the customer would just have to deposit Regulation T (Reg T; 50%) of the purchase. However, in an opening transaction for a long margin account, the investor must pay in full, deposit $2,000, or pay the Reg T amount. If the customer is purchasing less than $2,000 worth of securities, they'd have to pay in full.

If the quantity of securities purchased is greater than $2,000 but Reg T is less than $2,000, the customer would have to deposit $2,000. If the amount of securities being purchased is greater than $2,000 and Reg T is greater than $2,000, the customer would pay the Reg T amount.

The best way to deal with this situation is to take the three numbers — the value of the securities, Reg T, and $2,000 — and then choose the number in the middle. This will always work for an initial transaction in a margin account. For this question, you have $1,800 in securities, $900 Reg T amount, and $2,000. The middle number is $1,800, so that's the answer.

658. C. $13,500

This investor is opening a combined (long and short) margin account. The best way to deal with this is to treat each transaction separately. The investor is purchasing ($15) (1,000 shares) = $15,000 worth of ABC and shorting ($12)(1,000 shares) = $12,000. Assuming Regulation T at 50%, this investor would have to come up with 50% of each transaction.

($15,000)(50%) = $7,500

($12,000)(50%) = $6,000

$7,500 + $6,000 = $13,500

This investor would have to deposit $13,500 as a result of the two transactions.

659. C. $2,000

You have to pay particular attention to whether it's an initial transaction because different rules apply. Because this customer is opening the margin account, it's an initial transaction. This customer is selling short as an initial transaction, so they must deposit a minimum of $2,000. If the customer had an existing margin account, they'd have had to deposit 50% (Regulation T) of the $1,500 short sale, or $750.

660. A. open-end funds

New securities cannot be purchased on margin until they've been in the market for at least 30 days. Since open-end funds (mutual funds) are always new securities, they cannot be purchased on margin. However, once the mutual fund shares have been held for at least 30 days, they can be moved to a margin account.

661. D. $2,000

Normally, the requirement is 50% but since this is an initial transaction, there are other rules that come into play. If the purchase is greater than $2,000 but Regulation T (50%) is less than $2,000, the customer must pay $2,000. The customer purchased $3,200 worth of stock ($32 × 100 shares) and 50% of that is $1,600, so the investor must pay $2,000.

662. **B. The Fed sets Regulation T and maintenance, but they may be increased by the broker-dealer.**

The Fed sets Regulation T (50%) and minimum maintenance (25% for long accounts and 30% for short accounts), but the broker-dealer may increase them if they feel it's necessary.

663. **C. $2,500**

In an initial transaction for a short margin account, the investor has to deposit Regulation T (Reg T; 50%) of the amount of securities shorted, or $2,000, whichever is more. Because this investor is shorting $5,000 worth of securities, they have to deposit ($5,000)(50%) = $2,500.

664. **C. $3,800**

Normally, the customer would just have to deposit either $1,900 if it was an existing margin account or $2,000 for a new margin account. However, because the customer is shorting a low-priced security, different rules come into play. They are as follows:

Price per share	Margin and maintenance requirement
$0 – $2.50	$2.50 per share
$2.50 – $5.00	100% of SMV
$5.00 – $10.00	$5.00 per share

Because this investor is selling short stock at $3.80 per share, they're in that $2.50 to $5.00 range and must deposit 100% of the SMV (short market value) for a total of ($3.80)(1,000 shares) = $3,800.

665. **B. You may not make calls to potential customers before 8 a.m. or after 9 p.m. local time of the customer.**

The rule is that you can't call potential customers (cold calling) before 8 a.m. or after 9 p.m. local time of the customer. If a potential client doesn't want to be called anymore, you must place them on your firm's do not call list.

666. **D. Nobody from the rep's firm may contact the individual.**

If the individual has said that they're not interested in investing with the rep or the rep's firm, now or ever, the individual's name should be placed on the do not call list, and the individual should not be contacted in any way.

667. **D. Both (A) and (B)**

According to the TCPA (Telephone Consumer Protection Act of 1991), calls may not be made to potential customers (cold calling) before 8 a.m. nor after 9 p.m. local time of the customer. Exempt from that time requirement are calls to existing customers, calls from tax-exempt non-profit organizations, and debt collection companies.

Chapter 9 Answers

668. **D. Bond anticipation notes**

Market risk is the risk that the price of a security will decline due to negative market conditions. Because bond anticipation notes (BANs) are short term, they're not in the market as long and, therefore, are less subject to market risk.

669. **C. I, II, and III**

Your client would face political risk, market risk, and currency risk but not interest rate risk because they aren't buying fixed income securities. Political (legislative) risk is the risk that laws may change that may adversely affect the securities purchased. Market risk is the risk that the securities might decline due to negative market conditions. Currency risk is the risk that the security declines in value due to an unfavorable exchange rate between the U.S. dollar and foreign currencies.

670. **C. Variable annuities**

Purchasing power risk is inflation risk. Variable annuities provide variable payouts while fixed annuities provide fixed payouts. If anyone invests in a fixed annuity, although the fixed payouts are guaranteed, the money received is worth less as time goes on. A variable annuity gives investors the potential to outperform the inflation rate.

671. **A. reinvestment**

Reinvestment risk is the additional risk taken with interest or dividends received. Since zero-coupon bonds make no interest payments (they are issued at a discount and mature at par value), there is nothing to reinvest.

672. **D. all of the above**

Certainly, investors of foreign securities face all of the risks listed as well as others. Political risk is the risk that the politics of a particular nation affects the investments. Currency risk is the risk that the value of the value of the foreign security held will lower due to exchange rates. Regulatory risk is the risk that legislative changes may affect the market.

673. C. Liquidity risk

Liquidity or marketability risk is the risk of not being able to purchase or sell a security easily.

674. A. T-bonds

Inflationary risk is also known as purchasing power risk. It is the risk that the return on investment will not keep pace with the rate of inflation. Long-term, such as T-bonds (Treasury bonds) and fixed annuities, have high inflationary risk.

675. B. inflationary risk

All long-term bonds have inflationary (purchasing power) risk. Inflationary risk is the risk that the return on the investment doesn't keep pace with inflation. To limit inflationary risk, investors should purchase stocks. Over the long haul, stocks have more than kept pace with inflation.

676. D. regulatory risk

Regulatory risk is the risk that the price of a security declines due to new regulations placed on specific corporations.

677. C. II and III

Portfolio diversification doesn't reduce systematic (market) risk because a bearish market can affect all securities. However, portfolio diversification does reduce non-systematic (business) risk because some companies may perform better than expected, even though others may not be performing as well.

678. B. I and II

AA-rated corporate bonds and AAA-rated industrial development bonds are both considered safe investments. However, income bonds are issued by corporations in bankruptcy, and high-yield bonds are also known as junk bonds. This investor should definitely stay away from purchasing income bonds and high-yield bonds.

679. D. I, II, III, and IV

You'd do well to advise all your clients to have a well-diversified portfolio. Smaller investors can build a well-diversified portfolio by purchasing mutual funds. Diversification happens in many ways, such as buying different types of securities, buying securities from different industries, buying debt securities with different maturity dates, buying securities with different ratings, and buying securities from different areas of the country or world. Most investors diversify in several ways to limit their risk.

680. D. Treasury Strips

Reinvestment risk is the additional risk taken with interest and dividends received each year. All securities making interest or dividend payments have reinvestment risk. Treasury STRIPS have no reinvestment risk because they're issued at a discount and mature at par value without making interest payments along the way.

681. B. I and IV

Liquidity relates to how tradable a security is. Securities with low liquidity are hard to trade and, therefore, aren't desirable for most investors. This question asks for bonds with the least liquidity risk, so the correct answers are *bonds with a high credit rating* and *bonds with a short-term maturity*.

682. A. Treasury bills

Although your client has a main investment objective of aggressive growth, they may have to put that on hold for a short while because they're purchasing a home. Actually, Choices (B), (C), and (D) are ideal for an aggressive growth strategy; they're too risky for someone purchasing a home in the near term. In this case, you should let your client know that purchasing Treasury bills is a safe investment, which ensures that they have the funds available when needed to purchase the new home.

683. B. I, III, and IV

If one of your customers has a primary investment objective of *preservation of capital*, you wouldn't recommend speculative investments, such as an exploratory direct participation program. However, AAA-rated corporate bonds, blue chip stocks (such as IBM, Ford, and GE), and U.S. government bonds are all proper recommendations.

684. C. amount

When looking at a client's portfolio of securities, you should make sure that they're diversified. A client shouldn't have too many of their eggs in one basket, so to say. Relating to municipal bonds, diversification could be buying bonds of different types (revenue, GO, notes), buying bonds with different credit ratings (AAA, A, BBB), buying bonds from different geographical locations (New York, California, Guam), buying bonds with different maturities (short term, intermediate term, long term), and so on. However, buying a different amount of one security doesn't figure into the diversified portfolio mix.

685. A. Purchasing several different mutual funds

Because this investor has no other investments and has only $10,000 to invest, it's impossible to build a diversified portfolio without mutual funds. Mutual funds are designed for investors who don't have enough money and/or expertise to build a diversified portfolio. Each mutual fund in itself is diversified because the fund invests in several different securities.

686. D. All of the above

Diversification helps investors mitigate investment risk. All the choices listed are ways investors can lessen risk. When dealing with clients, you should always help them diversify their portfolio. It's the old "don't put all of your eggs in one basket" theory.

687. D. trend lines

Fundamental analysts decide what to buy, and technical analysts decide when to buy. A fundamental analyst compares the earnings per share (EPS) of different companies as well as balance sheets and income statements. However, trend lines are something that a technical analyst examines.

688. A. Earnings trends

Fundamental analysts compare companies to help determine what to buy. Technical analysts examine the market to try to determine when to buy. Knowing that, fundamental analysts are definitely interested in earnings trends. Technical analysts are interested in such things as support and resistance and the breadth of the market.

689. B. the support

Support is the lower portion of a trading range while the resistance is the upper portion of the trading range.

690. D. net income

The balance sheet is just a snapshot of the net worth (stockholders' equity) of a company. The balance sheet includes the company's assets, liabilities, and stockholders' equity. Net income is derived from a company's income statement. The income statement looks at a company's income minus expenses.

691. D. $40 million

To determine the working capital, you have to subtract the current liabilities (all the liabilities due this year) from the current assets (everything convertible into cash within one year). Current assets include cash, securities, accounts receivable, and inventory. Use the following equation:

Working capital = $60,000,000 – $20,000,000

692. C. II and III

If a corporation issues bonds, their working capital (the amount of money they have to work with) increases because they received cash by issuing the bonds. Their net worth remains the same because the money that they borrowed by issuing bonds has to be paid off at some time in the future.

693. B. utility

Proponents of the Dow Theory believe that both the industrial average and transportation average have to go in the same direction (advancing or declining) in order to confirm a trend. This makes sense because if corporations are producing more goods, they will have to be shipped.

694. A. equipment

Fixed assets are items owned by a corporation that are not easily convertible into cash. These include items such as land and equipment.

695. B. outstanding corporate bonds

Current liabilities are anything a corporation must pay within a 1-year period. These include taxes, accounts payable, wages, declared dividends, and so on. Outstanding corporate bonds are considered a long-term liability (something that must be paid off in more than a year).

696. A. Trademarks and patents

Intangible assets are items that don't have physical properties; included are items such as trademarks, patents, formulas, and so on.

697. D. Trend lines

Technical analysts look at the market and decide when to buy. Technical analysts look at things like trend lines, trading volume, and short interest. Fundamental analysts look at things like the price earnings ratio, income statements, and balance sheets.

698. C. In the stockholder's equity section

The balance sheet is comprised of assets, liabilities, and stockholder's equity (net worth). Treasury stock is stock that has been repurchased by the issuer and it's part of the issuer's net worth.

699. C. the earnings

Technical analysts look at the market and price movements. Corporate earnings is something that a fundamental analyst would examine.

700. D. Transportation

The Dow Jones Transportation Average tracks 20 stocks from the transportation sector.

701. **D. I, II, and IV**

When the company pays a cash dividend, it pays of debt because the dividend was declared previously. The net worth does not change since assets and liabilities decrease by the same amount.

702. **A. Assets = liabilities + shareholder's equity**

When looking at a corporation's balance sheet, the left side lists the assets, and the right side lists the liabilities and the shareholder's equity. Each side balances out so the left side equals the right.

703. **D. Lipper**

Lipper indexes allow investors to compare mutual fund investments against active indexes based on sectors, industries, countries, market capitalization, and so on.

704. **A. DJIA**

The DJIA (Dow Jones Industrial Average) is made up of 30 broad-based listed common stocks and is the most widely used to indicate the performance of the market. The DJIA is part of the Dow Jones Composite, which is made up of the industrial stocks, transportation stocks, and utility stocks.

705. **C. an increase in the DJIA and the DJTA**

According to the Dow theory, trends must be confirmed by the DJIA (Dow Jones Industrial Average) and the DJTA (Dow Jones Transportation Average). For it to be a real trend, both need to be going the same direction. This makes sense because it isn't enough that industries are selling and producing goods unless they're also being shipped.

706. **B. II, III, I**

If the economy is expanding, you would expect it to hit a peak at some point. After reaching the peak, the economy would start to contract until hitting the lowest point, which is the trough. After that, you would expect it to start all over again.

707. **A. I, II, and III**

If you're bearish, you want the price of the underlying security to decrease. Selling stocks short, buying put options, and buying inverse ETFs (exchange traded funds) are all bearish strategies. However, selling uncovered put options is a bullish strategy because the seller would like the price of the underlying security to increase, or at least not go in the money.

708. **D. Contraction**

During periods of contraction, inventories usually rise because consumer demand is not there.

709. **B. Increasing or decreasing government spending and changing tax rates**

The U.S. government by way of Congress and the president can vote to change government spending and tax rates. Reserve requirements and buying or selling U.S. government securities is controlled by the Fed (Federal Reserve Board).

710. **C. money available for bank loans**

An increase in the money available for bank loans would show an easing of the money supply, not a tightening.

711. **A. The Federal Reserve Board**

The Federal Reserve Board (Fed or FRB) is responsible for the U.S. monetary policy. They are responsible for trying to maintain a slow steady growth of the U.S. economy.

712. **D. increased consumer spending**

If the Fed (Federal Reserve Board) tightens the money supply, consumer spending will be reduced, not increased.

713. **D. an increase in foreign imports**

If the Fed eases the money supply, there will be more money available. If more money is available, the U.S. dollar will be weaker, and it will be more expensive to buy foreign goods. Therefore, there would be less foreign imports, not more.

714. **C. II and III**

If the U.S. dollar is strong, it will be cheaper to purchase foreign goods so there will be an increase in U.S. imports. If we're buying more U.S. goods, we have more money going out of the United States, which leads to an increase in the balance of payments deficit.

715. **D. All of the above**

The Fed (Federal Reserve Board) may use all of the choices listed as a way to tighten the money supply.

716. **B. I and IV**

The Fed has a few tools to help ease or tighten the money supply including: open market operations, adjusting the discount rate, changing reserve requirements, and raising or lowering Regulation T requirements. Out of the choices given, the two that would ease (add money to) the money supply would be inserting money into the system by purchasing U.S. government securities like T-bills and lowering reserve requirements (the percentage of customer deposits banks have to hold each night).

717. **A. Open market operations**

Although the Fed does control the discount rate and reserve requirements, the tool most commonly used by the Fed to control the money supply is open market operations. Open market operations is when the Fed buys and sells U.S. government securities, which happens on a continuous basis.

718. **B. setting the prime rate**

The Federal Reserve Board (FRB) is responsible for open market operations (buying and selling U.S. government securities), setting the discount rate (the rate the Fed charges banks for loans), and setting the minimum margin requirements. However, the prime rate is the rate banks charge their best customers (usually corporations) for loans. Although the prime rate would likely increase if the Fed increases the discount rate, the prime rate is ultimately decided by commercial banks.

719. **C. T-bonds**

T-bonds (Treasury bonds) have the longest-term maturity, so they'd decrease the most in price. Remember, when the discount rate (the rate the Fed charges banks for loans) changes, all rates across the board change, including yields on bonds. Bond prices and yields have an inverse relationship, so if yields increase, outstanding bond prices fall. Short-term debt securities, like T-bills will react quicker to rate changes, but overall, in most cases, long-term bonds will change more in price.

720. **A. I and III**

If the Fed (or Federal Reserve Board, FRB) is trying to tighten the money supply, it could increase the reserve requirements (the percentage of deposits banks must keep on hand), or it could raise the discount rate (the rate that the FRB charges member banks for loans).

721. **B. the interest rate that the Fed charges banks for loans**

The *discount rate* is the rate that the Fed charges banks for loans. The discount rate is the lowest of all rates. The *prime rate* is the rate that banks charge their best customers for loans. The *federal funds rate* is the rate that banks charge each other for overnight loans. The *broker loan (call loan) rate* is the rate that customers are charged on the debit balance in their margin accounts.

722. **D. inflation increases**

If the Fed increases the discount rate, you can assume that all rates will increase across the board. Therefore, bond yields and the federal funds rate would increase. When the discount rate is increased, it also tends to hurt the market and lower stock prices. Typically, one of the reasons the Fed increases the discount rate is to help curb inflation. This means that if the Fed increases the discount rate, the inflation rate would decrease, not increase.

723. **C. Utilities**

Utilities are most heavily affected by changing interest rates since they are highly leveraged (issue a lot of debt securities). If interest rates increase, they will have to issue debt securities with higher coupon rates.

724. **A. the interest rate that banks charge each other for overnight loans**

The Fed Funds rate is the interest rate that banks charge each other for overnight loans to help them meet their reserve requirements. The Fed Funds rate is the most volatile of all interest rates.

725. **D. All of the above**

The Federal Reserve Board was established to help stabilize the country's financial system. All of the choices listed are in the Fed's toolbox.

726. **C. II and III**

The Fed could lower bank's reserve requirements to ease the money supply, because it would allow banks the ability to lend out more money. The Fed could also buy U.S. government securities from banks to increase the money supply.

727. **A. inflation increases**

The Fed typically increases the discount rate in order to slow the economy down and lower inflation. So, inflation isn't likely to increase, it's likely to decrease.

728. **D. Increase taxes**

The federal government controls taxes and spending. If the federal government increases taxes, it will pull more money out of the economy and slow it down. All of the other choices would put more money into the economy.

729. **B. I and IV**

What you have to do with questions like this is look at which way the money is flowing. The question indicates a trade deficit, meaning that more money is going to foreign countries than what's coming in from foreign countries. If that deficit is increasing even more, you have to look at which choices send more money out of the country. If the United States is buying more foreign goods, it has to pay for them, so that increases the deficit. Also, if U.S. investors are purchasing ADRs (American Depositary Receipts), they're buying interest in foreign countries and increasing the deficit more.

730. B. Declining GDP

If the GDP (Gross Domestic Product) is declining, it means that business is slowing down, and we could be heading toward a recession. In this situation, the Federal Reserve Board would likely want to stimulate the economy. They can do this by printing money, buying U.S government securities from banks, lowering reserve requirements, lowering the discount rate, and so on.

731. D. U.S. exports will increase.

Answers (A) and (D) are in opposition to each other so one has to be true and one has to be false. We're looking for the true answer in this case. If the U.S. dollar has been falling, it is cheaper for foreigners to buy U.S. goods. Therefore, U.S. exports will increase.

732. C. The Fed Funds rate

The Fed Funds (federal funds) rate is the rate that banks charge each other for unsecured overnight loans. Since they are overnight loans, which are based on current interest rates, plus supply and demand, the rate changes constantly.

733. A. An increase in U.S. exports and a surplus in the balance of payments

If the U.S. dollar is falling against foreign currencies, it will be less expensive for foreigners to buy U.S. goods. If it is cheaper for them to purchase our goods, more money will be coming into the United States, and there will be a surplus in the balance of payments.

734. B. I and IV

If the U.S. dollar is falling against the euro, it shows a weakening in U.S. currency. When the U.S. dollar is weak, it costs more to purchase foreign goods, and it costs foreign companies less to buy U.S. goods. Therefore, U.S. imports would likely decrease, and U.S. exports would likely increase. The weakening of the U.S. dollar typically happens during easy-money periods.

735. A. the prime rate

Leading indicators are those that help give an indication of how the economy is going to do. The main leading indicators are M2 money supply, stock prices, the Fed Funds rate, and the discount rate. The prime rate — the rate that banks charge their best customers for loans — is a lagging indicator. Lagging indicators go the same direction as the leading indicators but arrive a little later.

736. C. Building permits

Leading economic indicators are statistics that indicate how the economy is going to do. Leading indicators include the money supply, stock prices, the discount rate, the federal funds rate, reserve requirements, orders for durable goods, and so on. Industrial production and GDP (gross domestic product) are coincidental indicators, and the unemployment rate is a lagging indicator.

737. C. Prime rate

The prime rate (the rate banks charge their best customers for loans) is a lagging indicator. Lagging indicators go in the same direction as leading indicators, but they move a little later.

738. A. Personal income

Personal income is a coincidental (coincident) economic indicator. M2 money supply is a leading indicator and corporate profits as well as the unemployment rate are lagging indicators.

739. D. 2 consecutive quarters

A recession is a two-consecutive quarter decline in the GDP, increases in unemployment, falling retail sales, a lowering of income, and a decrease in manufacturing.

740. B. GNP

The GNP (gross national product) includes all the investments made by U.S. businesses and residents inside and outside the United States.

741. A. Buy U.S. government securities in the open market

The Federal Reserve attempts to have the economy grow at a slow steady pace. They also attempt to keep the inflation rate low (around 2% per year). If the inflation rate is lower than that, and we're in a recession, it means that people aren't spending money quickly enough. In order to encourage spending, the Federal Reserve will inject money into the economy by purchasing Treasury bills in the open market. Lowering the tax rate would also work, but taxes are controlled by congress, not the Federal Reserve Board.

742. C. CPI

The CPI is the Consumer Price Index. The CPI measures the price changes of a basket of goods over a one-year-period. The increase in price shows the inflation rate.

743. **B. Personal income**

Unemployment claims, reserve requirements, and the money supply are all leading indicators. Personal income is a coincident (coincidental) indicator, which gives helps give you a snapshot of how things are going right now.

744. **D. The GDP**

Both the GDP (gross domestic product) and GNP (gross national product) are measured in constant dollars. When measuring in constant dollars, they are factoring inflation into the equation to see if the economy is actually expanding or contracting year to year.

745. **C. Utilities**

Utilities are highly leveraged companies because they issue a lot of bonds (debt securities). If interest rates increase, they'll have to issue bonds with higher coupon rates, which affects their bottom line more than other companies that aren't as highly leveraged.

746. **B. Household appliances**

Household appliance companies are cyclical companies that perform poorly during periods of economic downturns. As you can imagine, if the economy isn't doing well, more people are going to wait to buy that new refrigerator, stove, or whatever.

747. **A. Discount retailers**

Countercyclical companies are ones that perform better when the economy isn't performing well. These include companies such as fast food, discount retailers, auto parts companies, and so on.

748. **C. technology**

Growth companies are ones that have a high chance to grow at a rapid rate. Technology companies fit into that category.

749. **B. Alcohol companies are defensive.**

Alcohol companies are defensive companies because no matter how the economy performs, they typically do pretty well. Other defensive industries are utilities, food, clothing, tobacco, and cosmetics.

750. D. countercyclical stock

Cyclical stock moves in the same direction as the economy. So countercyclical stock moves in the opposite direction of the economy. Investors buy countercyclical stocks to balance out their portfolios and to protect themselves in the event of economic decline. Precious metals stocks, such as gold, tend to be countercyclical because they usually do well when the market is doing poorly and vice versa. Defensive stocks tend to do well no matter what. Some examples of defensive stocks are food companies, alcohol, tobacco, pharmaceuticals, and so on. Blue chip stocks are from well-established companies (such as IBM, Ford, and Microsoft) with a history of good earnings.

751. B. III and IV

Defensive stocks are ones that perform consistently no matter how the economy's doing. Companies that sell goods such as alcohol, food, tobacco, and pharmaceutical supplies, issue defensive stocks. Automotive and appliance company stocks aren't defensive because when the economy is doing poorly, investors wait a little longer to purchase these items.

752. A. II, III, and IV

Defensive industries are ones that perform well no matter how the economy is doing. Utilities, food, clothing, alcohol, tobacco, cosmetics, healthcare, and pharmaceutical are examples of defensive industries. Household appliances are cyclical, and their performance depends on the economy.

753. C. supply-side theory

The supply-side theory is also known as Reaganomics. Supply-side economics lowers taxes and allows people to keep and spend more of their own money. The money spent by individuals helps stimulate the economy and create more jobs. When more people are working, tax revenues actually increase.

754. B. Keynesian theory

Proponents of the Keynesian (demand-side) theory believe that raising taxes, deficit spending, borrowing money, and printing currency are the best way to stimulate the economy.

755. D. the monetarist theory

Controlling the money supply implies a hands-on approach. That approach is called the monetarist theory.

Chapter 10 Answers

756. **A. a syndicate selling new issues of municipal GO bonds to the public**

Remember, new issues are always sold in the primary market regardless of whether they're municipal GO bonds or any other security. By contrast, sales of outstanding securities or previously outstanding securities (treasury stock) always take place in the secondary market. The secondary market is broken down into the following:

First market: Listed securities trading on an exchange

Second market: Unlisted securities trading over-the-counter

Third market: Listed securities trading over-the-counter

Fourth market: Institutional trading without using the services of a broker-dealer

757. **D. initial public offering**

An initial public offering (IPO) is the first time a corporation ever sells stock to the public.

758. **A. primary offering**

An initial public offering (IPO) is the first time a corporation ever sells stock to the public. Corporations typically hold back a lot of shares for future needs, this is known as shelf registration. The additional 5 million shares have never been issued, so it is a primary offering.

759. **C. I, II, and III**

The secondary market is the trading of outstanding securities whether OTC (over-the-counter) or securities listed on an exchange. The underwriting of new issues is executed in the primary market.

760. **B. I and IV**

Primary distributions are the selling of new shares being sold by the issuer. Secondary distributions involve the sale of shares that have already been issued and outstanding shares.

761. **D. unlisted securities trading OTC**

The second market, not to be confused with the secondary market, is unlisted securities trading OTC (over-the-counter). The secondary market is broken down into the first market, the second market, the third market, and the fourth market. The first market is listed securities trading on an exchange, the third market is listed securities trading OTC, and the fourth market is institutional trading without using the services of a broker-dealer.

762. **C. Listed securities trading OTC**

A third market trade is listed securities trading OTC (over-the-counter).

763. **D. fourth market trade**

A trade between institutions without using the services of a broker-dealer is considered a fourth market trade. Fourth market trades usually take place using ECNs (electronic communications networks).

764. **B. Designated market makers**

Designated market makers (DMMs) are responsible for maintaining a fair and orderly market on the NYSE floor and helping to keep trading as active as possible.

765. **A. auction market**

The New York Stock Exchange is an auction (exchange) market where buyers and sellers get together to execute trades.

766. **C. Listed securities can be traded on an exchange and over the counter; unlisted securities can only be traded over the counter.**

Listed securities can be traded on an exchange, such as the New York Stock Exchange, or over the counter. Unlisted securities can only trade over the counter.

767. **D. OTCBB**

OTCBB is the Over the Counter Bulletin Board, which is the quotation service operated by FINRA for unlisted (non-Nasdaq) securities.

768. **A. pink market**

The pink market (pink sheets) is for corporations too small to be placed on the OTCBB (Over The Counter Bulletin Board). Corporations on the pink market are not required to meet listing requirements or file with the SEC.

769. **C. broker or dealer**

Designated market makers work on an exchange and execute trades for their own accounts as a dealer and for others as a broker.

770. C. II and III

The capacity (whether the firm is acting as a broker or dealer) must be disclosed on the confirmation (receipt of trade). If the firm is acting as a broker, the commission must always be disclosed. If the firm is acting as a dealer, the markup or markdown does not need to be disclosed.

771. B. a negotiated market

The over-the-counter (OTC) market is a negotiated market where buyers and sellers negotiate the trading price of a security. Exchanges are considered auction markets where prices and trading volumes are shouted out on the exchange floor.

772. A. the difference between bid and asked prices of a security

The spread is the difference between the bid and asked price of a security.

773. D. market maker

A market maker (designated market maker) is responsible to keep trading as active as possible for a particular security. They execute trades for other firms and will purchase or sell out of their own account.

774. D. Under no circumstances

A firm cannot act as a broker and dealer for the same trade. This means they can't charge a markup or markdown plus a commission at the same time. If a customer places a trade for more securities than a broker-dealer has available, the broker-dealer can buy the securities in from another dealer for resale to the customer. In this case, the broker-dealer would be selling out of their own inventory and only charging the customer a markup.

775. A. agent

When a broker-dealer charges a customer a commission, they are acting as a middleman or agent for the trade. If charging a markup or markdown, they are acting as a dealer (principal or market maker).

776. B. I and IV

Most brokerage firms are broker-dealers, meaning that they act as a middleman and deal out of their own inventory. When acting as a broker, a firm is buying or selling a security for a customer through another dealer. If executing a trade as a broker, the firm charges the customer a commission. Firms also act as dealers if they are buying and selling out of their own inventory. If acting as a dealer, the firm charges a markup when the customer buys and a markdown when the customer sells.

777. **C. principal**

When broker-dealers make a market in a particular security, they're acting as a principal or market maker. This means that they're willing to buy securities for their own inventory or sell securities from their own inventory. Broker-dealers not acting from their own account are acting as a broker or agent.

778. **C. prime broker**

Prime brokers are mainly used by large retail clients or by institutional accounts. Prime brokers help clients with more complex financial needs. They can help combine several accounts into one statement, provide lending, leveraged trade execution, cash management, and so on.

779. **B. Clearing broker**

Some broker-dealers are also clearing (carrying) firms. This means that they not only handle customer's orders to buy and sell but also maintain custody of their assets (securities and cash).

780. **A. Introducing brokers**

Although introducing brokers (IBs) are more commonly referred to in commodities and futures trading, an IB is a member firm that even though they are a party to a transaction, they do not actually execute or clear the trades. An introducing broker would deal with customers and make recommendations and accept orders but then have the orders executed by a clearing firm.

781. **D. II and IV**

When a securities firm buys securities for or sells securities from its own inventory, it's acting as a dealer (principal or market maker). When a dealer sells securities from their own inventory, they charge a price that includes a markup.

782. **B. bearish**

Short sellers borrow securities for immediate sale in the market. Their hope is that the price of the security drops, and they can repurchase it in the market at a lower price and return it to the lender. Therefore, short sellers are definitely bearish because they want the price of the security to decrease. If they were neutral, they would want the price of the security to stay the same. If this were the case, they wouldn't make money, and they'd still have to pay a commission, which is a losing proposition.

783. **A. to take advantage of a bullish market**

Selling a security short is a bearish positon, not a bullish one.

784. **D. not price specific to sell at the highest bid price**

Market orders are not price specific. If someone places an order to sell a particular security, they will sell it at the highest bid price (the most a dealer is willing to pay).

785. **C. not price specific to purchase at the lowest ask price**

Unlike limit or stop orders, market orders are not price specific. Someone placing a market order to buy will purchase at the lowest ask price, whatever that may be. The majority of orders are market orders.

786. **D. II and IV**

Short sellers are bearish because they want the price of the security they're purchasing to decrease. Because short sellers can lose money if the price of the security increases, their maximum loss potential is unlimited because there is nothing from keeping the price of the security from increasing more.

787. **D. municipal bonds**

Although municipal bonds may be sold short, they typically aren't. The reason is that the security must be borrowed and later found to cover the short position. Because municipal bonds are usually thin issues, they're not very liquid and, therefore, not good candidates for selling short.

788. **D. OTCBB stocks may be sold short**

All short sales must be executed in margin accounts. Therefore, because OTCBB (Over-the-Counter Bulletin Board) stocks aren't marginable, they can't be sold short.

789. **D. Stop**

Stop (stop loss) orders become market orders for immediate execution as soon as the underlying security passes the stop price. Stop orders are used for protection.

790. D. All of the above

Stop orders are used to help protect investors from losing too much money when holding either long or short positions. For argument's sake, say that you purchased stock for $30 per share, so you could enter a sell stop order at $28. If the market price touched or passed through the $28 per share, your stock would be sold at the next price. By the same token, if you purchased the stock at $30 per share and the stock subsequently rose to $37 per share, you could enter a sell stop order below that price to protect your profit. Buy stop orders are used to limit the loss on a short position or protect the profit on a short position. Unlike sell stop orders, which are entered below the market price, buy stop orders are entered above the market price. Investors who sell securities short lose money when the price of security increases.

791. A. buy stop order on FFF

Remember that stop orders are used for protection, so you can cross off Choices (B) and (D) right away. Because your client has a short position on FFF, they'd have to buy themselves out of the short position. Therefore, the answer is Choice (A) Your client would enter a buy stop order above the current market price.

792. A. below the current market price

Investors who own a security use sell stop orders for protection. Because these investors are concerned about the price dropping, they enter sell stop orders below the current market price of the security. If the market price of the security hits or passes the sell stop order price, the sell stop order becomes a market order for immediate execution.

793. C. Sell stop at $46

Stop orders (not limit orders) are used for protection. Therefore, none of the answer choices that include the word limit would fit. A sell stop order would be entered below the market price of the security, so the correct answer is Choice (C).

794. C. An order to sell $1,000 shares of JKL at $40 stop, $39.75 limit

In this case, Melissa should enter a sell stop limit order. So, first it is a sell stop order to sell $1,000 shares of JKL when it drops to $40 or below. Now, stop orders are not price specific, so the sell order could take place at any price after it's triggered. In this case, with a stop limit order, when the stop order was triggered, it becomes a market order to sell at a specific price or better ($39.75 in this case).

795. **B. the short sale of securities**

Regulation SHO covers the rules for short sales. Under SHO rules, all order tickets must be marked as short sale as compared to long sale, which is when an investor is selling securities that are owned. In addition, all brokerage firms must establish rules to locate, borrow, and deliver securities that are to be sold short. All brokerage firms must make sure that the security can be located and delivered by the delivery date prior to executing a short sale.

796. **B. Buy limits and sell limits**

By placing a limit order, an investor guarantees that the order will be executed at a specific price or better if it ever hits that price. Stop orders are triggered when hitting the stop order price or better but may be executed at a price at, above, or below the stop price.

797. **A. I and III**

The customer specified a price, so it's a limit order. In this case, it would be a limit order to buy 100 shares at a price of 50 or lower. Market orders aren't price specific; they're used to buy or sell at the best price available. All stop and limit orders are good for the day unless the customer specifies that they want the order in place for a longer time. If the day order isn't executed that day, the order is canceled.

798. **A. I and III**

Open orders are orders that are good until cancelled. In real practice, most brokerage firms will cancel or reconfirm the orders with their customers after 30 days or so because many customers forget about them. Because it's a stop order, when the order is triggered (it reaches $35 or above), it becomes a market order for immediate execution at the best price available.

799. **B. the time at which a security is traded**

Not held orders have to do with the timing of an order. So, for not held orders, the customer must agree to whether they want to buy, sell, or sell short a security as well as the number of shares. A not held order is one in which the customer is giving you, their registered rep, discretion as to the time an order is placed. This may be a situation where you think that you can get the customer a better price later in the day.

800. **A. I and III**

Fill-or-kill (FOK) orders must be executed immediately in their entirety, or the order must be canceled.

801. C. II and III

An immediate-or-cancel (IOC) order must be attempted to be filled immediately by the firm handling the order but may be filled partially. It's a one-time order and doesn't allow the order to be executed in several attempts.

802. B. must be executed in their entirety, or the order is canceled

Unlike fill-or-kill (FOK) orders and immediate-or-cancel (IOC) orders, all-or-none (AON) orders don't have to be executed immediately. However, like FOK orders, they must be filled entirely, or the order is canceled. AON orders remain active until they're executed or canceled.

803. A. It is cancelled.

At-the-open orders must be executed at the opening price; otherwise, the order must be cancelled. At-the-open orders allow for partial execution.

804. B. Stop and limit

When customers place a stop or limit order, they are providing a price for the trigger or execution of the order. A DNR (do not reduce) order is used for stop and limit orders when the customers don't want the price of their order to be reduced for a dividend.

805. C. I, II, and IV

Discretionary orders are ones in which the customer gives the registered representative the authority to make trades on their behalf without consulting them first. As with all orders, they must be approved by a principal of the firm sometime that day. The order ticket must be marked as "discretionary" because it will require a little extra scrutiny from a principal. To give a registered rep discretionary authority over an account, there has to be a power of attorney from the customer on file.

806. B. It must be marked as unsolicited.

This order was unsolicited because the registered representative did not recommend the purchase. As such, the order ticket needs to be marked as unsolicited. All orders need to be approved by a principal whether solicited or not. The approval doesn't necessarily have to be before the trade takes place but must be done by the end of the day.

807. C. An alternative order

An alternative order is also known as a one cancels the other order or an either/or order. In this case, a sell limit order would be placed to sell 100 shares of MKR at 50, and a sell stop order to sell 100 shares of MKR at $45. If either order is executed, the other is cancelled.

808. D. I, II, and III

All the choices listed are discretionary orders and require a written power of attorney signed by the customer in order to be accepted. To not need a power of attorney, the customer must provide or agree to the number of shares (or bonds), whether to buy or sell, and the specific security. Discretionary orders don't require a customer's verbal approval to be executed.

809. A. I and III

Remember, you're looking for false answers to this question. Unsolicited orders are ones in which the investor tells the registered rep which securities he wants to purchase, sell, or sell short. Although orders must be approved by a principal, they don't have to be approved prior to the order being placed. In addition, there are no limits to the size of the order regarding unsolicited orders; they are only limited based on the investor's ability to pay.

810. D. DTCC

The DTCC (Depository Trust and Clearing Corporation) provides safeguards to the world's financial markets. They provide the following:

Clearing services

Matching, settlement, and asset services

Collateral management

Wealth management services

Derivative services

Data services

811. D. I, II, III, and IV

Actually, all of the choices listed are considered accredited investors. Accredited investors are able to handle more financial risk than average investors.

812. C. an accredited investor

Individuals making at least $200,000 ($300,000 joint) for the previous two years and are expected to at least make over $200,000 ($300,000 joint) this year, would be considered accredited investors.

813. A. joint investors

This one probably stuck out like a sore thumb. Certainly, joint investors are not institutional investors like insurance companies, hedge funds, or commercial banks.

814. D. I, II, III, and IV

All of the choices listed would be considered institutional investors. Institutional investors are the big guys. They are the ones that invest a lot of money on behalf of their entity.

815. D. All of the above.

Retail investors are the ones that most registered representatives deal with on a daily basis. They are the smaller investors who are trading for their own account instead of trading for a big institution.

Chapter 11 Answers

816. D. sales

Progressive taxes are taxes that increase depending on an individual's tax bracket. Progressive taxes affect individuals with high incomes more than individuals with low incomes. Personal income, gift, and estate taxes are progressive taxes. Sales tax and excise taxes (gas, alcohol, tobacco, and so on) are regressive taxes because everyone is taxed at the same rate.

817. C. II, III, and IV

Regressive taxes are ones in which all individuals are taxed at the same rate regardless of income level. Regressive taxes include sales, gas, and alcohol. Progressive taxes, in which individuals with higher income pay a higher rate, include income, gift, and estate taxes.

818. A. I and III

Property tax is a flat or regressive tax in which taxes are levied equally regardless of the individual's income level. Flat taxes include sales, gasoline, excise, payroll, and property tax.

819. A. capital gains

Earned (active) income includes salaries, bonuses, and any income received from active participation in a business. Capital gains are considered portfolio income.

820. B. II, III, and IV

Portfolio income includes net capital gains from the sale of securities (including municipal bonds), dividends, and interest. Income, gains, and losses from a DPP (direct participation program) are passive.

821. D. passive income

Income, losses, or gains from a partnership are passive. Passive income can only be offset by passive losses.

822. D. all of the above

Unlike investment income, earned income is money received from working. Earning income includes wages, tips, bonuses, commissions, and so on.

823. B. III and IV

Stock dividends and stock splits aren't taxable events. However, cash dividends and interest payments on corporate bonds are taxable.

824. A. I only

Passive losses (losses from a limited partnership) can only be written off against passive income.

825. C. exempt from federal tax

When an investor receives dividends from a municipal bond fund, the dividends are federally tax free. However, capital gains distributions are taxable on all levels.

826. B. I and IV

Municipal bond interest is exempt from federal tax. However, unless purchasing a municipal bond within your home state or from a U.S. protectorate (such as Guam, U.S. Virgin Islands, or Puerto Rico), the interest is subject to state tax.

827. B. federal tax but not state tax

Interest on U.S. government T-bonds (treasury bonds) is subject to federal tax but not state tax.

828. D. Running a business

Dividends from stocks and interest from bonds are both investment income. However, any earnings made from running a business is considered earning income.

829. A. I and III

Dividends received from stock which was held for more than 60 days during a 121-day holding period prior to the ex-dividend date are taxed as qualified dividends (0%, 15%, or 20%). Passive income is income that an investor receives from limited partnerships only. Long-term capital gains are for securities held for longer than one year. Because this investor held the stock for exactly one year, it's taxed as a short-term capital gain.

830. **A. Interest received from corporate bonds, interest received from T-bonds, and cash dividends**

Interest received from corporate bonds, T-bonds (Treasury bonds), and cash dividends are all taxable for the year they were received. Investors are not taxed for stock splits or stock dividends because the investor didn't receive a cash payment.

831. **B. Their cost basis on the stock owned will be reduced.**

Unlike receiving a cash dividend, receiving a stock dividend is not a taxable event. When receiving a stock dividend, the market price and the cost basis of the stock will be reduced.

832. **D. $4,500**

Cash dividends are always fully taxable for the year in which they were received.

833. **C. Appreciation**

At this point, the investor just has appreciation of securities. You don't know whether the investor is going to have a profit or loss until the securities are sold. Capital gains or losses take place when a security is sold, and ordinary income would be from interest or dividends received.

834. **C. one year or less**

To have capital gains, you have to be selling the security at a profit. Short-term capital gains or losses would be on securities held for one year or less.

835. **A. I and III**

This is a short-term capital gain because when a security is sold up to and including one year from the purchase date, it would be a short-term capital gain or loss. Since it is short-term, the gain would be taxed at the investor's tax bracket.

836. **C. all gains or losses are considered short term**

Short selling is selling a borrowed security. Investors are hoping that the price of the security drops so that they can purchase the securities in that market at a lower price and return the securities to the lender. Short selling is a bearish strategy because investors want the price of the security to decrease. Because the investor isn't actually holding the securities, all gains and losses from selling short are considered short term, and the investor is taxed at their tax bracket.

837. **C. October 1 of the following year**

This is somewhat of a trick question. Securities become long term after holding them for more than a year. In this case, you may think that September 31 would be the answer. However, September has only 30 days, so there's no September 31; the correct answer is October 1 of the following year.

838. **C. They have a $3,000 loss for the current year and $3,500 carried over to the following year.**

Capital losses can be used to offset capital gains. In this case, your client had losses exceeding gains by $6,500 ($21,000 losses – $14,500 gains). Out of the $6,500, the client can write a total of $3,000 against ordinary income each year. This means that your client would be carrying a $3,500 loss ($6,500 – $3,000) into the following year.

839. **D. DEF preferred stock**

The IRS wash sale rule states that investors can't sell a security at a loss and buy back the same security or anything convertible into the same security for 30 days (before or after). If an investor violates the wash sale rule, they wouldn't be able to claim the loss on their taxes. (It would increase the cost basis of the securities repurchased.) In this case, DEF convertible bonds are convertible into DEF common stock, DEF call options give the holder the right to buy DEF common stock, and DEF warrants give the holder the right to purchase DEF common stock at a fixed price. DEF preferred stock is allowable because it's a different security and isn't convertible into DEF common stock.

840. **C. I, II, and III**

You need to remember that Marty sold LMN at a loss; therefore, he can't buy back the same security or anything convertible into the same security within 30 days to avoid the wash sale rule. Buying warrants and call options gives Marty the right to buy LMN common stock, so they would be a violation. However, LMN preferred stock is a different security (unless convertible), so it wouldn't violate the wash sale rule.

841. **A. The customer cannot purchase call options on the same security for 30 days before or after the sale and be able to claim the loss.**

According to the wash sale rule, an investor who is selling a security at a loss cannot purchase the same security or anything convertible into the same security for 30 days prior or 30 days after the sale and be able to claim the loss. However, the loss isn't gone completely, it just means that the cost basis for the new securities purchased will be adjusted for the loss. So, for example, if the investor sold ABC common stock at a loss, they wouldn't be able to purchase ABC call options on the stock because call options give the investor the right to purchase the underlying security.

842. B. 30 days

According to the Wash Sale Rule, if an investor sells a security at a loss, the investor is restricted from buying the same security or anything convertible into the security for 30 days and to be able to claim the loss.

843. A. The loss will not be allowed because it is a violation of the wash sale rule.

When the investor sells a security at a loss, they cannot buy the same security nor anything convertible into the same security for 30 days (before or after). The idea behind this is that the IRS doesn't want investors to be able to claim a loss on a security while still maintaining the same position. What would happen is that the cost basis would be adjusted to reflect the loss. Since this investor had a loss of $8 per share on the original purchase ($48–$40), the cost basis on the new purchase would be adjusted so that the investor had a built-in $8 loss. So, the cost basis for the $42 purchase would be adjusted to $50.

844. C. Retirement plans

Revenue bonds are types of municipal bonds. Revenue bonds have a federal tax advantage because the interest received is federally tax-free. Therefore, because retirement plans already have a nice tax advantage (money isn't taxed until it's withdrawn), it wouldn't make much sense to purchase low-yielding municipal bonds.

845. D. Municipal bonds

Because pension funds and other retirement plans are tax-deferred, it wouldn't make much sense to purchase municipal bonds because of their low yield. Remember, because the interest in municipal bonds is federally tax-free, they typically have the lowest yields of all bonds.

846. C. payroll deduction plans

Payroll deduction plans are non-qualified plans that aren't required to include all full-time employees. ERISA (Employee Retirement Income Security Act) regulates only qualified plans that are available to all full-time employees of a company.

847. A. private pension plans

ERISA (Employee Retirement Income Security Act) regulations cover private pension plans only.

848. A. I and III

Contributions to IRS qualified retirement plans are made with pretax dollars, and the distributions are 100% taxed at the holder's tax bracket.

849. D. deferred compensation

Tax-qualified plans are ones that meet IRS standards for favorable tax treatment. If the plan is tax qualified, contributions are made from pre-tax dollars. However, when the money is withdrawn, the entire amount, including the initial contributions plus any gains, is taxable. Tax-qualified plans include IRAs, 401(k)s, profit-sharing, money-purchase, and so on. Nonqualified plans are funded from after-tax contributions and include deferred compensation, payroll deduction, 457 plans, and so on.

850. C. 401(k)

Deferred compensation, payroll deduction, and 457 plans are nonqualified because they don't meet the IRS standards to receive favorable tax treatment. However, a 401(k) plan, which is available to many individuals at their place of work is a tax-qualified plan. Tax-qualified plans allow investors to deduct payments into the plan against their taxes.

851. B. $6,500

For investors under age 50 with no other retirement plan, the maximum an investor can contribute to a traditional or Roth IRA is $6,500 per year as of 2023.

852. C. $1,000 per year for investors aged 50 and older

Investors age 50 and older may contribute an additional $1,000 above the $6,500 maximum contribution limit to their traditional or Roth IRA each year.

853. B. $6,500 combined

The maximum an investor can contribute to a traditional and Roth IRA combined is $6,500 as of 2023. If 50 or over, that number increases to $7,500.

854. A. I and III

401(k) plans are corporate retirement plans. They are defined contribution plans in which the employee chooses the amount (percentage) of their pay they want contributed to the plan. Typically, the employer will do some sort of match, like 50% of what the employee contributes. Contributions are made from pretax dollars meaning that the money that is contributed is not taxed until withdrawn.

855. A. Contributions to the IRA are fully deductible.

An investor can always contribute money into an IRA even if covered by an employer pension plan. However, whether it's deductible or not depends on the investor's earnings. As of 2023 (the amount increases yearly), an investor who makes up to $73,000 can contribute to an IRA and be able to deduct the full amount from their taxes.

856. **D. April 15 of the following year**

Investors can deposit money into a traditional IRA up to April 15 (tax day) of the following year and claim it as a write-off on the previous year's taxes.

857. **A. Withdrawals from both are tax-free provided that investors have held the accounts for at least five years and have reached the age of 59½.**

Contributions to both Roth IRAs and Roth 401(k)s are made from after-tax dollars. So, withdrawals are tax-free provided that investors have held the accounts for at least five years and are at least 59½ years old.

858. **C. Within 60 calendar days**

Rollovers must be completed within 60 calendar days.

859. **C. Contributions to the IRA may be taxable.**

If an investor is covered by the 401(k), they may still contribute to an IRA. However, depending on their income, the contributions to the IRA may be pre-tax, after-tax, or partially taxed.

860. **B. 100% taxable at the investor's tax bracket**

403(b) plans are also known as tax-sheltered annuities (TSAs). TSAs are available to school employees, tax-exempt organizations, and religious organizations. These are salary reduction plans in which the contributions are made on a pre-tax basis. Because the investor didn't pay any taxes on the contributions, the distributions are 100% taxable at the investor's tax bracket.

861. **C. 403(b)s**

403(b) plans are set up for public school employees (elementary, secondary, college, and so on) and certain charities. They are considered salary reduction plans because the amount contributed by the employee reduces their salary so that they aren't taxed on the money contributed until it's taken out at retirement.

862. **A. I and III**

The money deposited into both Roth 401(k)s and Roth IRAs (individual Retirement Accounts) is from after-tax money. (You can't write off the deposits on your taxes.) However, qualified dividends are not taxed on the money originally deposited (that was already taxed), nor on the amount the account hopefully went up in value (appreciation).

863. **D. On April 1 of the year after the investor turns age 73**

For most qualified retirement plans, investors must take minimum distributions by April 1 of the year after they turn age 73. The IRS has a minimum distribution table to make sure investors will start withdrawing money at some point. If investors don't take their minimum distribution, they will face a tax penalty.

864. **C. 60 days**

After withdrawing money from a pension plan, individuals have 60 days to roll over the money into another retirement plan or IRA without being taxed as a withdrawal.

865. **A. No consequences**

Since this investor owns a Roth IRA, the amount of money deposited was taxed, but any money taken out (deposits plus appreciation) is not taxed. Since the IRS will not make any money on withdrawals, there is no required minimum distribution (RMD).

866. **A. private pension plans**

ERISA regulations cover private pension plans only.

867. **C. The $30,000 withdrawn is taxed as ordinary income.**

IRAs are usually qualified plans where investors make pre-tax (tax deductible) contributions. Since taxes are not paid on the money contributed, all withdrawals are fully taxable. All taxable withdrawals from retirement plans are classified as ordinary income, not capital gains since retirement accounts are not taxable when investments are sold.

868. **B. 59½**

Investors may start withdrawing money from an IRA at age 59½ without facing a 10% penalty for early withdrawal. The 10% penalty may be avoided for first-time home buyers, in cases of death, in cases of disability, and so on.

869. **A. All employees are fully vested immediately.**

All employees who have had their employer contribute to a SEP (Simplified Employee Pension) IRA in their name are fully vested immediately. What that means is that if the employee leaves the company for whatever reason, the full account goes with them.

870. **A. There is a 6% penalty on the amount over contributed.**

If investors over contribute to an IRA for a particular year, they will face a 6% penalty on the amount over contributed.

871. **C. The withdrawal is taxed at their tax bracket plus a 10% penalty.**

Since the investor is under age 59½, they will be charged at their tax bracket plus a 10% penalty. As with some other plans, the 10% penalty is often waived for first-time homebuyers, death, and disability.

872. **D. 25% of an employee's pay**

The maximum employer contribution per employee is 25% of the employees pay, which includes salary, bonuses, commission, and overtime.

873. **D. They receive a 50% penalty on the amount that was supposed to be withdrawn.**

If an investor fails to take their required minimum distributions (RMD), there will be a 50% penalty on the amount that was supposed to have been withdrawn.

874. **B. The contribution amount is fixed, and the benefit amount is variable.**

As the name might imply, the contribution is defined (fixed). However, the benefit amount is variable based on how the investments picked for the plan perform.

875. **D. 403(b), 401(k), traditional IRA**

403(b)s, 401(k)s, and traditional IRAs are qualified plans, which require holders to take minimum distributions by April 1 of the year after turning age 73. However, Roth IRAs are not subject to the minimum distribution laws because the money withdrawn is tax-free.

876. **B. Contributions can be made by the employer only.**

SEP (Simplified Employee Pension) IRAs allow for contributions from the employer only.

Chapter 12 Answers

877. **A. I, III, and IV**

The Securities and Exchange Commission (SEC), which was created under the Securities and Exchange Act of 1934, regulates the trading of securities. Commodities aren't considered securities and, therefore, aren't regulated by the SEC. A Series 7 license doesn't allow you to trade commodities, which is something you should keep in mind when answering Series 7 questions.

878. **B. The Securities and Exchange Act of 1934**

The Securities and Exchange Act of 1934 created the Securities and Exchange Commission (SEC).

879. **C. To help promote fair and equitable practices among its members**

Self-regulatory organizations (SROs) such as FINRA, MSRB, NYSE, and so on, make sure there are fair and equitable trading practices among its participants. They establish rules and regulations to make sure broker-dealers, registered reps, principals, and so on treat each other and their customers fairly and do not violate any securities laws.

880. B. It regulates trades of securities in the primary market.

The Securities Act of 1933 regulates trading of securities in the primary (new issue) market. The Securities Exchange Act of 1934 regulates trades of outstanding securities in the secondary market.

881. D. the full and fair disclosure required on new offerings

The full and fair disclosure that's required on new offerings is covered under the Securities Act of 1933, not the Securities Exchange Act of 1934. The Securities Act of 1933 deals with the registration of new issues, and the Securities Exchange Act of 1934 deals with the trading of outstanding issues.

882. C. SEC

SROs are self-regulatory organizations that are unaffiliated with the federal government. The SEC (Securities and Exchange Commission) is a government agency.

883. D. MSRB

Yes, believe it or not, the MSRB (municipal securities rulemaking board) does not enforce MSRB rules, they just make them. FINRA and the SEC enforce MSRB rules for broker-dealers; and the FDIC, the FED, and Comptroller of Currency enforce MSRB rules for bank dealers.

884. A. corporate bonds

The Trust Indenture Act prohibits bond issues of more than $50 million from being offered without an indenture. The bond indenture is a written agreement that protects bondholders by disclosing the particulars of an issue (coupon rate, coupon dates, maturity date, collateral backing the bond, and so on).

885. D. Investment Company Act of 1940

The Investment Company Act of 1940 regulates the registration requirements and the activities of investment companies, such as mutual funds.

886. C. The State Administrators

The State Administrators of each state are responsible for the state registration of securities, broker-dealers, registered reps, investment advisers, and so on. The North American Securities Administrators Association (NASAA) is devoted to investor protection.

887. A. I and III

Investment advisers charge a fee for giving investment advice. If they have under $25 million under management, they only have to register with the state(s) where they are doing business. If they have $25 million or more under management, they have to register with the SEC and states. Rules for investment advisers are covered under The Investment Advisers Act of 1940.

888. D. economists

According to the Investment Advisers Act of 1940, lawyers, accountants, teachers, and engineers are professionals excluded from the definition of investment adviser. Therefore, an economist is not specifically excluded based on the law.

889. D. FINRA

FINRA (Financial Industry Regulatory Authority) is a self-regulatory organization that is responsible for the operation and regulation of the over-the counter (OTC) market, investment banking, NYSE trades, investment companies, and so on.

890. A. Department of the Treasury

The U.S. Department of Treasury (USDT) was established to manage U.S. government revenue. As such, the USDT oversees the printing of all currency and minting of coins. In addition, it is responsible for collecting taxes through the IRS, managing U.S. government debt securities, and assisting other branches of the U.S. government in helping set fiscal policy.

891. B. II, III, and IV

As self-regulatory organizations (SROs), FINRA and the NYSE can fine, expel, and/or censure members. However, because FINRA and the NYSE aren't affiliated with the government, they can't imprison members.

892. C. I, II, and III

The SEC has the authority to punish individuals inside or outside of the brokerage industry. The NYSE and FINRA may penalize an individual within the industry. However, because the MSRB doesn't enforce MSRB rules, the MSRB may not punish any individual for rules violations.

893. C. I and IV

An individual who has been convicted (not charged) within the past ten years of any felony is prohibited from working in the securities industry. In addition, an individual who has been convicted of any securities- or money-related misdemeanors can't work in the securities industry. Just because an individual is charged doesn't mean that they'll be convicted.

894. B. II and III

Answers II and III are definitely reasons why a person would be statutorily disqualified. However, Answer I doesn't fit because the person would be statutorily disqualified if they had a felony conviction in the last 10 years, not 15.

895. D. I, II, III, and IV

The U-4 form is the form that must be filled out by all registered reps. At the time it is filled out, all information must be accurate. If anything changes, the U-4 form must be amended. It includes all of the information listed plus also a criminal history (if any), disbarments, suspensions, and so on. The form also includes what states the rep will be registered in.

896. A. No, they must go through arbitration.

As part of the U-4 form, the registered rep will have agreed to settle any disputes between them and their firm through arbitration (arbitration disclosure).

897. C. two years

If a registered rep leaves the brokerage industry for more than two years, they will be required to take their exams all over again.

898. A. Their license will be suspended until they meet the requirements.

If a registered rep fails to meet the regulatory element within 120 days of their second anniversary (and every three years after), their license will be suspended until they complete the requirements.

899. B. They must notify their firm.

If a registered representative wishes to moonlight at another job, they may do so by notifying their firm. They do not need permission. If the firm believes it to be a conflict of interest, they may restrict or reject outside employment.

900. D. All of the above

All of the employees listed must be fingerprinted as well as employees having access to the firm's books and records. Fingerprints must be submitted within 30 days of the time the U-4 form was submitted.

901. B. I and IV

If an associated person, such as a registered rep, at one firm wishes to open an account at another firm, the associated person must get written permission from their firm. In addition, if the associated person's firm requests it, duplicate confirmations and account statements must be sent to the firm.

902. C. Member firms must have annual meetings, and registered persons must take the regulatory element within 120 days of their two-year anniversary and every three years after that.

Member firms must have meetings at least annually (the firm element). They must cover services and strategies offered as well as covering any recent regulatory developments. They must also allow people to ask questions. Registered persons must take the regulatory element within 120 days of their two-year anniversary and every three years after that.

903. D. The firm files a U-5 form, and the registered representative has up to two years to get registered with another firm or their license will expire.

When a registered rep starts working for a broker-dealer, they must fill out a U-4 form. When leaving the broker-dealer for whatever reason, the firm will fill out a U-5 form. The registered representative has up to two years (unless in the service) to get registered with another firm, or their licenses will expire.

904. A. I, II, and III

Choices I, II, and III are exempt from registering with FINRA because a clerical person is not handling a customer's business by way of sales or dealing with securities. Commodities are not securities and aren't controlled by FINRA. Municipal securities are exempt, so if a registered individual only deals with municipal securities, they don't have to be registered with FINRA. However, reps involved in options transactions must get registered.

905. A. a principal

New account forms and order tickets must be signed by a principal (manager) of the firm. Order tickets don't have to be signed prior to placing the order for trade but must be signed by the end of the day. This means that you can do trades while your principal is out to lunch.

906. D. I, II, III, and IV

When you become a registered rep, you receive your own unique identification number. This number has to be placed on any order ticket you fill out along with a description of the securities (such as ABC common stock), the time the order was placed, and whether the order was solicited or unsolicited. An unsolicited order is when a client tells you the securities they want to purchase or sell without your input.

907. **D. the investor's occupation**

The investor's occupation is something that's on the new account form, not the order ticket.

908. **B. take the order and mark it as "unsolicited"**

You probably want to let your client know about the risks of investing in low-priced stocks and let them know that it doesn't fit their investment objectives. However, you should definitely take the order and mark the order ticket as "unsolicited." By marking the order ticket as "unsolicited," you're putting the responsibility for the order on your client's shoulders.

909. **D. I, II, III, and IV**

All order tickets need to include the items listed in the question plus the client's account number; the number of shares or bonds purchased or sold; whether the client is buying, selling, or selling short; for options whether the client is covered or uncovered; whether it is a market order, good-till-cancelled, and so on.

910. **C. take the order but mark it as "unsolicited"**

Even though the shares of Biff Spanky Corporation may not fit into Gina's investment objectives, you can still accept the order. However, to protect yourself, you need to mark the order ticket as "unsolicited." The only unsolicited orders that you wouldn't be able to accept are on options (unless Gina's options account was approved) and DPPs (direct participation programs).

911. **D. Take the order and mark the order ticket "unsolicited."**

You do not have to refuse the order unless the order is to purchase a direct participation program. In this case, you just have to mark the order ticket as "unsolicited" and take the trade.

912. **C. the same day as execution of the order**

Principals (managers) must approve trades on the same day as execution but not necessarily before execution. This would allow the order to be entered as quickly as possible. Principals must approve trades as soon as possible after execution but no later than the end of the day at the latest.

913. **D. II and III**

A registered representative may open a joint account with a client if obtaining approval from a principal of the firm. In addition, the registered representative and the client must agree in writing to share gains and losses based on the percentage of money invested.

914. **B. Tuesday, October 7**

The settlement date for stock purchases is two business days after the trade date (T+2). Remember, Saturday and Sunday aren't business days, so the settlement date would be Tuesday, October 7.

915. **B. Two business days after the trade date**

Regular way settlement for corporate bonds is two business days after the trade date (T+2). Payment is due four business days after the trade date.

916. **D. II and IV**

For municipal bonds, regular way settlement is two business days after the trade date (T+2), and payment is due two business days after the trade date.

917. **B. Tuesday, September 16**

The last day that an investor can buy the stock "regular way" and still receive the dividend is on the business day before the ex-dividend date. Since the ex-dividend date is on Wednesday, September 17, an investor must buy the stock no later than Tuesday, September 16 to receive the dividend.

918. **A. one business day after the trade date**

U.S. government securities such as Treasury bonds (T-bonds) settle in one business day after the trade date (T+1), and payment is due within one business day after the trade date.

919. **D. on a date to be assigned**

When issued (when, as, and if issued) is a method of delivery used for securities that have been authorized and sold to investors prior to the certificates being ready. This is typically for stock splits, new issues of municipal bonds. The settlement date is a date to be assigned, two business days after the securities are ready for delivery, or on a date determined by FINRA.

920. **A. T+1**

Regular way options transactions settle in one business day after the trade date (T + 1).

921. **A. I and III**

Regardless of the type of security, any trades for cash settle the same day, and payment is due the same day.

922. C. Regulation S-P

All brokerage firms must have safeguards to protect customer records from unauthorized use (Gramm-Leach-Bliley Act). The safeguards must be disclosed in writing to all new customers at the time of the opening of the account and to all existing customers annually. Non-public information includes customers' Social Security number, transaction history, account balance, and so on.

923. B. Regulation BI

SEC Regulation BI (Best Interest – Rule 15i-1) was recently established to enhance the Securities Exchange Act of 1934. All broker-dealers are required to act in the best interest of their customers. As part of the rule, all broker-dealers must provide a customer relationship survey (Form CRS) to each client prior to the initial recommendation.

924. D. I, II, III, and IV

When a client receives a confirmation (receipt of trade), the confirmation has to include the trade and settlement date, the name and type of the security, how many shares were traded, and the amount of commission if traded on an agency basis. In the event that the trade was made on a principal basis, the amount of markup doesn't need to be disclosed.

925. A. Regulation S-P

Under Regulation S-P, all broker-dealers, investment companies, and investment advisers must have written policies to protect customer's records and private information. This would include things like social security numbers, bank account numbers, and so on.

926. A. at or prior to the completion of the transaction

For member-to-customer transactions, the member firm must send the trade confirmation at or prior to completion of the transaction (the settlement date). For member-to-member transactions, the firms must send each other confirmations no later than one business day after the trade date.

927. C. the customer's signature

A customer's signature is not included on a trade confirmation. The trade confirmation is what is sent to a customer after the trade is made. It includes items specific to the trade like the number of securities, the price of the security purchased or sold, the name of the security, the date and time of trade, the commission if on an agency basis, and so on.

928. **C. II, III, and IV**

A confirmation must include the amount of commission charged for an agency transaction, a description of the security purchased or sold, the registered representative's identification number, and so on. However, the markup or markdown doesn't need to be disclosed for principal transactions.

929. **C. confirmation**

All member firms are required to send a trade confirmation to a customer at or prior to the completion of each transaction. The confirmation provides all the specifics of the trade, such as the trade date, whether the customer bought or sold, the quantity of securities, the name of the security, the price of the security, and so on.

930. **D. whether the trade was executed on a dealer or agency basis**

MSRB (Municipal Securities Rulemaking Board) rules require that confirmations include whether a trade was executed on a principal (dealer) or agency (broker) basis. The amount of the commission on an agency trade does need to be disclosed, but the dealer's markup or markdown on a principal trade doesn't have to be disclosed. The trade date (the day the transaction was executed) would need to be disclosed but not the settlement date because that's assumed to be three business days after the trade date.

931. **A. named "Trusted Contact Person"**

All accounts for specified adults (natural persons aged 65 and over, and natural persons aged 18 and over who have physical or mental impairments that render them unable to protect their own interests) must have a named "Trusted Contact Person" who can be contacted in the event that the specified adult's account is or may be exploited.

932. **C. Place a temporary hold on the disbursement of funds or securities from the account**

Rule 2165 allows member firms to place a temporary hold on the disbursement of a specified adult's funds or securities. After a hold is in place, the member has up to two business days to contact all parties involved in the transaction as well as the trusted contact person (unless the member believes that he or she is involved in the exploitation) to describe the reason(s) for the temporary hold. The hold may last up to 15 business days while being reviewed.

933. **D. all of the above**

Rule 2165 covers the rules regarding the financial exploitation of specified adults. Specified adults include those aged 65 and older and natural persons aged 18 or older with mental and/or physical impairments that render them unable to protect their own interests.

934. **D. I, II, and III**

All of the choices listed are possible as well as if the registered representative and customer have a personal relationship outside the broker-customer relationship (boyfriend, girlfriend, fiancée and so on). Additionally, if the customer and registered person are both registered under the same firm, it is also acceptable.

935. **B. Quarterly**

For accounts, like Declan Smith's, the brokerage firm must send out account statements at least quarterly (every three months). For mutual funds, every six months.

936. **B. The most recent balance sheet**

If a client requests a copy of a broker-dealer's balance sheet, the brokerage firm must send a copy of the most recent one to the client immediately.

937. **A. II, III, IV, I**

First MKR Corporation will announce the dividend on the declaration date. After that, you have the ex-date (ex-dividend date), which is one business day before the record date. Then, the record date and finally, the payment date.

938. **B. the date on and after the date the seller is entitled to the dividend**

The ex-date or ex-dividend date is one business day before the record date and is the date that the buyer would be purchasing the stock without a dividend. On the ex-date, the stock is reduced by the amount of the dividend. The corporation is still responsible for paying the dividend, and because the buyer isn't entitled to it, the seller is.

939. **A. one**

The ex-dividend date is the first day that the purchaser of a stock will not receive a previously declared dividend. The ex-dividend date is one business day before the record date. As a reminder, Saturday and Sunday are not considered business days. So, if the record date was on Monday, the ex-dividend date would be on the previous Friday.

940. **D. quarterly**

A brokerage firm must make sure that customer account statements are sent out at least quarterly (once every three months) whether any trading has been done in the account or not.

941. C. semiannually

According to the Investment Company Act of 1940, mutual funds must send out customer account statements at least once every 6 months (semiannually).

942. B. Thursday, October 7

The first day the stock trades without the dividend is on the ex-dividend date. The ex-dividend date is one business day before the record date . . . in this case, Thursday, October 7.

943. B. accept the complaint and write down any action taken

After receiving Meisha's written complaint, the broker-dealer must accept the complaint and write down any action taken to resolve the complaint. All broker-dealers should keep a complaint file for each client and keep accurate records of any communications or actions taken regarding a complaint.

944. D. The DBCC

Most brokerage firms have their customers sign an arbitration agreement because it is less costly and decisions are binding. However, in this case, the customer is taking the firm through the court process (Code of Procedure). The DBCC (District Business Conduct Committee) has the first jurisdiction over complaints.

945. C. Arbitration decisions are binding and non-appealable, but mediation decisions are appealable.

Arbitration decisions are binding and non-appealable. Mediation is conducted by an independent third party. Unlike arbitration, mediation decisions are nonbinding and appealable.

946. B. Institutional, retail, and correspondence

The three types of communication recognized by FINRA are correspondence, retail communication, and institutional communication.

947. D. all of the above

Retail communications are any written communications (including electronic) distributed to more than 25 retail investors within a 30-day period. They must be approved by a principal and filed with FINRA at least 10 business days prior to first use.

948. B. I and III

All legal disputes between members of FINRA and disputes between FINRA members and their registered representatives must be handled through arbitration. However, unless the customer (whether a bank or retail customer) signed an arbitration agreement, they can take the FINRA member through Code of Procedure (COP) or through arbitration — it is their choice.

949. A. members may take non-members to arbitration

Members can't force non-members to submit a dispute to arbitration. The non-member (customer) decides if the dispute is settled through arbitration or COP (Code of Procedure). However, many firms require customers to sign an arbitration agreement when opening an account that requires disputes to be settled through arbitration only.

950. C. Arbitration

Arbitration decisions are binding and non-appealable. Arbitration is certainly less formal and less costly than going through the court system. As a matter of fact, many brokerage firms have customers sign an arbitration clause as part of a new account form stating that the customer agrees to have disputes handled through arbitration.

951. C. $50,000

Simplified arbitration is used for disputes of up to $50,000. One person decides the dispute solely based on written evidence by both parties involved in the dispute.

952. D. a lifetime

Documents that establish the broker-dealer as a corporation or partnership must be kept for the firm's lifetime.

953. D. I, II, and IV

U-4 forms of terminated employees must be maintained by brokerage firms for only three years. All other choices listed must be maintained by brokerage firms for a minimum of six years.

954. C. I and III

Blotters, which includes records of all trades executed by the brokerage firm; ledgers, which include customer account statements; general ledgers; position records; account records; and information on closed accounts must be kept for a minimum of six years. U-5 forms and sales literature must be kept for a minimum of three years.

955. A. ledgers

Ledgers, which are customer account statements, must be kept on file for a minimum of six years, not three. As a reminder, all records must be easily accessible for two years.

956. B. two years

All broker-dealer records must be kept easily accessible for a minimum of two years.

957. B. three years

Brokerage firms must keep trade confirmations, order tickets, and advertisements for a minimum of three years under FINRA rules.

958. D. The over-the-counter sale of outstanding non-exempt securities

The 5% markup policy doesn't apply to primary (new issue) offerings, mutual funds (continuous offering of new shares), or Regulation D (exempt) offerings.

959. D. All of the above

The 5% markup policy is a guideline for broker-dealers to use when executing trades of outstanding securities for public customers. For a standard-sized trade of non-exempt securities, broker-dealers typically shouldn't charge a commission, markup, or markdown that is greater than 5%. However, some situations may warrant a charge more than 5%, such as a small trade or extra work involved in executing the trade. The 5% policy applies to both commission charges on agency transactions and to markups and markdowns on principal transactions, including proceeds transactions, and riskless (simultaneous) transactions.

960. A. dealer cost

The 5% markup policy states that a firm may use all relevant factors of a trade to determine the markup or commission charged to a customer except the price that the firm paid to have the stock in inventory (dealer cost).

961. C. Sales of outstanding shares of corporate stock

The 5% markup policy covers the over-the-counter trades of outstanding, nonexempt securities with public customers. Securities sold with a prospectus are not outstanding shares; they're new shares. Municipal bonds are exempt securities, and mutual funds are always new securities when purchased.

962. **C. the 5% policy**

Municipal bonds are exempt from SEC registration, so they're not subject to the 5% markup policy.

963. **B. $250**

Municipal finance professionals (MFP) are limited to donating up $250 per municipal candidate, per election, for candidates they're allowed to vote for.

964. **D. all of the above**

The 5% markup policy is a guideline for broker-dealers to use when executing trades of outstanding securities for public customers. In most cases, for a standard-sized trade of nonexempt securities, broker-dealers should not charge a commission, markup, or markdown that is in excess of 5%. The policy applies to both commission charges on agency transactions and to markups and markdowns on principal transactions, including riskless and simultaneous transactions.

965. **C. commingling**

Mixing a customer's securities with that of the broker-dealer is a violation called commingling.

966. **D. All of the above**

All of the choices listed are violations. Commingling of funds takes place when a firm combines a customer's fully paid securities with margined securities, or when a firm combines its own securities with a customer's securities. Interpositioning is when two securities broker-dealers act as agents for the same trade, thus requiring the customer to pay more than one commission. Signatures of convenience are ones in which a customer's signature is forged.

967. **B. freeriding**

Clients must pay for trades even if selling the securities at a profit shortly afterward. You can imagine the problems that would occur if clients never paid for trades and just waited to see whether there was a profit. In this case, the client's account would be frozen for 90 days, and they wouldn't be able to purchase securities without paying for them first.

968. **B. the illegal manipulation of a security**

Matching orders is when broker-dealers trade securities back and forth with no real change of ownership. This would create higher trading volume on a security than expected and would garner investor interest. Matching orders is the illegal manipulation of securities.

969. **B. a gift of theatre tickets for a client and daughter for a total of $250**

Gifts may be given to clients of up to $100 per person per year. However, wedding gifts and gifts for the birth of a child are exempt from FINRA restrictions. In addition, business expenses are exempt from restriction. For sports and entertainment ticket contributions to be legal, the rep must attend or intend to attend the event.

970. **C. A registered representative encouraging clients to buy equity securities just prior to a dividend being paid so that they will receive the dividend**

Selling dividends is a violation because it is meant to entice investors to purchase securities right before a previously declared dividend is paid. Remember, that the price of a security is reduced by the dividend on the ex-dividend (ex-date), so there's no advantage for investors to purchase right before a dividend.

971. **B. hypothecation**

All of the choices listed are violations except for Choice (B). Hypothecation takes place when a broker-dealer lends money to a customer when purchasing securities in a margin account.

972. **A. the profit or loss**

Churning is the excessive trading of a client's account for the sole purpose of generating commissions and is a violation. Yes, believe it or not, when FINRA (Financial Industry Regulatory Authority) is looking to see whether an account has been churned, the client's profit or loss doesn't come into play.

973. **C. Pump and dump**

All of the choices listed are violations. However, pump and dump is the only violation listed that is a form of market manipulation. Pump and dump is fake news typically regarding penny stocks that is designed to drive the price of a particular stock up so that the firm can sell their stock at a large profit.

974. **D. prohibited**

This is a violation because if the registered rep purchases back the securities so that customer doesn't take a loss, is the rep is making a guarantee against loss, which is a violation.

975. **A. the SDN list maintained by OFAC**

All financial institutions, such as banks and broker-dealers, must have customer identification programs (CIPs) in place. As part of that program, the names of all new customers must be checked against the SDN (Specially Designated Nationals) list maintained by OFAC (Office of Foreign Assets Control).

976. **A. money laundering**

Although the depositing of large amounts of cash in itself isn't illegal, it may be a sign of the possibility of money laundering.

977. **B. intermediation**

The three stages of money laundering are placement, layering, and integration. Placement is when illegally obtained money is placed into a financial institution. Layering is an activity intended to disguise an illegal activity. Integration is when illegal money is mixed with legal money.

978. **C. A cash deposit of $15,000**

A Form 112 is used to report cash transactions or money order transactions of $10,000 or more. Cash deposits greater than $10,000 in one day may be an indication of money laundering and must be reported to FinCEN (U.S. Treasury Financial Crimes Network) by filling out a currency transaction report (CTR).

979. **A. The Bank Secrecy Act**

The Bank Secrecy Act established the U.S. Treasury Department as the regulator of anti-money-laundering programs. All broker-dealers are required to develop programs to detect possible money-laundering abuses.

980. **A. I and II**

Structured transactions are an indication of money laundering. Transactions of $10,000 or more in cash, money orders, wires, and so on in once day must be reported as possible money laundering. Since statements I and II are regarding deposits of just under $10,000 and there are multiple deposits, it looks suspicious and is considered structuring.

981. **D. All of the above**

All of the choices listed may be signs that your customer is planning on laundering money.

982. **D. I, II, III, and IV**

All of the answer choices listed are potential indications of money laundering.

983. **A. structuring**

Structuring is an indication of money laundering. Structuring occurs when an investor makes deposits just under $10,000, which don't need to be reported to the U.S. government.

984. A. contact a principal immediately

If you suspect that one of your clients is using inside information, you must immediately inform a principal. Any further action will be decided by your firm. The Insider Trading and Securities Fraud Enforcement Act of 1988 requires all broker-dealers to have written supervisory procedures that address insider information.

985. D. I and II

Inside information is information about the company that has not been released to the public, which might affect the price of the securities. Changes in management and undisclosed financial difficulties would be considered inside information if not already disclosed to the public through the media. If a dividend has been declared already, it isn't inside information. Also, if Moody's is downgrading their bonds, it would already be known.

986. C. II and III

Contemporaneous traders are investors who can sue insiders in court for insider trading violations. Investors can only accuse insiders if they were trading the opposite way of the insiders. Therefore, investors can sue insiders if they were buying when insiders were selling or selling when insiders were buying.

987. D. II, III, and IV

Civil penalties for insider trading may be imposed on anyone violating insider trading rules, whether registered or not. So, if Roman numeral I is out, the only answer that works is Choice (D).

988. C. Both (A) and (B)

When a trade takes place based on material nonpublic information, both the tipper (the one spreading the material nonpublic information) and the tippee (the one who traded based on the material nonpublic information) are liable.

989. C. Both the CEO and the lifelong friend

Because the friend used the inside information (information not yet released to the public), both the CEO and the friend violated insider trading rules.

990. B. I and IV

The maximum penalties for insider trading are $5 million per individual per violation ($25 million per business) and up to 20 years in prison per violation. Although not part of this question, the maximum civil sanctions are three times the gain or three times the loss avoided plus disgorgement of profits.

991. **B. two**

Because of the possibility of an emergency, all firms are required to have business continuity plans and provide emergency contact information. In addition, all firms must provide the emergency contact information for two principals to FINRA.

992. **A. annually by a principal of the firm**

Business continuity plans must be reviewed annually by a principal of the firm.

993. **C. The firm may hold the client's mail up to three months.**

If a client is traveling, moving, or whatever, the firm may hold their mail up to a period of three months or a little longer if needed.

994. **D. SIPC funding is made by member assessments.**

SIPC (Securities Investor Protection Corporation) is funded by annual fees paid by brokerage firms. SIPC isn't a U.S. government agency. Banks and investment advisers aren't required to purchase SIPC insurance.

995. **A. depositor for up to $250,000**

The FDIC (Federal Deposit Insurance Corporation) provides depositors insurance against failed (bankrupt) banks for up to $250,000. SIPC protects investors from broker-dealer failure up to $500,000, of which no more than $250,000 can be cash.

996. **A. $500,000 in cash and securities with no more than $250,000 cash**

SIPC (Securities Investor Protection Corporation) covers investors in the event of broker-dealer bankruptcy. SIPC covers each investor up to $500,000, of which no more than $250,000 can be cash.

997. **D. All of the above**

SIPC (Securities Investor Protection Corporation) provides coverage for all types of securities held in customer accounts. SIPC provides protection for customers in the event of broker-dealer bankruptcy. SIPC coverage covers each separate account up to $500,000, of which no more than $250,000 can be cash.

998. **C. four**

The customer has a cash account and a margin account in their name, which counts as one separate customer according to SIPC. The joint account with the wife, the joint account with the son, and the corporate account are three other separate accounts.

999. B. $1,300,000

SIPC (Securities Investor Protection Corporation) covers each separate customer account up to $500,000, of which no more than $250,000 can be cash. So in this case, Mike's account would be covered for $450,000 ($200,000 stock + $50,000 bonds + $200,000 cash); Mary's account would be covered for $350,000 ($100,000 stock + $250,000 cash); and the joint account would be covered for $500,000 ($100,000 stock + $350,000 bonds + $50,000 cash). Added together, that's $450,000 + $350,000 + $500,000 = $1,300,000.

1000. B. general creditor

SIPC (Securities Investor Protection Corporation) protects each separate account only up to $500,000, of which no more than $250,000 can be cash. If the investor had more held in the account than would be covered by SIPC, they would become a general creditor of the firm for the remainder.

1001. D. FDIC

The FDIC (Federal Deposit Insurance Corporation) is the guarantor and insurer of bank savings account. The FDIC insures each bank account up to $250,000 in the event of bank failure.

Index

C

D

E

F

G

H

N

O

P

Q

R

S

About the Author

After earning a high score on the Series 7 Exam in the mid 1990s, **Steve Rice** began his career as a stockbroker for a broker dealership with offices in Nassau County, Long Island, and in New York City. In addition to his duties as a registered representative, he gained invaluable experience about securities registration rules and regulations when he worked in the firm's compliance office. But it was only after Steve began tutoring others in the firm to help them pass the Series 7 exam that he found his true calling as an instructor. Shortly thereafter, Steve became a founding partner and educator in Empire Stockbroker Training Institute (`www.empirestockbroker.com`).

In addition to writing *Series 7 Exam For Dummies, Securities Industry Essentials Exam For Dummies,* and *Series 7 Exam: 1001 Practice Questions For Dummies*, Steve developed and designed the Empire Stockbroker Training Institute online *(Securities Industry Essentials, Series 7, Series 6, Series 63, Series 65, Series 24, Series 66,* and more) exams. Steve also has coauthored a complete library of securities training manuals for classroom use and for home study, including the *Securities Industry Essentials, Series 6, Series 7, Series 24, Series 63, Series 65,* and *Series 66.* Steve's popular and highly acclaimed classes, online courses, and training manuals have helped tens of thousands of people achieve their goals and begin their lucrative new careers in the securities industry.

Dedication

I dedicate this book to my beautiful wife, Melissa. Melissa was the love of my life, my joy, my inspiration, and my best friend. Unfortunately, Melissa lost her long battle with cancer and is no longer in my arms. She was the most joyous and loving person I've ever met. I will carry her love in my heart for the rest of my days.

Author's Acknowledgments

A phenomenal team over at Wiley made this book possible. I would like to start by thanking my acquisitions editor, Lindsay Lefevere, for seeing something in me that told her that I was the right person for the job. She is a professional through and through, and I appreciate all of her help and guidance.

A load of thanks also goes to my development editor, Tim Gallan, for his rapid-response emails, which provided guidance and helped to keep me moving in the right direction. Tim and I have worked on many books together and hopefully many more.

I would also like to thank my copy editor, Kelly Henthorne, for making suggestions and tweaking my writing to make it more in line with Dummies style. Her input ultimately made this book more fun to read for all of you.

Next, I would like to thank the entire composition team and the technical reviewer, David Lambert. Although I didn't get a chance to communicate with any of them directly, this book wouldn't be possible without every one of them. I sincerely appreciate all of their hard work.

Publisher's Acknowledgments

Executive Editor: Lindsay Lefevere
Development Editor: Tim Gallan
Copy Editor: Kelly D. Henthorne
Technical Editor: David Lambert

Managing Editor: Kristie Pyles
Production editor: Saikarthick Kumarasamy